LIFE ENERGY

John Diamond, M.D.

DODD, MEAD & COMPANY
NEW YORK

Also by John Diamond, M.D.
Your Body Doesn't Lie

Serious diseases should always be treated under medical supervision. Nor should there be any delay in seeking medical advice whenever the symptoms of an ailment persist.

The material in this book is for educational purposes only and is not intended for use in diagnosing or treating any individual.

Published by Dodd, Mead & Company, Inc.
79 Madison Avenue, New York, N.Y. 10016

Distributed in Canada by
McClelland and Stewart Limited, Toronto
Manufactured in the United States of America

Designed by Denise C. Schiff
First Edition

Library of Congress Cataloging in Publication Data

Diamond, John.
  Life energy.

  Includes index.
  1. Emotions. 2. Acupuncture. 3. Thymus gland.
4. Psychotherapy. 5. Health. I. Title.
BF531.D53 1985   152.4   84-24701
ISBN 0-396-08489-3

PHOTO CREDITS:
Wilhelm Furtwängler: from *Furtwängler—Great Concert Artists* (Geneva: Kister, 1956), photo by Roger Hauert. With kind permission from Elisabeth Furtwängler. Artur Rubinstein: Photo by Louis Ouzer, Rochester, NY (copyright 1979), with permission. Winston Churchill: Wide World Photos, with permission. John Chambers, portrait by Hans Holbein: Kunsthistorisches Museum, Vienna, with permission. Bartok: courtesy of International Museum of Photography at George Eastman House. Babe Ruth: courtesy of International Museum of Photography at George Eastman House. Freud: courtesy of Mary Evans Picture Library, London. Model's face (circulation-sex meridian): courtesy of J. Frederick Smith. Portrait of a Member of the Wedigh Family, by Hans Holbein the Younger: courtesy of The Metropolitan Museum of Art, Bequest of Edward S. Harkness, 1940. Liv Ullmann: from *Without Makeup: Liv Ullmann*, A Photo-Biography compiled by David E. Outerbridge. 1979, with permission. Botticelli Venus: courtesy of Uffizi Gallery, Florence. Ingrid Bergman: from *Movie-Star Portraits of the Forties*, John Kobal. The Gold Mummy Mask: courtesy of The Egyptian Museum in Cairo. All photos of model courtesy of J. Frederick Smith.

Contents

Acknowledgments

I wish to express my thanks to my students and patients, from whom I have learned so much over the years, and hope that to some extent I have repaid that debt. Much of the information in this book has been their gift to me, for which I am most grateful.

I would like to thank Virginia Rohan Mann for her help with the early draft; Dr. Gloria Schwartz for her assistance in the earliest stages of research on the relationship between the meridians and the emotions; Victoria S. Galban, my research assistant; and Harvey Klinger for his continuing advice and support.

My thanks as well to J. Frederick Smith for his kindness and his excellent photographic work. My continuing gratitude goes to Dr. George Goodheart, the originator of kinesiological muscle testing.

Finally, I wish to express my special love and gratitude to my wife, Betty. This book, like nearly all my writings, is a joint effort. The research and the initial writing is my work. That to me is the easy part. Putting it all together and making it coherent has been her heavy task. It is only her modesty that prevents me from designating her as co-author.

John Diamond, M.D.
Valley Cottage
June, 1983

Before You Read This Book . . .

Get yourself a partner, friend or family member, and try the following simple test.

1.   Have your partner stand erect, right arm relaxed at his side, left arm held straight out, parallel to the floor.

2.   Face your partner and place your left hand on his right shoulder to steady him. With your right hand, grip his extended arm just above the wrist.

3.   Tell your partner that you are going to push on his arm, as he tries to resist with all his strength.

4.   Push down on his arm quickly and firmly, just hard enough to feel the spring and bounce in the arm. In nearly every case, the muscle will test strong.

Now perform the test again as your partner does one of the following things:

- Thinks of something unpleasant
- Thinks of his job
- Thinks of needing money to repair his car
- Looks at a fluorescent light
- Eats some refined sugar

The result will be dramatic. In nearly every case your partner will be unable to resist the pressure. His arm will go down easily. Although you are using the same amount of pressure, the arm goes weak.

What has happened? Somehow the thoughts and the external stimuli have reduced the life energy and caused the muscle to test weak. The same phenomenon would occur with any other muscle in the body. (This particular muscle, the deltoid, is used because it is convenient to test.) As you will learn in this book, by testing this muscle, a procedure that takes no more than a minute, it is possible to assess accurately and then to correct instantly the negative emotional attitudes affecting us at a given time. The test is basically a test of life energy.

In this book you will be shown points on the body that you can test by using the indicator muscle (the deltoid is used throughout) and one of these points. Each of these body test points, which are acupuncture meridian points, relates to a specific emotional state. Thus you will be able to determine with just a minute of testing which organs of your body are under stress; but more importantly, *you will know the specific emotional attitudes affecting you at that moment.* You can refer to the chart given you, say the corresponding positive affirmations, and reinforce them in the ways outlined—and *instantly overcome your negative mental attitudes.*

As an example, test your partner's thymus gland. See page 18. Use the deltoid muscle of your subject's left arm as the indicator, and have him place his right hand on his thymus test point. If his thymus tests strong, have him think of someone he hates, or a situation of great fear. On retesting you will find that now he tests weak. You can test other points on the body, with your partner thinking the same thoughts, and the indicator muscle will not be weak, showing us just how accurately and precisely the body points relate to specific emotional states.

Now test your partner again while he is looking at the fluorescent light. He will most likely test weak. Perform the same test again, but ask him also to think of someone he loves while you are testing him. Now you will most likely find that he tests strong!

In this book you will learn how to correct negative emotional states. For example, if your thymus tests weak, stop and think of someone you love. You will probably find that it will then test strong. There are positive thoughts and affirmations for each body point, each emotional state.

Carried out regularly, the program outlined here will not only help to keep you in correct mental balance, both in terms of correcting your emotional states and balancing your cerebral hemispheres, thereby increasing your creativity, but it will also keep your physical body healthier because all the meridians relate to your physical state as well. Therefore, with these simple techniques, which take but minutes each day, you can be well on your way to achieving positive health and optimum life energy.

Introduction

I write this book from twenty-five years of psychiatric and preventive medicine experience. Having at last reached the top of some small hill on my professional journey, I can now for the first time clearly see the goal that lies ahead of me for the attainment of perfect health for my students, and I look back into the valley from which I have thankfully arisen. Many of my years in medicine were times of disappointment, regret, and unhappiness. You will later learn precisely the meaning of these emotional states as they affect each of us and how they affected my mental and physical well-being.

I was experiencing these negative emotions because I recognized that what I was doing, and what my colleagues were doing, was not really getting anyone well. Thus it is that when I test my professional colleagues—and now I have tested many thousands of them—I find that they, too, hold negative emotions about their profession. When they think of their work experience, the job to which they are dedicated—helping mankind to reduce suffering and increase happiness—negative emotional attitudes are produced. They are not necessarily identical to those that I felt, but they are similar. Doctors go into medicine with a deep concern and love for mankind and a wish to help them overcome their suffering in the same way that a Yehudi Menuhin takes up the violin out of a great love for music and a wish to express this to the world. Yet we find today that when we test doctors, as you will be able to test yourself after reading this book, their work takes away their life energy and devitalizes them. Imagine if the same were true for Yehudi Menuhin. Imagine that every time he thought of playing the violin, of carrying out his task in life, he lost life energy!

This was the state I was in. My life energy was draining away, and I was descending lower and lower into the valley, becoming more disillusioned, knowing that I was not achieving what I had set out to do in medicine. I was "successful" with my patients, but the positive results I achieved were basically short-lived. Too much depended on me, on the visit to my office, and so little depended on the people I was treating. Something was missing in the doctor-patient relationship.

A turning point for me occurred one day when I was in the doctors' lounge of the hospital talking to a fellow psychiatrist. He announced that the only reason a certain patient of his was still alive was because of what he said to her. In essence, he believed that he was keeping her alive! Suddenly my disappointment, my regret, and my unhappiness reached a peak (or depth, as you wish), because I realized that this was what we were *all* doing. We had this idea that what *we* did kept the patient alive, or cured him. Yet we all found that most of our patients who were sick enough to be hospitalized would later need to be rehospitalized. The pattern seemed to be set. The hospitalization had helped to allay or overcome the effects of the stress of their lifestyles on them, but it was the rare case where we could raise the life energy enough to make the patient so invulnerable to stress that when he returned to his domestic and work situations he was able to remain centered and strong. The disappointment over this was one of the factors leading me into my present investigations and the writing of this book.

I had walls and walls of psychiatric and medical books and journals reminding me of how much I had learned. But in order to implement this knowledge with the patient, I first had to activate his own will to be well. I had to activate his life energy. As I later discovered, this is a property of the thymus gland. We shall discuss this relationship later.

As I continued in my practice, I watched the lines on my face develop. The line of unhappiness appeared, and the lines of self-doubt, of professional guilt, of wondering constantly what I was doing wrong. I kept asking myself why my patients were not fully matured, adult, evolved, healthy and strong, invulnerable to stress, and able to face the world with a physical and psychological shield protecting them from major environmental assault. This is what I knew was their lot, and this is what I yearned for, and worked for, and was so anxious for them to have. But it did not occur. Hence the unhappiness and the sense of professional unworthiness and guilt.

This was my valley of disillusionment, of discontent, of unhappiness, and even depression concerning my work. But nearly all the thousands of my colleagues whom I have tested are to some degree experiencing a similar valley. Soon you will understand the precise meaning of these emotional states, and you will learn how to overcome them, whatever the particular causes may be.

Some years ago my life changed, and for this I am eternally grateful. When you learn what the feeling of gratitude does to raise life energy, you will recognize the importance of that statement. For the first time, I discovered that it was possible for me accurately and instantly to find the precise emotional attitudes affecting myself or my patients, and in fact, to pinpoint them for anyone, including my professional colleagues. With a few moments of very simple testing, anyone could learn for himself or herself the emotional attitudes that were holding him or her back. Thus it was that I discovered the negative emotional attitudes in my life that were holding me back personally and professionally. This is quite remarkable. It was the first time that I or anyone could learn his or her own conscious and unconscious attitudes—accurately and instantly. And the technique is so simple.

After all my years of psychotherapeutic and psychoanalytic experience, once I was able to identify my own negative emotional states, through testing I could then discover precisely which aspects of my personal and professional life were causing them. Just as importantly, I learned how I could very quickly, almost instantaneously, overcome those hindrances. The change in my outlook on my profession was immediate and striking. At this point I began to emerge from the valley. I was beginning to find the answer to assessing and enhancing life energy.

I then started to implement this testing with patients. To my great joy—and you will learn exactly what that state implies—I found that my patients, even those cases that I had been treating for years, began making dramatic improvements and recoveries. This was primarily due to the fact that I was able to help them discover the basis of their problems.

The basis of all physical and, of course, mental problems is the emotional attitude. As long as we can keep our emotional attitudes positive, as long as there are no negative patterns holding us back and draining our life energy, then we will be, and will stay, healthy and vital. We are now able to do this. Patients can be shown exactly what their negative emotional attitudes are. I have learned and shown them that with the *power of the word* (and this you will realize when you test for yourself), they are able instantly to transmute their negative emotional states into positive ones, to completely turn around the flow of their life energy from negative to positive.

It is not a question of "working through" some psychiatric problem such as why they hate their mothers, or why they couldn't get along with their fathers, why they are impotent, or whatever. It became a question of discovering the precise negative emotional state and, through the power of the word and its underlying thought, through the positive affirmation, then instantly transforming the negative framework into the positive. After seeing by testing that it worked, that it had made the difference to them, they then carried out a simple daily program to keep themselves well. And the results I found in psychiatric cases as well as with many types of disease were quite remarkable.

The big breakthrough had occurred. It was no longer a question of my doing the work *for* the patients. Instead I now showed the patients what their negative emotional attitudes were, and through testing I showed them where the stress problems were in their lives. More accurately, *their bodies showed us.* They saw instantly what their true wishes and desires were, and they saw how they could overcome any negative obstacles. Then they had to use their own willpowers to maintain a positive balance and thus to have a complete life change. It was a matter of their assuming responsibility for themselves, of saying, in essence, "Here I am at this point in my life; I now realize things are wrong with me and that is why I have come to the doctor. My body, through his assistance and testing, has shown me the attitudes and stresses that are holding me back. Now I make the decision that I really want to be well because I have seen how it can be done." The patient would then in a sense roll up his sleeves and say, "Let's get down to work. I see what's wrong. I see what *I* have to do to correct it, and I would like your assistance in doing it."

No more was it a matter of my feeling that it was what I did that kept a patient alive. Furthermore, if the patient did not improve, I no longer felt it was my fault. The factors that were causing my professional disappointment, unhappiness, and guilt were now abolished. Instead, there was contentment with my work, happiness, and a sense of worth, fulfillment, and purpose. My major role was to help the patient's body show him what he was doing to contribute to his illness and then to help activate his willpower, his desire to get himself better.

One of the biggest problems facing present-day psychiatry is the fact that throughout all the interviews the patient is encouraged to dwell on the negative, to tell the psychiatrist about all the bad that has befallen him, enumerating this in great detail. Such psychotherapy and psychoanalysis may continue over a period of years. The end result of this for most patients is that they become more aware of what is wrong with them, but their life energy stays low —as does that of the psychiatrist. The insalubrious effects of this have previously been discussed in my book, *Your Body Doesn't Lie.* What is required is not the dwelling on the negative. We must, of course, recognize and understand the negative. But then we give it up, transmute it into the positive. In this way it is possible to heal oneself, quickly and very effectively. It will not be accomplished by continually dwelling on the negative. One of the primary forces leading me out of my own valley was the change from dwelling on the negative to embracing the positive. When this happened, the patient's life energy increased and so did mine. We each began our ascent.

The testing that I have mentioned has now been taught to many thousands of patients and students with wonderful, rewarding results, some of which you will read about in this book. We have also taught many practitioners of all branches of the healing arts with similar results. What you will learn can change your life, whether you be a layman or a professional, whether you be sick or well. For the first time you will learn of the stresses, conscious and unconscious, that are creating in you certain emotional attitudes that are holding you back. "Unconscious" means that you are not aware of these factors, but now you can find out for yourself the unconscious, unknown attitudes—the answer that is within yourself. This knowledge can take some years of psychoanalysis to discover. Now you can do it instantly. *For the first time, you can find your unconscious motivations, your true desires in any situation.*

From the little hill on which I find myself after emerging from the valley, I now see a goal in the distance, which I hope this book will help to accomplish—and that is the emancipation of mankind from doctors, in the sense of the doctor-patient relationship as we know it today. Except in traumatic and acutely ill cases, I hope to see the end of "patients" and the beginning of "students." In this way the doctor can accomplish his calling as teacher (the Latin *doceo* means I teach), and the patient can be transformed from the sufferer (the Latin *patior* means to suffer) to the student (the Latin *studere* means to study, be diligent), wanting to learn more about himself, wanting to help himself become mentally, physically, and spiritually as well as he can possibly be. This goal is becoming more and more attainable, possible, and realistic. I have written this book in an attempt to help you become a student—to share with you the results of my years of experience in medicine, psychiatry, and this newer work.

As you read this book you will learn many things about yourself and about the wondrous functioning of your own mind and body. You can learn how to be master of yourself, to find out exactly your level of emotional functioning, and what you can do to improve yourself. There is no need for you to stay in your valley. You will learn what you, and others, really think and really desire. You will be able to discover your true wishes, not just those in that small part of you of which you are consciously aware, but also those in that infinitely larger part, your unconscious. Once you know this, you will be in a position for the first time to make creative decisions about your life, all decisions—major and minor. You will be able to move in harmony with your true wishes and desires. You will be able to find your real self, to achieve your own individual goals on this earth. And you can determine these goals simply, easily, and accurately.

By learning your negative emotional states, you can transform or transmute them into positive ones. You will be able to release the energy that is now blocked inside you, trapped by your own thoughts, and become free and vigorous. This freedom will allow the emergence of your true self. Through understanding the incredible functioning of your own mind and body, you will learn of the power of thoughts to heal or to weaken. Through getting in touch with your own mind and body, you will find new freedom. You will discover what it feels like to have your whole brain working, to be on the path of creativity and health.

Most of our daily stresses, the factors that gradually wear down our energies, affect us unconsciously. Since they are not really known to us, we find it difficult to confront and surmount them.

Now, through simple testing techniques, you can identify your own unconscious stress areas and overcome them. For example, thinking itself is often a stress factor! When we have a problem, we think on it to try to solve it, yet that very act of thinking may for many people introduce a new stress—and thinking about the problem actually becomes a problem! This can be overcome—you will learn how to make your thinking creative. You can solve problems rather than perpetuate them. Furthermore, your aspiration to be creative, healthy, and fulfilled will be rekindled and you will *want* to make the choices that will be most beneficial.

You will learn how to be creative in all aspects of your life. You will be able to apply *all* your mental energies to your daily tasks rather than using predominantly one cerebral hemisphere as 95 percent of us do 95 percent of the time. Daily activities as well as life patterns become harmonious, flowing, and energizing—not just for ourselves but for others as well.

Most important of all, you will learn the power of love, how love will activate your life energy as no other force can and how it will overcome any imbalances and disharmonies in your mind or body, how love can restore you and keep you in perfect health. This is the supreme answer that is within us.

All this and more is what I mean by *psychobiological harmony.* *Harmony* is when "all parts are joined together for the good of the whole." I use the word *psycho* first since it refers to mental activity and, in the older sense of *psyche*, means soul. By *biological* I refer to all the physical properties and functions of life. By *psychobiological harmony* I refer not only to our totality of body, mind, and soul—the harmony between these three interdependent parts (if we can separate them at all)—but also to the harmonious working of all the parts within each. When all the parts of our psychological functioning are coordinated and whole within themselves, then the energy flow through our bodies will be balanced and coordinated.[1] In this state, can there be perfect health, happiness, and love.

I have learned from my years in psychiatry that illness is basically a problem of loving and of being loved. This was perhaps first stated by the Greek philosopher Empedocles about twenty-five hundred years ago.[2] What Empedocles said is so basic and yet at best we pay it lip service. He said that there were two forces that controlled the entire function of the universe, be it the universe of an individual—his body, mind, and soul, what we might call the micro-universe—or the macro-universe of the total universe. These two forces were love and hate, if you will, the positive emotions and the negative emotions.[3] When hate is operant there is chaos and disharmony. The parts that make up the total world, the sphere, are not working together for the common good. There is fragmentation, scattering, and chaos, disharmony and ill health. But when love is operant there is integration, health, and harmony. This is my philosophy and what I hope to teach with this book— how to determine the specific areas of stress, chaos, negativity that are holding you back and preventing you from being totally healthy by preventing you from totally loving, and then how to transmute these into perfect harmonious balance.

While in this brief introduction we have covered many areas generally, the details to come will clarify any questions you are beginning to form. The goals described above are immediately attainable. The ultimate beauty of this work is that you need not take my word for any of it. Everything you learn from reading this book will be a result of the testing that *you* do. Do not take my word for it—test and prove it for yourself. After all, this is the ultimate scientific proof, whether you, in your own home—your laboratory—with yourself and your friends as your research subjects, can reach the same conclusions and achieve the same results that I and my professional colleagues have been achieving with our patients and ourselves for quite some years. The final arbiter is your own body.

One of the findings that is especially exciting in this work is that we can now demonstrate specific relationships between the mind and the body—that specific emotional states affect specific body organs.[4] All doctors, particularly those concerned with psychosomatic medicine, have been interested in this concept for many years. Now it is possible to see how this occurs.

The connecting link is the acupuncture system. I am well aware that modern Western medicine has not yet "scientifically validated" the acupuncture theories to its own satisfaction, but remember that they have been practiced successfully in China and other Eastern countries for many thousands of years. Once you have seen a major surgical operation performed solely under acupuncture anesthesia, questions of the Western acceptance of acupuncture become insignificant. It is there and you see it. Through our research we have been able to demonstrate that each acupuncture channel, or meridian, relates to a specific emotional state, and by the very simple testing of these channels we can learn what our own emotional states are. This is a major breakthrough.[5] Once you have learned the simple testing techniques and balancing methods, you will have another tool to use in practicing positive health.

I shall delineate precisely and exactly each emotional attitude for each channel of acupuncture energy. You will learn the explicit meaning of the words describing these emotions, because I have found that the more clearly we understand these words, the better equipped we are to differentiate between them in our own minds. If we understand the difference between, for example, the states of unhappiness and depression, then when we find on testing that one of these states applies to us, we will be in a better position to correct the imbalance. Contained in the heritage of our language are the emotional truths of our civilization. When we know the words, we know ourselves and can help ourselves as never before.

It is my hope that as you read this book you will for the first time gain an awareness of your precise emotional balance—something almost as individual as a fingerprint. Through discovering your true self and applying your knowledge about your own mind and body, you can begin to heal yourself. So it is that I would like to see my own profession—that of doctor and particularly of psychiatrist—disappear. My colleagues and I want to be *teachers* for you. We want to teach you the wonders of your own mind and your own body, and how they interact, and to show you how to discover for yourself those factors that are holding you back, preventing the optimal expression of your true self. After you have demonstrated these findings to yourself, you will have the strength of will to release the negative emotions and embrace the positive. Then you will be truly creative and on the path to positive health and maximum energy.

While this book may appear "easy," it has important psychiatric implications. Much of the work here corroborates some of the deepest, most profound, and fundamental theories of psychoanalysis and psychotherapy. So at the same time it is both apparently superficial and yet theoretical and academic. I believe scholars in psychology, psychoanalysis, communications theory and all members of the healing profession can derive much from these findings. But the book is written for *you* to help you to maximize your potential, release your energies, and become truly creative, balanced, and of greatest service to your fellow man.

All aspects of *you* will be harmoniously integrated, balanced between body and mind (both the conscious and the unconscious facets), and spirit—psychobiological harmony. It was expressed so well by Empedocles long ago:

> in the strong recess of Harmony,
> established firm abides the rounded Sphere,
> exultant in surrounding Solitude.

I hope that you will learn how to achieve this as you correct your negativities and activate your life energy.

GOAL
Positive Health
Harmony
Creativity

THYMUS
Love   Hate
Faith   Envy
Gratitude   Fear
Trust
Courage

LEFT HEMISPHERE
Reality
"Maths"
Conscious
"Neurosis"

RIGHT HEMISPHERE
Fantasy   Dreams
"Music"
Unconscious
"Psychosis"

Organ	Positive	Negative
CIRCULATION-SEX	Renunciation of Past, Generosity, Relaxation	Jealousy, Sexual Tension, Regret, Remorse
HEART	Love, Forgiveness	Anger
STOMACH	Contentment	Disappointment, Disgust, Greed
THYROID	Lightness	Heaviness, Depression
SMALL INTESTINE	Joy	Sorrow, Sadness
BLADDER	Peace, Harmony	Restlessness, Impatience

Organ	Positive	Negative
LUNG	Tolerance	Intolerance
LIVER	Happiness	Unhappiness
GALL BLADDER	Love	Rage
SPLEEN	Faith in Future	Anxiety about Future
KIDNEY	Sexual Security	Sexual Indecision
LARGE INTESTINE	Self-Worth	Guilt

Part I

The Goal

THE GOAL

Life Energy
Positive Health
Harmony
Creativity
Effective Communication
Insight

The Goal

It is every person's birthright to develop their true potential and aspire to evolve fully. This is our goal along the path of life and it is toward the goal that we may move if we cultivate only positive emotional attitudes and positive physical, mental and spiritual health.

Reaching toward the goal can be achieved by reducing stress, raising life energy, balancing the cerebral hemispheres, gaining true creativity, activating the thymus gland, and balancing the acupuncture meridians. In sum, eliminating the negative and promoting the positive will help bring about the attainment of the goal.

Among the most important measures we can take in order to achieve the goal is to reduce stress. This is vital. Depending on the nature of the stimulus, there are basically three effects of stress on the body: reduction of thymus activity and overall life energy, cerebral imbalance, and meridian imbalance caused by a specific negative emotional attitude created by the stress. And over the years, stress allows negative emotional patterns to be established and set. This is the root of all disease, the diminution of life energy.

But it is to health that we aspire and so our goal is to raise the life energy, not permit it to dwindle. And so our research includes the study and delineation of emotional attitudes, stress, and other factors that lead to a diminution of life energy. From this, we can develop methods for overcoming these factors and raise the life energy.

How Do We Define Life Energy?

It is life energy that causes us to grow. It is life energy that enables us to heal. Hippocrates called it the *vis medicatrix naturae* —the healing power of nature. Paracelsus spoke of it as the Archaeus. It is Prana, Chi, Spirit. It evokes the true and only healing, that which occurs from within. A drug may relieve the symptoms of a disease but it does not cure. The true cure always involves a major change in the person's attitude toward himself and toward life.

Life energy enters our body through the breath. It is life energy that flows through the acupuncture meridians and vitalizes the organs and tissues. An imbalance of the flow of this life energy leads ultimately to disease. As you will learn, these imbalances come about as a result of physical and psychological factors. Through your mental powers you have the ability to rebalance the flow of life energy throughout your body and thus combat disease and keep yourself well. Life energy is breath.[1] Life energy is spirit.[2]

According to the *Oxford English Dictionary, spirit* is the animating or vital principle in man and animals; that which gives life to the physical organs; the breath of life. Thus Milton in *Paradise Lost* wrote, "The pure breath of Life, the Spirit of Man." This life-giving essence, this activating factor underlying our maturation and our vitality, our very being, is mentioned in Genesis: "Then the Lord God formed a man from the dust of the ground and breathed into his nostrils the breath of life. Thus the man became a living creature." That which causes us to live is life energy, the spirit.

Throughout the Bible we find references to the relationship between breath and spirit. The Hebrew term *rûah* comes from a Semitic root, *rûh*, signifying "to breathe," "to blow." The primary signification of *rûah* is "air in motion," as wind or breath, and the general idea which is common to nearly all its usages is "power in manifestation, or energy."[3] In Ezekiel 37:5 we read, "I will put breath into you, and you shall live," and in I Corinthians 6:10, "Do you not know that your body is a shrine of the indwelling Holy Spirit, and the Spirit is God's gift to you?"

When we are healthy we are filled with life energy, with spirit, with love. As Shakespeare wrote, "O spirit of love, the spirit which heals." It is the spirit pervading the mind and body which is the healing force within us. When we are diseased, there will be an imbalance of Chi, of life energy, of spirit, affecting a specific acupuncture meridian, leading to particular psychological and physical problems and ultimately to disease. In this book you will learn how to overcome these energy imbalances and reactivate the life energy.

Our English word *spirit* comes from the Latin *spirare,* to breathe. The Latin word *spiritus* means breath, breath of a god, inspiration, breath of life, the soul. There would appear to be a primary root, what you might call an *sp* root, from which so many words relating to spirit have derived—spread, spray, spatter, spittle, spume, spit, spurt, sparse, sprinkle, spring, spry, disperse, esprit, spiratic, spray, sprinkle, spur, sputter, spirtle, splutter, split, sperm, speech, inspiration, aspiration, respiration, and many others. We see clearly in spit, spark, sperm, and speech, the prevailing underlying idea of the movement of organic, living matter by a breathlike expulsory act to a new site where it may grow and develop. Water springs from the ground and gives forth life. A spark is struck and starts a fire where it lands. A seed sprouts. Sperm are released and create new life, as may our speech. The spirit is the vital principle of life itself which by breathing life into us causes us to live and grow and love.

The Research procedure involves the accurate testing of the strength of an indicator muscle to assess the effects of nearly all stimuli—physical or psychological, internal or external—on the human body. It is basically a test of life energy, and can be used to gauge the relative functioning of the acupuncture meridians. Each acupuncture meridian is associated with specific muscles of facial expression, gesture, and vocalization.[4] Most importantly for our present purposes, each meridian is also associated with a specific negative and a specific positive emotional state. Thus, through implementing this testing technique, it is possible to determine which emotional states are most affecting each of us, both mentally and physically, at any given time. We have found that, by bringing this to the person's attention and by using imagery techniques, the changes that can be produced are immediate and immediately apparent.

Five of the primary tenets upon which our approach to positive health rest recognize:

1. *the critical importance of the reduction of stress* and the concomitant emotional attitudes. Disease is seen as arising from stress that causes a general reduction in life energy and specific energy imbalances throughout the body.
2. *the essential role of primary prevention*—prevention *before* pathological change, either mental or physical. At this early stage the energy imbalances may be described as fluid or dynamic and readily amenable to correction. If the stress is prevented, if the mental attitudes are changed, then primary prevention will be operant and disease will not occur.
3. *the individual's responsibility for taking charge of one's own health,* and one's own way through life. In this context the role of the so-called doctor is that of teacher—to explain and to help the individual to see exactly what he is doing to lower his own healing energies. The individual has superimposed maladaptive behavioral patterns upon himself which have pulled him away from his natural, "normal" state, and he must recognize and alter them.
4. *that great healing forces exist within us* and in nature to enable repair to occur once the stress is reduced and the negative attitudes are corrected. It is recognized that natural methods are essential since unnatural methods often diminish life energy. While these unnatural methods may provide symptomatic relief, they ultimately lower the life energy, retard the true healing process, and do nothing to correct the stress and the attitudinal problems that are at the base of the disease patterns.
5. *that most problems begin at an energy level.* The first physical manifestation of imbalance within the body is at an energy level and corrections can be made at this level. On top of this are the metabolic, structural, and nutritional problems that also require attention.

From these five tenets we can see how disease begins. The specific negative emotional attitudes that we harbor give rise to stress. Stress, in turn, causes a reduction of life energy and energy imbalances which ultimately lead to disease. The disease did not just "appear" from nowhere. It actually began at an energy level.

For example, suppose that someone has a predominant emotional attitude of unhappiness. (I will give an exact definition of this emotional state later.) In other words, whenever this person is placed in a stressful situation, he will tend to react by becoming unhappy.

Now, if this emotional state continues, there will be a breakdown of the harmonious functioning of his cerebral hemispheres—that is, his body will be under stress. He will therefore be both physically and psychologically unable to cope with the stress as well as he could if that emotional attitude did not exist. Finally, the stress on his body will lead to a dimunition of energy in the specific acupuncture meridian that relates to unhappiness. This meridian, as you will soon learn to test, is the liver meridian.

I am not suggesting that all liver disease is caused by unhappiness. But I am stating that in most cases of liver disease we do find impairment of the liver meridian as well as the specific emotional state of unhappiness. More importantly, I am proposing that if we can instantly correct the emotional state of unhappiness—as we can—we will function better at all times, we will not be stressed, and we will not interfere with the energy flow in the liver meridian. By preventing the stress, we will thus prevent energy impairment in the liver itself, which may ultimately have led to liver disease.

By applying what you have learned, you will be able to find out specifically how to eliminate or at least reduce the effects on you of the trouble spots in your life—those factors that are lowering your vital life energy day after day.

Remember, *it is not normal to get sick*, but unfortunately it is very common. Gradually people begin to expect poor health. They take out insurance policies in anticipation of a heart attack, arthritis, diabetes, or cancer that they feel is inevitable.

One very striking example of the way in which "normal" and "average" have become confused is apparent to me every time I look at a lab report detailing certain findings, such as the serum cholesterol level. Just a few years ago the acceptable range of this measure was 150–220 mgm percent. Then it became 150–250. Now it is 150–300. Imagine my dismay when I heard of a doctor telling his patient, "Well, your cholesterol is two-ninety, but don't worry. It's normal now." A few years ago it would *not* have been considered normal. As the level of serum cholesterol for the general population continues to increase, the accepted upper limit also increases. This does not mean that suddenly it is "normal" to have a cholesterol measure of, say, 285. It means only that it is becoming average. What does this say about our overall level of health?

Many people today tend to view disease as some foreign assault that suddenly "attacks" us almost without reason. We speak of a heart *attack*, or of being *stricken* with pneumonia or cancer. We find it very hard to realize that we create our own diseases—that a disease, when it occurs, is a result of our whole style and pattern of life. Everything we have inhaled, eaten, done or not done, and thought or not thought over all the years of our lives culminates in the illness. So, far from feeling as if we were just walking down the street minding our own business when suddenly a falling piece of masonry hits us on the head, we must recognize that most disease is of our own doing. Certainly some of the more virulent and dangerous elements in our environment that are now assaulting us are not of our own particular doing. But even there, to some extent, if we were to raise our life energy through positive health practices, we could prevent at least some if not most of the deleterious effects.

The first stage in prevention is to assume responsibility for ourselves and to accept our part in whatever happens to us. If we are in an accident, then we must ask at what level we were actually responsible for that accident. In the Australian army, no matter how innocent a driver would be found in civilian court, the army held him negligent for having become involved in that accident. He was deemed negligent for not having driven more defensively, for not having thought, in essence, more "preventively."

Thus whenever I or my patients and students become sick, I ask, and I suggest that they ask, "What have I done to produce this? What imbalances have I produced in the energy systems throughout my body that ultimately have manifested themselves in this physical disease?" Of course it may take many years for a physical disease to manifest itself. In all the time preceding this manifestation, the patterns are being formed in the same way as patterns of our future careers are laid down in our early years of schooling—which children shall have further academic education, which shall attend technical school, and so on. As we are thus *streamed* through life in terms of our employment, so we also have streams throughout life in terms of the diseases that we are likely to develop. These patterns of predisposition to disease are a result of specific energy imbalances in specific acupuncture meridian systems throughout the body.

The precipitating factor causing the initial energy imbalance will always be stress, physical or mental. The first result of that stress will always be a reduction of life energy. Coincidental with this, a specific negative emotional attitude will be created. It may be that of unhappiness, depression, anger, or any of the others that you will find described in later chapters. Each of these emotional attitudes relates to a specific acupuncture energy channel, or meridian, in the body, tending to cause an imbalance of life energy in the organs subserved by each meridian. (Remember that each me-

ridian serves one or more organs and is called by the name of the
organs. Hence we have names such as spleen meridian, bladder
meridian, and so forth.)

If these negative emotional attitudes persist, the energy imbalances in the associated meridian(s) will persist and ultimately lead
to disease. Let me give you a specific example. In my years in
psychiatry and psychosomatic medicine, I found, as many other
psychiatrists and cardiologists have found, that cardiac patients
have great difficulty in dealing with anger. This is so before they
have the heart attack and is more pronounced after the heart attack,
when many of them fear that to become overtly angry could precipitate another heart attack. I remember one patient who got married
for the first time when he was in his forties. He married the widow
of one of his best friends. He had promised his old army mate as
he lay dying that he would look after his widow. She, as he well
knew, had always been a difficult wife to his friend. Now she pro-
ceeded to be the same with him. She was constantly shouting at
him, berating and ridiculing him, continually comparing him un-
favorably with her first husband, criticizing his subordinate position at work, condemning his sexual performance, and so forth. If
he had known the phrase, he would have called her "a regular
Xanthippe."[5]

I saw him only a few times before his heart attack. Whenever I
tried to get him to see that underneath his very calm exterior he
was very, very angry whenever he mentioned his wife, he would
protest that he did not feel angry with her at all. Although he certainly had anger toward her surging through his body, he did not
feel it. However, it was so obvious—in his white face and clenched
knuckles, particularly whenever he talked about how she belittled
his sexual performance, what she referred to as his "husbandly
duties." The heart attack occurred shortly after one of her attacks
on his sexuality. I next saw him some months later, when it was
even more difficult for him to recognize his anger toward her.
Whenever I tried to bring it up in our discussions no matter how
subtly, he would make a movement with his head of both turning
away and sort of nodding, half-saying yes and half-saying no, while
simultaneously doing his best to dismiss it. He could not deal with
his internal anger. When I pointed out to him how much his wife
had mistreated him, he would say, "Well, Doc," with that flick of
the head, "she's had a hard life and who am I to judge her?" or
some equally ineffectual platitude.

It took quite a time in therapy before this man finally came to grips with his anger toward his wife. This was primarily because he was, of course, haunted by memories of his heart attack and fearful that he would have another. The memory of his heart attack —with him lying on the floor of a train clutching his chest in pain, staring up at all the passengers looking down at him from what seemed to be a very great height—was so fixed in his mind that he dared not ever face up to his anger. He feared he would precipitate another heart attack and he would have to relive that nightmare.

This story, with perhaps a few minor changes, could be told by any psychiatrist who has tried to work with cardiac cases.

The underlying specific emotional state in most if not all such cases is that of anger—chronic, ongoing, festering anger. This anger is often conscious, but also frequently unconscious—that is, not known to the patient. I say unconscious because he is so unable to deal with it that he represses it, pushes it down, out of his mind.

What we will find in most people who have cardiac problems is that one of the acupuncture meridians that constantly tests weak will be the heart meridian. This is not surprising. What is surprising is that whenever this meridian tests weak, if the patient then says, "I am not angry, I forgive," it will instantly be found that the meridian tests strong. If this affirmation is repeated often enough, with feeling, over a period of time, the heart meridian will cease to test weak, indicating that the energy has rebalanced and the body is now going about repairing any damage as best it can.

In people who do not seem to have cardiac problems it will also be found that if they say, "I am angry," then their heart meridian (which previously tested strong) will test weak. Thus all of us have a tendency to heart-meridian energy imbalances whenever we feel angry.

From the above example comes a very important finding. Just saying we are angry, or conversely, that we forgive, somehow creates within us a negative or positive emotional state and causes a change in the specific acupuncture meridian involved. The emotion of anger creates a negative energy imbalance in the heart meridian; merely by saying "I am angry" you can create a negative energy imbalance in that meridian. We must not underestimate the power of the word and its great potential for good, as we have demonstrated. Saying "I forgive" restores the heart meridian to its proper energy balance.

I do not mean to imply that any time someone's heart meridian tests weak it means he or she has heart disease or is going to have a coronary occlusion. What I am saying is that you will always find in such cases that there is the negative emotion of anger which is interfering with life energy, which is affecting the heart meridian and to some extent the heart, and which can be corrected by the appropriate affirmation. Should this energy imbalance, this unconscious emotional attitude of anger, persist for a long period of time, then it can lead, and often does lead, to cardiac disease. This is the basic premise of psychosomatic medicine.

Now we can see *how* the emotion leads to the heart disease—through the acupuncture system. We can also see how to prevent it. If we overcome our anger, which can be very simply accomplished as we will learn, then we will never hold the energy problems for long in the meridian, therefore we will not be predisposed to a heart attack.

This is what I mean by prevention. *By continually monitoring our meridian states, and instantly correcting, through the appropriate positive thought, any that are out of balance, we can keep our life energy high and balanced and thus prevent disease.* In this context I should point out again that the ancients knew psychosomatic medicine. As the Greeks knew that the life energy *(thymos)* was related to the thymus gland, so it was known that angry people were predisposed to heart disease.

There is a common origin through most of European civilization in the history of the words *anger* and *angina*. This is true not only in the history of the word throughout our Indo-European civilization, but also in terms of the history of the disease in the individual.

Having overcome the negative emotional states, you are in a position to practice true prevention. You will find that the thymus gland tests strong, that the life energy has been raised, and that the cerebral hemispheres are balanced in their functioning, thus allowing creativity. You are on the road to positive health—not just preventing yourself from being sick, but starting to be positively well.

For most of us this is the first time we really feel energy surging through our bodies. We begin to be alert, suddenly able to be creative in all our daily activities. The change is beautiful and gratifying. I have seen it so many times in patients and students, and it is a wondrous and inspiring experience when a patient who has been struggling with the handicap of cerebral imbalance, struggling with his formal education or struggling to solve his problems at work, or struggling with life in general, begins to experience this phenomenon. He becomes truly creative. He walks easily where before he stumbled. Life becomes exciting, full, rich, and manageable.

This is what we are trying to achieve. First we recognize the specific emotional states that are depleting our life energies, deactivating our thymus glands, and leading to cerebral hemisphere functional imbalances. We recognize that this makes it hard for us to solve our problems and creates other emotional imbalances, which then lead to specific energy imbalances in the acupuncture meridians supplying energy to all the organs and muscles of our bodies. If we correct these emotional imbalances early, we stay healthy. If we do not correct them, we sink into a state that is now considered normal but which is far from normal—the state of going from illness to illness, from operation to operation, living short, unproductive, uncreative, disease-ridden lives. None of this is normal. None of this is what was intended for us.

Our heritage is to lead long, healthy, happy, fully productive and creative lives. We must get away from the working model of disease and non-disease and create for ourselves a new health model in which illness as we now know it has no place. This we can do when our life energy is high and when the energy systems of our bodies are balanced. The easiest way to achieve this is to correct the specific emotional attitudes that are a result of stress and lead to energy imbalances throughout the body.

What we must now learn is how to identify and correct these emotional attitudes early. But before we learn this, we must first turn our attentions to the controller of the energy of the body, the thymus gland.

Part II

The Thymus

THYMUS

Love	Hate
Faith	Envy
Gratitude	Fear
Trust	
Courage	

The Thymus Gland

Medical science is at last recognizing what the Greeks knew thousands of years ago, that the thymus gland controls the life energy of the body. In fact the Greek word *thymos* actually meant life energy. According to far Eastern teaching, "there is a subtle energy manifestation circulating in the viscera, in the flesh, and ultimately permeating every living cell and tissue. The name given to this energy form, at this particular level, is translated as Life Force (Vital Force, Vital Energy)." [1]

The thymus gland lies just beneath the upper part of the breastbone in the middle of the chest. Until the 1950s little was understood about the thymus, although there had been clues to its function for many years. The standard teaching was that the thymus gland had no function at all in the adult, a delusion fostered by the fact that during autopsy the thymus was usually found to be quite small and atrophied. This is because the thymus gland, in response to acute stress such as an infection, can shrivel to half its size in twenty-four hours. Eventually it was realized that the thymus shrinks rapidly during serious illness or great physical stress. The thymus plays a vital role in the body's immune system.

The thymus gland monitors and regulates energy flow throughout the body's energy system, initiating instantaneous corrections to overcome imbalances as they occur so as to achieve a rebalancing and harmony of life energy. Further, it is the link between mind and body, being the first organ to be affected by mental attitudes and stress. A healthy, active thymus gland makes for vibrant and positive health.

15

But here I want to concentrate exclusively on the mental aspects of the thymus gland because, as we know, most disease starts at the mental level, before it becomes physical.

As I write, I learn of the sudden, tragic, accidental death of the young adopted daughter of a dear friend. When I first knew her, whenever her father or I tested her, she was weak on test-touching her thymus gland. (You will know shortly what this means and how you can do it for yourself). In Betsy's case, this diminution of life energy came, as she readily admitted, from the extreme anger—in fact even hatred—that she felt toward her older sisters. This hatred was reflected in many of her actions toward them and was a cause of great concern to her parents. When I first tested Betsy I explained that the thymus testing weak indicated that she probably felt very angry (I declined to use the word "hateful") toward someone. She readily said, "Yes, toward my sisters." Then I asked her to think about loving them. Suddenly her thymus tested strong. She turned to me and, with her bright, sharp eyes focused intently on me, asked, "What did that mean?" I explained, "Betsy, it means that whenever you are holding such thoughts about your sisters, you are suffering much more than they are. If you are going to be healthy and strong and have a happy, contented, fulfilled life, you should, as your body is telling you, think of loving your sisters. You saw for yourself the difference it made to your energy." Being young, and relatively free from all the overlying webs and nets of restriction against change under which adults labor, she said, "Okay, I'll try it. If it makes me strong, I'll do it." When I tested her again later that same day, her thymus was strong.

Over the next year or so whenever her father or I tested her, her thymus always tested strong. The change in her behavior and in all aspects of her life—both in school and at home—was dramatic. She had turned from hate to love; from underactive thymus to active thymus; from going downhill to going uphill; to embracing life at its fullest. And now she is suddenly dead. Her family and I take some consolation from the fact that she died in a much better state than had this occurred a year or so before. She died a better person; she died, even at such a young age, in many ways fulfilled. She had risen above the greatest obstacles that she had to face in her life— that of being adopted and that of feeling rejected by her older sisters. And she rose above these magnificently.

What am I to tell her parents? How am I to counsel them? What is to be done in such a situation? Throughout my years of practice, I have always looked in times of tragedy for what is positive, for what we can do to gain from and learn through the experience. We cannot bring Betsy back to life, and we have to wait for time and life energy to repair the physical damage done to the other family members. But we can work with their spirits, their emotional attitudes.

Most people when faced with tragedy—be it personal illness or the death of a close relative—respond to the event with underactivity of the thymus, with reduction of life energy. They therefore intensify the very pathological processes that they most need to overcome. An important question for the parents is how to keep their thymus glands active, how to keep their life energy up. To some extent it is being done and will continue to be done by recognizing how much Betsy herself, in her brief life, overcame her own problems. They can use her as an example to help themselves overcome their loss. This is not to say that they should not face up to the tragedy and acknowledge the seriousness of the situation; of course they should. But there are, even in this great tragedy, positive aspects.

There should be legitimate pride and satisfaction in the way in which they brought her up, for the love and respect the family and all of their close friends had for her. The love that they have for her will sustain them, and their thymus glands will test strong during this time of crisis. As long as this is the case, they will more readily and easily recover from this tragedy. Otherwise, the aftereffects will linger on and on, will become reflected in fixed emotional attitudes, fixed meridian imbalances, and then perhaps—as is so often the case—in physical disease.

The first response of the body to stress, as Hans Selye showed in *The Stress of Life*,[2] is shrinkage of the thymus gland. But even before this physical response, there is an immediate reduction of life energy. The thymus gland will test weak. When the stress is removed, the thymus gland will test strong again. Wherever we find an emotional imbalance, or any energy imbalance, or any disease process, we will almost invariably find the thymus gland testing weak. As the thymus gland is activated a change in the life energy of the individual occurs. But the healing forces within, the true healing power of nature, can effect the true cure.

Let me explain now how to test the thymus. I will begin with a review of the testing technique described at the beginning of this book. As you will recall, it takes two people to perform the deltoid test.[3] Choose a friend or a family member, whom we will call your subject, for testing.

1. Have the subject stand erect, right arm relaxed at his side, left arm held out parallel to the floor, elbow straight.
2. Face the subject and place your left hand on his right shoulder to steady him. Then place your right hand on the subject's extended left arm just above the wrist.
3. Tell the subject you are going to try to push his arm down as he resists with all his strength.
4. Push down on his arm fairly quickly, firmly, and evenly. The idea is to push just hard enough to test the spring and bounce in the arm, not so hard that the muscle becomes fatigued. It is not a question of who is stronger, but of whether the muscle can "lock" the shoulder joint against the push.

    Note: Do not smile when you are conducting the test or are yourself being tested, as the thymus will then test strong.

    Unless there is a physical problem with the muscle, it will test strong. (Any muscle may be used for testing. The middle part of the deltoid is the easiest and most convenient one to use as an indicator of the body's energy supply. A single muscle used for testing is called an *indicator muscle*.)
5. Have your subject place the fingertips of his free hand on the skin over the point where the second rib joins the breastbone (the sternomanubrial joint). This point (see p. 19) is directly over the thymus gland. Now, with your subject touching the thymus point, test the indicator muscle again. Is it still strong, or has it gone weak? Suppose it has gone weak. What does that mean?

What has happened is this: You have found a muscle, called an indicator muscle, to be strong "in the clear"—that is, without the subject's touching any part of his body with his free hand. However, when you had the subject put his hand on the specific test point, the indicator muscle tested weak, meaning that the energy supply to the subject's thymus gland is insufficient and his thymus gland is underactive at the moment. If his indicator muscle remained strong when he touched the thymus point, there was no evidence of energy imbalance involving his thymus gland, as revealed by the test, at that time.

How do we know it is the thymus gland that we are testing? All we need to do is to have the subject chew one tablet of thymus extract. The indicator muscle will now test strong. Other glandular extracts will not have this effect.

It requires experience and practice to do the testing reliably and accurately. It is simple, but it must be done precisely.

Try this test: Instead of having your subject test-touch the thy-

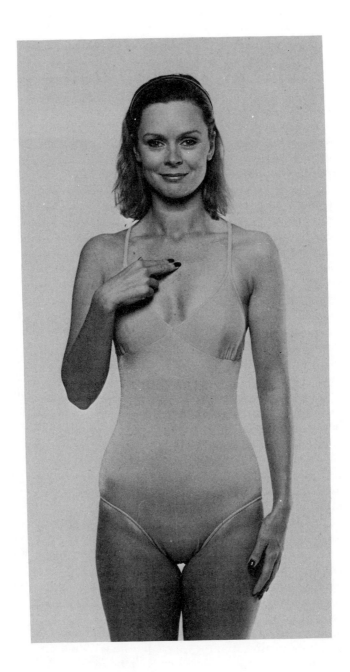

The test point for the thymus gland.

mus point, have him test-touch other places on the body at random. In other words, test the indicator muscle each time your subject touches a different point. Chances are that touching these other points will not cause the indicator muscle to go weak. It is where the fingertips are placed—the exact test-touch position—that is critical. A weak muscle reaction to test-touching shows that this specific point on the subject's body is functioning under the stress of an energy imbalance.

Suppose your subject's thymus gland point tested strong initially. Test again to confirm this result. Then have him think of a catastrophe, such as being in an automobile accident, and test again. What has happened? Usually, if not invariably, the thymus gland will test weak. Next, ask your subject to think of someone he hates. The thymus gland will continue to test weak. Then ask him to think of someone he loves. Instantly, he will test strong. You can see how quickly we can make significant findings about the mind and the body through the implementation of this test.

How do we know that the thymus controls all the acupuncture energy throughout the body? As you learn how to test for the energy in the acupuncture meridians, you will find that any meridian whose energy tests imbalanced will be automatically corrected and rebalanced when the thymus is activated. Whether it be activated by techniques such as I have described in *Your Body Doesn't Lie* —for example, the thymus thump or reading of poetry to balance the hemispheres—or whether it is activated by saying or even thinking the positive emotional affirmations for the thymus gland as described in this book, as a result of this activation you will find that any energy imbalances in the body will be automatically corrected. This is why we call the thymus the master switch, the master controller, of the acupuncture energy system of the body.

The thymus also reflects our will to be well. Whenever the thymus tests weak, it means we don't have sufficient will to be well. Our life energy is not high enough to carry out the healing processes. This finding has been of great value in clinical practice. The doctor's first goal must be to activate the patient's will to be well. Unless this is done, then all we can do, which is what medicine seems to be achieving at the moment, is produce a society of "walking dead." The wondrous advances of modern medicine are keeping people alive, but they have no life within them. They have no vitality. They still move, they still breathe, but they are not really alive. This is because we have forgotten that the true healing power comes from within. Medications are of value when used in conjunction with measures that activate the patient's life energy. That is why I advocate that the first treatment should be to get the patient's will to be well activated—to activate the thymus gland. Then the specific treatment should be given. Much more dramatic changes can occur because the will to be well has been mobilized. We do not want to create a species of zombie, having no life and vitality, existing from illness to illness, from wonder drug to wonder drug. The true wonder drug is the power and the vitality that is within us, our will to be well.

I have seen time and time again the difference that this can make in clinical practice. I recall the first two patients I ever had as an intern. They were in beds side by side. Both were paraplegic as a result of automobile accidents; both developed the same infection from the same organism. Each patient was given the same antibiotic. In a week one was cured and the other was dead. I asked my senior, "Why, why this difference?" He shrugged and said, "That's what patients are like. Some have it and some don't." He did not know, nor did I know until much later, that what he meant by "it" was life energy, the will to be well.

When I sat down and thought about these two patients very carefully, it was quite obvious which one had "it" and which one did not. The one who survived had gone ahead with his plans to marry his fiancée. He did his correspondence courses; he was bright and cheerful in the ward, always doing his exercises, always participating fully in his therapy, thinking and planning for the future.

The one who did not have "it" literally turned his face to the wall, away from the world. His one major activity was his correspondence with his lawyer. He was trying to get more money as compensation for his accident—with which he was becoming more and more obsessed. He broke off his relationship with his girlfriend, he would not participate in his therapy, nor would he participate in any correspondence courses. In essence, he had lost the will to be well. And when he was given the equal stress, the same organism, he succumbed and the other lived. These two people are good examples of what we could call high-thymus and low-thymus types. One has the will to be well and one does not. One can survive stresses that may overwhelm the other.

I knew a devoted couple who had been married for fifty-five years. I visited the husband a few months after the sudden death of his wife. He was as vigorous as ever, even more so. In addition to tending to his half-acre vegetable garden plot and taking care of all the maintenance on the house and the car, he assumed and managed his deceased wife's chores. He had taught himself to cook and delighted in showing me how to bargain-hunt in the supermarket. Of course, he was at times a little sad, a little tearful, but he was an amazing man and an example to his community of how one can rise above tragedy. In my practice I have often seen cases where, after long years of marriage, the surviving partner, within months or sometimes even weeks of the partner's death, also died. But here was the opposite. When I tested him his thymus was strong. I asked him his secret. Basically a very religious man, he answered, "Well, God has given me this new task, to manage on my own, and it's up to me to do it." So he rolled up his sleeves and went about his extra tasks, secure in his faith. He was a high-thymus man, living a highly exemplary life.

I remember a dear patient who had a series of tragic illnesses befall him. In particular, he had an un-united fracture of his arm. For the past three years he had been forced to use a sling and cast arrangement on his arm that considerably reduced his activity. Numerous means had been tried to stimulate the bone to grow together again, but all had failed. In his heart of hearts he knew that for the rest of his life his arm would be useless. Tragically, he also developed leukemia, which he knew in view of its fulminating nature would probably be fatal.

When I first met him, he was incredibly depressed. He saw no point in living and was really not far from suicidal. He was very angry, difficult to manage, and deeply resentful of what had happened to him. Naturally, his thymus tested weak. When I went through the usual procedures with him—as you will learn to do for yourself—he changed very rapidly. Thereafter, his thymus tested strong.

One day he said to me, "I don't know whether I'm going to live or die, whether I'm going to be able to activate my life energy to overcome these very serious illnesses, but I do know I have a different attitude toward life and death." He said, "I recognize that what I must do is to live my life as best I can, to get on with my daily work, and not to be angry and resentful for what has happened to me, but to try somehow to grow with this, to see this as some part of my ongoing evolution." That same day someone remarked to me, "I don't know how long he will live, but he certainly will die a saint."

It has been some years now since he died, but we who knew him still think of him with great love and respect. He spoke to me from his hospital bed shortly before he died. His spirits were high, and he said he had developed new faith and trust. He died a brave and courageous man, a saint, and as such we remember him.

I have never yet tested a smoker whose thymus tested strong and active. Every time a smoker lights up he knows, as it says on the package, that it will damage his health—yet he chooses to smoke. The will to be well has been replaced by the desire to go with the immediate gratification. I have found that the way to help people give up smoking is not to terrorize them with what will happen to them if they continue to smoke, thereby heightening their fears, because it is deep and unconscious fear that is keeping their thymus activity low. This fear is destroying the will to be well and thus actually influencing them to continue to smoke. Fear plays into the hands of the negative. Instead I point out to them the positive sides and discuss the concepts of life energy and optimum health.

I remember a man who consulted me after having been told that he had an untreatable disease which was almost always fatal. I suggested to him that even so, there were many things he could do to raise his life energy and which could only be of benefit to him— for example, improving his nutrition, stopping drinking, and stopping smoking. He said, "Well, I'm going to die from the disease anyway, so why not at least do the things that I find pleasurable until I die." This is a common occurrence in cases that have been diagnosed as fatal. It is the absence of the will to be well, the resignation, as demonstrated by this remark, that in my opinion lowered his life energy, or at least predisposed him to the illness in the beginning.

There are no magic pills. What is required is hard work—doing all the things that can raise one's life energy so the body can set about healing itself. As long as we subscribe to the hedonistic course, as long as we say, "Well, I'm going to die anyway so I may as well enjoy myself," then there is little that can be done. The man in our example does not even realize that real pleasure comes from doing things that *are* good, not from doing things that *feel* good. As Sir Walter Scott said on his deathbed to his biographer, "Lead a good life, Lockey. When you are where I am, that's all that matters."

In my practice I have rarely had a patient stay in treatment who did not stop smoking after a few weeks of thymus activation. Once the will to be well is activated, we no longer want to do the things that reduce our life energy.

The primary aim of my medical work for many years has been to activate this will to be well, this life energy, this *thymos*—to activate the thymus gland so that people will truly want to be well. It is easy to want to be well when we are not sick, but as soon as our energy starts to slip, so does our motivation. In fact, we could say that the first symptom of illness is the loss of the will to be well. For example, a patient told me, "Doctor, I know Vitamin C will help me when I have a cold, but when I'm sick I just feel too ill to reach over from my bed to get them." How many doctors have had patients tell them, "I was too sick to come for treatment"?

High-thymus types, high life-energy types, are those who are dwelling in the positive. With any tragedy, they are trying to see what they can salvage, how they can gain and prosper. Recently, a middle-aged female friend of mine who has been chronically ill for many years was told that her mother had died suddenly from a heart attack. I saw her just a few moments afterward as she was on her way to the family home. Her thymus, as you might expect, tested weak. I pointed out to her that if her life energy was low, she could be of little help to those around her, particularly her elderly father, who would most need her strength and her assistance. In this time of tragedy, she then found a definite goal for which to strive. That was for her first to remember all the wonderful attributes of her mother and how much she had loved her, and then to assume her new calling, to come forward and take over the role as the responsible senior female in the large family circle—from being the little daughter to being the substitute mother. Instantly her will to be well, her will to triumph over the tragedy, asserted itself. Her thymus tested strong. With a smile on her face and a look of quiet, placid determination, she left to arrange for the funeral, assuming her new role. She has continued to act in this role. Her father has told me that he was amazed at how much strength she had gained since her mother died and how she seemed like a new woman. Out of the tragedy she grew anew; she triumphed. This is what the high-thymus type can do.

In contrast, the low-thymus type is well known to us all. He seems to have chosen what he feels is the easiest path, the path of least resistance, the path of passively accepting what is known to be beneath his optimal level of functioning. Years after a tragedy such as described above, the low-thymus type is still depressed, still has not recovered from the tragedy. I know a woman whose husband died twenty-five years ago. She has virtually been a recluse since he died. She still has his bed, which is beside hers, made up as if waiting for him to return. She still talks incessantly of the past when he was alive. His death killed her. This is low-thymus activity. Finally, after all these years, she is now beginning to activate her thymus; through her work with me, she has made a decision to find a new life for herself. She said, "You know, there are things I'm doing today, wonderful things, that I couldn't have done when my husband was alive." She has developed from a low-thymus type to a high-thymus type.

If, as I suggest, disease occurs as a result of long-term thymus underactivity, then imagine how much worse it is once the patient has been given a diagnosis by the doctor—what a terrible "gift." In addition to his own internal energy problems, which have led to the thymus underactivity and ultimately to the disease, he has to cope with the added fear and dread of the diagnosis. Thus, I know that any patient who comes to me with a medical diagnosis is going to have thymus underactivity. The first task is to overcome the fear of the disease that has been unfortunately and unintentionally given to him by his doctor. Until this fear is recognized and overcome, there can be no will to be well because the will to be well means a conquering of fear, a conquering of all negative emotions. As Friedrich Hoffmann said in 1695, "Unrestrained emotion disturbs the mixture of the blood and humors, brings about an uneven movement of the spirits, produces disproportion and obstructions, and thus may act as the cause of severe diseases. . . . Nothing shortens life or increases diseases more than distorted emotions."[4]

Love and Hate, The Two Primary Emotions

While there are many emotions, there are essentially only two primary ones. These are love and hate in their various and deepest manifestations. And while the organs of the body are each associated with specific and what we might call superficial emotions, the thymus gland, the master controller of the life energy, not surprisingly, is the gland that is affected by these deepest emotions. We can easily demonstrate this. Just test someone, and if his thymus is testing strong, ask him to think of hating someone. Instantly his thymus will test weak. Conversely, test someone whose thymus is weak and have him think of someone he loves. Instantly his thymus will test strong.

A young male patient who had been "given" a diagnosis of cancer came to me for help. In the course of the interview I asked him, "Do you hate anyone?" He said, "I loathe and detest my mother." When he test-touched his thymus, it was weak. I said, "As long as you hate your mother, this hatred will so diminish your thymus activity, your life energy, that you will never get completely well." He said, "I would sooner die than give up hating my mother."

It is reasonable that these basic emotions affect the basic controller of our life energy. Let us take this one step further. Whenever we find a meridian imbalance, and an associated emotional imbalance, deep down we will find thymus underactivity. Beneath the more superficial emotions such as joy and happiness there will be love, and beneath sadness and unhappiness there will be a latent deep fear or hate.

I use *hate* in a very definite sense of the word. I am not necessarily stating that everyone whose thymus tests weak (and up to 95 percent of the thousands of people my colleagues and I have tested do test weak), is a hateful person. Nor are these envious people. (The relationship between hate and envy will be discussed later.) But there is a third emotion that accompanies these two, and possibly arises from them, that of *fear*. Our society at the moment seems to have a basic pervading attitude of fear. We fear every crisis ahead of us. It seems that deep down we fear for our very existence. Superficially we are optimistic and outgoing—we have our recreational vehicles, our bowling, our baseball, and all the other attributes of our present materialistic and hedonistic society. But underneath is a deep sense of fear and unease—a sense that what we have cannot last. We fear inflation, we fear taxes, we fear political ideologies, a depression, the energy crisis. And so it goes on. The newspapers are full of fear. Everywhere we are confronted with it.

We all have become so accustomed to reading terrifying articles about nuclear disaster and the collapse of the world banking system and the like that somehow we don't appear to be as affected by them as perhaps we should. They do not incite me to telephone my congressperson, write an indignant letter, or complain to a government agency. They don't mobilize me to do anything. So we could say that we have become so resigned to living with these fears that they no longer affect us, but that's not true. When I read such articles my thymus tests weak. When you read them, your thymus will test weak. They are subtly adding to the tremendous burden of fear that we are carrying unconsciously, regardless of how much we *appear* to have become accustomed or insensitive to bad, or terrifying news. Underneath, these fears are gnawing away at us diminishing our life energy, and they are mounting each day, adding yet another stress factor.

Add to this our fear of illness. We take out life insurance policies because we expect to die young and to leave behind dependents who will need to be supported. We take out health insurance because we expect to get sick. Such deep fear is ultimately debilitating.

Primitive hate arises out of the basic fear of death and is a retaliation[5] against it. This primary fear is so primitive and fundamental that we are not aware of its existence on a conscious level, but it is a part of us from earliest childhood. We hate, for example, the countries that we fear. Look at two young children. One has high-thymus activity, love, trust. If you throw him lightly up in the air, he laughs and smiles and gurgles with glee. The other one, having basic fear and distrust, responds to the same treatment with fearful and frightened screams. At that moment he hates you for what you have done to him, but his deepest fear is not primarily directed at any person. It is directed at the world. This fear pulls us down, depletes our life energy, makes us vulnerable to stress. Very few of us have the courage to come to grips with this deepest and most basic of all fears, the fear of death.

Let us look now at the other side of the coin. Whether we are religious or not, most of us have deep in our unconscious an expectation that after death we will be either in heaven or in hell—either we will be experiencing love and all that that implies, or hate and all that that implies.

Perhaps this was best expressed to me by a deeply religious and unassuming man. His religion is one of utter simplicity, joy, and perfection. He is now in his mid-eighties. He said that he was saved—he had a rebirth—when he was in his forties. Looking back, he said, he realized that until he was saved he was very frightened of death. Since his rebirth he is not the least frightened of death. He told me, "I have faith in the Lord. I have tried to do what I believe He wanted me to do, and I have no fear of death. I walk without fear in this life, because I believe that what is said in the Bible is true, that when I die I will go to heaven. I have faith in the Lord, and I know that I have tried to do the best I can."

This really sums it up. If we have faith that when we die we will go to heaven, why do we need to fear death? Fear of death, the ultimate fear, can only exist when we are unhappy with ourselves, our lives, and our deeds. Somehow we fear hell.

Freud spoke of a life instinct and a death instinct.[6] He said that we are continually at war within ourselves until eventually the death instinct triumphs. Probably no part of his writing has caused more contention than the invocation of this "death instinct." Whether or not it is a true instinct seems irrelevant in this context. What concerns us every day of our lives is that at all times there are tendencies toward our own undoing, competing with our drives to realize, to grow, to achieve, to love. There is this deep love-versus-hate fight occurring within us, in a sense within our thymus glands, all the time. There is the will to be well, and then fighting against this is the desire to turn to the wall and die. When the thymus tests strong, when we are of high-thymus activity, love is triumphant, life is triumphant. When it does not test strong, our will to be well is low—if you like, the death instinct is ruling us—the negative emotions have triumphed over love. The "death instinct," the wish to die, is the manifestation of this hatred turned on ourselves.

In the December 1979 issue of *New Age*, George Lakey described how he recovered from cancer. Among other techniques, he used a specific meditation technique and dream analysis. He wrote, "To my surprise, I located deep inside me a wish to die. It was hidden from me by my physical bounciness, my enthusiasm for political work, my zest for intellectual challenge, my love for my family and friends. But along with the positives, there was a hope which had turned to despair—a despair which even now I do not know how to name." It will be found in every such case there is a deep, hidden wish to die. Even though we are reluctant to recognize it, once we do, then, as Lakey found, we can go about the healing process, which is what his body, mind, and spirit have now been able to do. But first, before a healing process can really start, we have to locate that deep, all-powerful wish to die.

Later you will see just how appropriate was Lakey's use of the word *despair*. It has been pointed out that hopelessness, which is related to the thyroid meridian, or despair, is a prerequisite psychological condition for the development of cancer. In fact, one doctor has shown clinically that there is a direct relationship between thyroid activity and the development of cancer—his opinion being that if thyroid activity is normal there will be no cancer.[7]

This triumph of the death instinct may be difficult for us to understand or to accept, but this is the deep malaise of our society. As Freud pointed out then, and as many analysts, particularly Melanie Klein, have pointed out since, there is a drive for destruction within us. We see this every day in the pollution of our environment, for example, and in the destruction of our soil and water. The ethologist knows that a bird that fouls its own nest is soon to die, and this is what we are doing to our planet. We live in a time where the forces of destruction are very powerful. All the more reason for us to strengthen our thymus and activate our life energy, to dwell in the positive. And as you can now prove for yourself, positive thoughts raise your life energy.

One of my deepest disappointments with psychoanalysis is how little attention it pays to love and kindness, the positive thymus qualities. Most psychiatrists have been so involved with looking at the negative because that is what their patients talk about and it is where they feel they must dwell if they are to help them. We pay too little attention to the healing power of pure, altruistic love, the highest manifestation of life energy. In fact, my own feeling is that the fundamental problem with psychoanalysis may be that a psychoanalyst rarely, if ever, sees normal parents or a normal child. By "normal" I mean very high life energy, full of love, with little if any negativity—in other words, in a state of full and blooming positive health. The negative qualities which the psychoanalyst attempts to treat arise out of a family situation in which there is low life energy, fear, envy, and hate. When there is pure love, these qualities are not operant. Such negative patterns are merely manifestations of low thymus activity in the parents and therefore in the child. What we must strive for is normal, healthy, high-thymus parents who will nurture high-thymus children, all-loving people.

I wonder if there would be any discussions of a death instinct if we had truly loving parents and if we ourselves were truly loving. We would not need to attribute a death instinct to ourselves any more than an analyst feels bound to attribute it to a tree or a flower. Death would be accepted as part of the ongoing cycle of the universe.

As the thymus emotions are predominantly love and hate, it is not surprising that the supreme gesture of love, the open-armed embrace of a mother toward her child, is a thymus-strengthening gesture. I call it the *thymus gesture*. Whenever this heart-opening gesture is adopted and held for a brief period of time, it will be found that the energy imbalances throughout the body will be corrected and the thymus will test strong and active. The body gesture has said, "I love you," and this has corrected the energy imbalances, the negative emotional attitudes, throughout the body. Love really is prevention; love really is positive health. Swedenborg wrote in *True Christian Religion* that "love in its essence is spiritual fire." Conversely, if we closed in our arms to ourselves and refused to put ourselves out we would be "turning away without love."[8] This negative gesture diminishes our life energy. Perhaps this is the reason for the gesture in which corpses like Egyptian mummies are frequently placed. We have termed the high-thymus gesture the "madonna gesture," and the low-thymus gesture the "Egyptian mummy gesture."

We must always remember that in terms of ourselves as individuals and as a species, positive thymus attitudes, high life energy, and love are all compatible with our survival. Fear and hate kill. As Stokes says, "Love integrates, hate decomposes."[9] Johnson's Dictionary of 1755 has one of the best definitions of hate: "contrary to love." He also relates hate to envy when he defines envy as "to hate another for excellence, happiness, or success." In I John 4:18 we read, "There is no fear in love; but perfect love casteth out fear."[10] When the thymus is strong and active and our life energy is high, there is no intense fear such as is basic to all of our negative emotions.

John Preston wrote in *The breast-plate of faith and love* (1628), "Love and hatred are . . . the great Lords and Masters, that divide the rest of the affections between them." Here he is stating in essence that love and hate are the primary emotions and that all the other emotions are more superficial to them.

By examining a few quotations about love we will perhaps better understand this deepest and most basic of all positive emotions.[11] For example, Proverbs 10:12 reads, "Hatred stirreth up strifes: but love covereth all sins."

We could say with Bernard Leach that "nothing coming out of the mouth has more life [life energy] than to say, 'I love it.' "[12] This you can find for yourself through testing. If your thymus tests weak,

Low-Thymus Gesture

Egyptian Mummy Gesture, Closed to the World: Test while looking at this picture and you will find that your life energy has been depleted, and your thymus now is underactive.

High-Thymus Gesture

The Mother's Gesture, Open to the World: Test while looking at this, and you will find that all your energy imbalances have been corrected.

just say, "I love," or "I am full of love." Instantly your life energy will be raised and you will test strong. You will have moved from the dark into the light as quickly and positively as that.

In essence the thymus test is really a test of how much love we have at a given time, bearing in mind all the factors in our environment and the fears to which we are heir, that are mitigating against this love. When you test someone and he tests strong, then you know you are with someone who has the capacity for great love, whom you can trust, and who can love you.

Christ taught in the Sermon on the Mount, "Love your enemies, bless them that curse you, do good to them that hate you, and pray for them who despitefully use you, and persecute you; That ye may be the children of your Father which is in heaven." According to Octavio Paz,[13] our society does not adhere to this. He says, "One of the bases for our civilization has been the idea of love. It is not love for the body, it is not sex only, it is also attraction for a soul. The idea of love was founded on our loving a mortal person forever. This brought us to terms with the idea of death. It is a way to face death. . . . If our society is going to recover, we must recover this idea of love. . . . If we don't find this, life is going to be a desert. We must re-invent love."

Positive Thymus Attributes

There are other deep, positive emotional states very closely related to this concept of basic, all-encompassing love, which I will now discuss.

Faith

Faith[14] is related to love, so it is not surprising to find the saying, "Love is where there is faith." John Henry Newman wrote, "To have faith in God is to surrender oneself to God."[15] Jonathan Swift defined faith as, "an entire dependence upon the truth, the power, the justice, and the mercy of God; which dependence will certainly incline us to obey Him in all things."[16]

In studying the etymology of the word, we find that its primitive hypothetical so-called Indo-European root (I-E root)[17] from which our modern word *faith* has arisen is *bheidh,* which meant "to believe." Thus we have the idea of belief giving rise to faith. If your thymus tests weak, you can activate it by saying "I have faith."

Trust

"In Thee, O Lord, do I put my trust." Psalm 31:1

The thymus gland is also strengthened on testing when we say, "I have trust." Wyclif wrote, "Have trust in the Lord with all thine heart." *Trust* comes from the I-E root *deru,* which means to be firm, solid, steadfast. This became in Old English *treow,* which was loyalty and fidelity, from which we got our words *true* and *tree.* It also gave rise to the old Norse *trost,* meaning security, from which we get our word *trust.*

We can see through the history of this word how the concepts of trust, truth, solidity, and having a treelike [18] quality, of always being there, of being steadfast and maternal, are basic. One psychoanalyst, Erik Erikson, has referred to the most primitive stage of the infant's development as being the stage of basic trust vs. basic mistrust.[19] He says that early in life the infant is caught between wanting to completely trust his mother and yet perceiving that she cannot attend to him in every way. He has to realize that when he wants food and attention it does not always come automatically. In point of fact, he learns that her love is not complete. He learns that her feelings toward him are mixed and that there is always some hate with her love, because her thymus is never as active as it should or could be, that she is never totally treelike, that there is always some part of her feelings toward him that are negative— when she is angry with him, when she feels imposed on, and so forth. So the baby never fully develops a basic trust. There is always some mistrust. In some children, this mistrust becomes stronger than the trust, and these are often the children who later become psychotic. This first stage of ego development, what we would term envy vs. trust, is critical. Overcoming the envy leads to overcoming mistrust and the development of basic trust.

Once again we see the primary importance of this connection between trust, love, and faith in even the earliest phases of life. These words—although they have slightly different meanings— are very closely related and essential for our mental and physical well-being and functioning.

With great love, trust, and faith, there will be little or no fear and hatred. Imagine the child who has been brought up in a perfect family environment, experiencing full, complete, undiluted love from his parents. He would never experience fear. His birth would have been a beautiful experience, not the traumatic experience in the cold hospital labor ward that it was for nearly all of us, with the mother apprehensive and frightened, straining to release the baby and yet frightened to let the baby go. There would be no fear at his birth—and there would have been no fear when he was being carried in the womb. His entry into the world would have been a time of complete peace, tranquility, and love. This is what the French Buddhist obstetrician Frederick Leboyer has been trying to teach us. If there is, as he put it, birth without violence,[20] and if the child is carried prenatally with complete love, the child will be born knowing only love. He will know no distrust, no great fear, and will grow into a normal, high-thymus person—someone we all should have had the opportunity of being.

Gratitude

Another positive emotional state that is a thymus quality is *gratitude*. The primitive Indo-European root from which this comes is *gwere*, which means to praise aloud. From this root we get words in English such as *grace* and *gratitude, agree* and *congratulate*. In the early Sanskrit language, another word derived from the same root was *gir*, which meant a song of praise. A later Sanskrit root relating to gratitude is *gurtas*, which meant celebrated (in a religious sense), pleasing, and dear. The Latin root *gratus* meant received with favor or conscious of favor.

According to the *Oxford English Dictionary*, gratitude is "a warm sense of appreciation of kindness received, involving a feeling of goodwill towards the benefactor and the desire to do something in return." If we feel gratitude toward someone it is not enough just to feel it, it must also be expressed. A song of praise must be sung aloud back to the giver. Thus it is not insignificant that the root *gwere* also gave rise to the English word *bard*, the singer, basically the singer of praise. So many times we say we are grateful, but we don't tell the other person that we feel grateful. Gratitude is only complete when it is expressed. When someone's thymus tests weak, if he says "thank you," his thymus will now test

ENERGY

strong. As John Page Hopps, author of *First Principles of Religion and Morality* (1878), said, gratitude urges us to repay kindness. When we say "thank you," we are recognizing that we have received love and are now giving it back. "Thank you" is the repayment for the love offering,[21] returning love with love.

Gratitude is a desire to do something in return. We give back, we praise aloud, we return our thanks. Gratitude is thus the rounding of the circle. We experience love and kindness and return this as gratitude. And if we think of this when we visualize gratitude, we have a better understanding of the word.

Samuel Johnson, defined gratitude as "a desire to return benefits." South wrote, "Gratitude is properly a virtue, disposing the mind to an inward sense and an outward acknowledgment of a benefit received, together with a readiness to return the same, or the like."

Several years ago, I treated a young man who had been referred to me by his firm because of frequent, although minor, sexual offenses that he had been committing. The firm very generously offered to pay for his treatment. After several sessions, I was not satisfied with his progress and decided to try another approach. But at the end of a few months, he still had not shown any indications that he wanted to improve. Not surprisingly, he had absolutely no sense of gratitude toward the firm and little if any toward me, and I had gone out of my way to try to help him. Further, he had no sense of concern or even feeling for the people he had hurt by his offenses. I recognized that he was taking no responsibility at all for his predicament or his life.

At about this time, I discovered that his firm, due to an accounting error, had never paid my bill. I discussed this with the patient and told him that I would cancel the entire debt owed to me by his firm if he would, out of his own pocket, pay me one dollar. What I was trying to do was to activate his sense of responsibility for the situation he was in and also to activate his sense of gratitude, both to me and to his firm. In a way, although I didn't realize it at the time, I was trying to use this means to activate his thymus. But he refused to pay the dollar, arguing that the firm had arranged to pay for my services and it was their responsibility, not his. Needless to say, he didn't improve.

Courage

"Wait on the Lord: be of good courage, and he shall strengthen thine heart." Psalm 27:14

The fifth positive thymus emotional state is that of *courage.* The word *courage* comes from the Latin, *cor,* which means heart. Thus we get the idea of courage being seated in the heart—as in *lion-hearted.* The Greeks referred to the thymus gland as the protector of the heart. The *Oxford English Dictionary* defines courage as "that quality of mind which shows itself in facing danger without fear or shrinking." When we have high-thymus activity, when we are full of love, then we have courage to face our adversity, courage to go on, courage and the will to change from the negative to the positive.

There is a specific instance of courage that I wish to discuss. It is what I call the courage to have insight, the courage to sit down and draw up an inventory of ourselves, to look at ourselves as we really are—not as we would like to be, but as we really are. It is only when we recognize who we really are and the things that are wrong with us that we can do something about it. Most of us would prefer to practice what is called *denial*—to pretend that everything is all right.

I know of many women with lumps in their breasts who took a long time to go to the doctor. By the time they did, it was too late. They pretended that the problem would go away, or they convinced themselves the lumps were benign. They did not have the courage to face up to the fact that it might be serious: "I'd better get something done about it right away."

Many surveys have shown that it can be some months or even longer before a patient goes to the doctor with a complaint. As Dr. Jerome Mittelman says, the five most dangerous words are "Maybe it will go away." In this context of courage and insight versus denial, I am not speaking only in the framework of medicine, but also about the courage to examine everything in our lives, from the pollution of our environment to the general destruction of our way of life to our value systems, and so forth.

The most basic and primitive emotion is love in its various manifestations. This has been neglected in medicine, neglected in psychiatry, and neglected in our society. We don't read in the newspapers about love. We don't read in the medical textbooks about love. We don't read in the psychiatric textbooks above love, except to study it in a pathological way. We must realize that love can activate our life energy and promote healing. This is a matter of vital medical importance. Medicine today pays little if any regard to love and its power to heal. Perhaps what is needed more than anything else is to put love back into medicine and to reunite the professions of doctor and priest as they were in the past.

To summarize, there are five affirmations, any one of which will activate the thymus gland. (Of course, it is preferable for all five to be affirmed.) These affirmations will activate our life energy and help us to overcome the stress and emotional and energy imbalances that affect us. These affirmations may best be said as follows: "I am full of love. I have faith, trust, gratitude, and courage." The more fully we understand these words, the better our image of these concepts, the more we will be helped by them. Saying these affirmations with feeling several times throughout the day can activate our life energy and help us to change, to make better choices for life.

Negative Thymus Attributes

As we come to consider the negative thymus attributes—those basic emotional attitudes that destroy life energy—I do not want to sound like someone passing judgment, I wish merely to state that these are the negative emotional attitudes that demonstrably diminish our life energy. When we think of someone we hate, or when we think of a fearful situation, the thymus gland will test weak, and our life energy has been diminished.

Melanie Klein has said that the basis of hatred and envy and thus of all the other negative emotions is a deep primitive fear.[22] This probably is related to what has been called "birth trauma"—the baby is seen as living in a beautiful paradise inside the womb and then suddenly being forced out with earthquakes and convulsions into a cold and hard external world, cast out from his Garden of Eden into the most frightening and forbidding terrain imaginable. It took Leboyer to point out to us that the trauma of birth was of our own making and not necessarily part of our heritage.

The baby's state of existence changes from that of an internal, fluid environment to the external environment, but it should still maintain its close relationship with its mother, only now from the outside rather than from the inside. Birth is a stage of its evolution, not a time of trauma from which it seems never to recover. Leboyer has shown how our present birth practices—with the mother either screaming and straining or anesthetized (and thus the baby anesthetized with her), bringing the newborn into a harsh, sterile environment of stainless steel and white walls, plucked out, turned upside down, slapped, placed on cold scales, and then taken away —are so terrifying. In his first moments, the child has experienced fear which stays with him for life.

Leboyer showed us that there is another way. The baby can be born in quietness and semidarkness so it is not traumatized by noise and light. The umbilical cord can be left pulsating to continue the last link with the mother's internal world for as long as possible. The baby then can be placed in close relationship with the mother to allay any of its fears, so it can still hear its mother's heartbeat.

In my experience, and in the experience of others who have participated in or observed Leboyer births and the subsequent development of the children, there is a great difference. These children do grow up to be more loving, with fewer fears. And a similar experience occurs with the parents. They are bonded in a most loving and beautiful relationship. Such a nontraumatic birth can activate the *thymos* of the parents and the child in a way that we psychiatrists never thought was possible.

Leboyer's work may be one of the most important and fundamental contributions of modern times. If a baby can be born without this deep fear, there will be no death instinct, there will be no hatred; he will grow up in a beautiful, loving household, a high-thymus household. His experience of negative psychopathological states, so fully described in the psychiatric and psychoanalytic literatures, will be minimal. He will be creative. He will evolve.

But what of us? My own delivery was a traumatic experience for my mother, as I am certain it was for me. I am equally certain that your birth experience was little easier than mine. Thus, we probably started off with the great fear from birth trauma as we have described. It has been stated by one school of osteopathy that most births are so traumatic that at birth the baby never takes the full, natural breath that expands his whole body, in particular, his skull bones, which have been enfolded to facilitate his passage through the birth canal.[23] With a Leboyer birth, for example, the first breath opens up all these skull bones and opens up the whole body so that the baby's normal development can take place. It is said that such an occurrence is rare, that the first breath is delayed, or even precipitated by the shock and pain of a smack on the bottom. The baby gasps for breath, he does not take that full, deep, relaxed, natural breath as he enters the world. It is also said that most of the structural problems that we develop throughout our lives are a result of this trauma. But a beautiful, natural delivery will be a time of love for all, a high-thymus time.

Fear

Let us examine the word *fear*. In studying its origins we discover the unconscious connotations of fear which still operate within our psyches and are powerful determinants throughout our lives. Fear is defined, for example, as "alarm or disquiet caused by expectation of danger, pain, disaster." Now we are not aware that we feel this fear every day, but it is gnawing away at us unconsciously.

The primitive Indo-European root from which *fear* arose is *per*, meaning to pass through or to travel, which gave rise in English to such words as *peril* and *experience*—experience having to do with the idea of traveling through life. From this root in Old English a word developed, *var*, which meant to ambush. The same thought occurred in the word in Old High German, *faren*, which meant to lie in wait. The original meaning of fear, then, was seen in terms of danger of being suddenly ambushed while traveling. We have mentioned previously this concept of a sudden attack as it relates to how most of us view the origin of disease—we are traveling through life, minding our own business, when suddenly we are struck down by illness. This is what we fear, we never know when it might occur.

Instead of trying to restructure our lives to prevent ourselves from becoming sick, we donate to such organizations as the Arthritis Society, the Diabetes Society, or the Cancer Society, as some form of insurance, thinking that if we are suddenly struck down with one of these diseases, our best protection will be what researchers have learned about its cure. But if we traveled carefully, perhaps we would not be ambushed. If we travel negligently, foolhardily, then we are inviting it. We are thus haunted by this terrible fear, the fear of death through the unknown.[24] And this fear has haunted us since we were brutally separated from our mothers at birth.

When we test someone and find that the thymus is underactive, we know that deep down there is this constant fear of never knowing when disaster may strike as we travel through life—the fear and uncertainty of never knowing when we may be ambushed by disease and ultimately by death. Some people will acknowledge and respond to this fear by working harder to overcome it. Others will say, "You can never know when you're going to be attacked, so what's the point in trying? I've got to die of something, so I might as well take a few chances (such as smoking) and enjoy myself." But remember, "He that fears death, lives not." As long as this deep fear is operant, our thymus will never achieve optimal activity. We will never really have life energy. We will be alive, but not really living.

Hate

Hate arises out of the deep fear we have discussed and from the traumatic birth experience. As we know, we tend to hate those who hurt us and traumatize us. We hate those we fear.

The origin of the word *hate* is both fascinating and essential, so we will discuss it in some detail. It illustrates what Freud wrote many years ago in "The Antithetical Meaning of Primal Words."[25] He showed that, for example, in the Egyptian hieroglyphs, the symbols for *weak* and *strong* were the same. He stated that this phenomenon was quite a common occurrence in primitive languages and therefore perhaps also occurs in our unconscious.

When we go back to the primitive root from which the English word *hate* arose, we see how the ideas of love and hate are combined. The primitive root was *ka,* which meant to like or desire. This gave rise to the hypothetical root *karo,* from which we have derived such words as *care, caress,* and *charity.* It also gave rise to the primitive word *kamo* from which *kama* was derived in Sanskrit, which meant love and desire. The primitive root verb *kad* was also derived from *ka.* As they have the same root they may psychologically be related. The first meaning for *kad* was to fall or to die, from which we get in English *cadence* and *cadaver.* It also gave rise to words meaning "to cover or to shelter." Eventually we see these words coming through in English as *hat* and *hood*. We might note here that the related root *kam* meant to cover over, devolving, as we shall see when we work with the word later, to *shame* and *chemise*. There was another side to the meaning of the root *kad* that implied hatred. Thus we have such words as *hate* and *heinous*.

The primitive root meant love and desire, and yet this deviated in one direction into words having to do with death and falling and being covered over (as if in death) as well as meanings of hatred. It seems to me that in the origin of this primitive, very basic word we have the essence of the emotional states of the thymus. The baby grows in the womb with love, but then the birth trauma is experienced almost as a form of death, which takes away the beautiful life he once had—and this then gives rise to hatred through fear.

We may state that hatred arises out of the primitive fear of death which is initiated by the birth trauma and other fearful experiences through the early stages of infancy. If the early environment is completely nurturing, sheltering, and loving, then the infant will grow with that love. If it is not, then he will experience fear and hate. This hatred will manifest itself in numerous ways; for example, it will reveal itself when the baby begins, either in fantasy or in reality, to turn on the very breast that feeds him. This state is that of *envy*.

Envy

I once wrote a psychiatric textbook on envy. In it I pointed out the virtually universal occurrence of envy as a major underlying emotional state in nearly all psychiatric patients, in fact in most physical illnesses as well. I gave hundreds of examples from the psychiatric and general medical literature as well as examples from everyday life, mythology, and throughout recorded history, showing how envy has been an all-pervasive, negative factor working against the vital life factors of our existence.

The book was over four hundred pages, but I never published it. I realized that I had written a book that was completely negative, because apart from perhaps one particularly involved, very deep, and extensive form of psychoanalysis—that pioneered by Melanie Klein—there was no "cure" for envy. My book delineated how destructive a force envy was, but there was no solution for the problem. Thus I decided not to publish it. Society has gone out of its way to deny the existence of envy as a basic and influential negative attitude. What was the point of my awakening people to the presence of envy if there was nothing that could be done about it? Why add to their already-present fears, why make them feel even less self-worthy, why add to their negativity?

But with the new techniques that we have developed for thymus activation, the whole picture has changed. Now, when I see envy in people, and in particular my patients, students, and myself, it no longer alarms and grieves me. I know that there is something we can do about it. I no longer feel that Francis Bacon was right when he stated, "Nothing can reconcile envy to virtue but death" *(Rhetoric)*.[26] I know now that envy can be eliminated; envy can be abolished, stopped dead in its tracks, in but a minute. Thymus activation overcomes envy.

I feel free to talk about envy now because I know that we can do something about it. While I don't want to dwell on hate and fear and envy and other negative qualities, I do feel I must show you and describe to you the presence of these negative qualities and the power of our thoughts and feelings to make us sick. More importantly, I want to demonstrate the power that we have within us to overcome them instantly. This is the power of the thymus, the power of our life energy, which we can use for good whenever we desire.

Have you ever wondered why there are so many jokes about psychiatrists going mad? I know that when I was practicing psychiatry it intrigued me a great deal; in fact, I made a collection of well over a hundred of these jokes. In my practice, I sometimes experienced the feeling (and I do not think it was a paranoid one) that my patients wished I were crazy. They did not wish that they were sane, but wished me to be crazy, recognizing, of course, that if I were crazy as well, I could do nothing to help them. This is the basic expression of envy. Rather than their wishing to be sane, as they presumed I was, and rather than wishing that my sanity could help them regain theirs, they became envious of my sanity and wished to destroy it. It was more important to them for me to be insane than for them to be sane. This is exactly what envy is like. The envious person feels, "If I can't have it, no one will have it." Common examples of envy are seen in the plain girl who disparages the beautiful one or the vandal who scrapes the paintwork of the Rolls Royce—"If I can't have one and enjoy it, then I am going to stop him from enjoying it." He does not even steal the car for himself; his wish is not to possess it, but to destroy the pleasure of the man who does have it. Envy is not a wish to possess, but a wish to destroy.

There were many cases of envy in my psychiatric experiences. I once had to take over a unit of a large psychiatric hospital because the psychiatrist in charge had a mental breakdown. One of my first duties was to tell the patients that this doctor had become mentally ill. The reason I told them something of the nature of his illness was that we were all living within a hospital community and it would have been only a question of time before they discovered for themselves. Furthermore, I felt it was fair to let them know of the problem because many of them may have detected that something was wrong with him in the days prior to his breakdown. To give them the reality of what had happened would, I felt, assist them in sorting out what was reality and what was not in their own experiences. This would give them feedback and help them evaluate their own intuitions and feelings. But I found a distressing situation instead. Only two or three of the patients were sympathetic to the doctor who had done a great deal for them over the years, who had worked with them and cared for them and worried over them. Most of them openly expressed delight. Many of them smiled and some even broke out into laughter. It was then that I started to see why at least some of these patients were still in the hospital even after many years. They had, in a sense, resisted every effort on the part of the doctor to help them. They preferred that the doctor be a "nut case" like them than to allow him to help them. Their envy had destroyed them.

Melanie Klein developed her own technique of child analysis which enabled her to explore the deepest workings of the minds of young children. She found that[27]

> Envy stirs as soon as the infant becomes aware of the breast as a source of life and good experience; the real gratification which he experiences at the breast, reinforced by idealization, so powerful in early infancy, makes him feel that the breast is the source of all comforts, physical and mental, an inexhaustible reservoir of food and warmth, love, understanding and wisdom. The blissful experience of satisfaction which this wonderful object can give will increase his love and his desire to possess, preserve and protect it, but the same experience stirs in him also the wish to be himself the source of such perfection; he experiences painful feelings of envy which carry with

them the desire to spoil the qualities of the object which can give him such painful feelings.

The word *envy* comes from the Latin, *invidia,* meaning a hostile stare [28] from which we get all the expressions having to do with the evil eye. We see this in our everyday expressions such as, "If looks could kill." A woman goes to a party and someone else is wearing a more beautiful dress than hers. If looks could kill, she would destroy the other woman, not to have the dress for herself (that could be jealousy) but to destroy the other woman and her dress (and that is envy). (Frequently we find that envy is confused with jealousy. I have found in tracing the evolution of the word that there is an increasing tendency to do this. Always the attempt is to water down the severity of envy and to equate it more with jealousy. Jealousy is the state of, "I believe this is mine and I want it for myself," whereas envy is, "If I can't have it, I am going to destroy it." "Jealousy is based on love and aims at the possession of the loved object and the removal of the rival." [29] Because envy is such a powerful, destructive impulse, we find it difficult to accept, acknowledge, and live with, so we tend to dilute its definition.) It has been said that the concept of the evil eye has developed from the time when the baby is envious of the breast and glares at it intently while he is feeding.

We also have the expressions, "biting the breast" and "biting the hand that feeds you." Those who most supply us with our needs are those on whom we often turn, not because we feel that what they give us is bad, but because we want to control it for ourselves, we do not want to be dependent—we want to be both donor *and* receiver. Therefore, we are often disappointed when we do things for other people or when we give them things and then find that they are not grateful (a high-thymus quality), but are instead envious and turn on us. We wonder, "Why is he being so nasty to me after all I have done for him?" Well, he is being nasty *because* of all you have done for him; he is envious of the fact that you have it and you have done it, rather than his being able to do it himself— rather than being autonomous, independent, controlling.

Consider envy and gratitude as two sides of the same coin in medical practice. The envious patient will not get well, does not have the will to get well, and will tend to destroy what the doctor is trying to do to help him, by refusing to take medication or do exercises for instance. On the other hand the high-thymus, grateful patient carries out the suggestions, has the will to get well, and *does* get well.

Remember the story of the judgment of Solomon. The true mother was prepared to let her child be given to the impostor rather than have him killed. She acted out of supreme love for the child. This is, of course, what led Solomon to make the decision that she was the rightful mother. But what of the other woman? She preferred to see the child killed rather than let him be restored to his rightful mother: "If I cannot have the child, no one will have him." She allegedly was acting out of love for the child, but you can see here how much she envied the other woman the child. Her main purpose was not to get the child for herself, which would perhaps be jealousy, but to deprive the other woman of him. This is envy, this is destructive hatred.

In her book on envy and gratitude, Melanie Klein explores some of the characteristics of envy. She writes, "It could be said that the very envious person is insatiable, he can never be satisfied because his envy stems from within . . ." Later she continued, "I would even suggest that it is unconsciously felt to be the greatest sin of all, because it spoils and harms the good object which is the source of life." [30] Even in the young children she treated, envy was apparent and was the basis for most of the psychopathology. It often manifested itself in cleverly disguised behavior, and it was always the most difficult aspect of any patient to treat.

That envy is a primary and very debilitating condition is not a recent discovery. In "The Parson's Tale," Chaucer wrote, "It is certain that envy is the worst sin that is; for all other sins are sins only against one virtue, whereas envy is against all virtue and against all goodness."

Envy defeats creativity. This negative aspect of the thymus gland destroys its positive side. Adrian Stokes wrote, "A fresh mind, ear, eye, are means of creativeness, of the propensity most deplored by envy." Creativity cannot occur in a setting of envy or fear—only high-thymus activity will allow creativity to be manifest. Just how important creativity is will be explained in the chapter, "The Cerebral Hemispheres."

To summarize to this point: The thymus controls our life energy. If we want to be well, if we want to have all our mental and physical energies high and balanced, if we want to be invulnerable to stress, we must be in a high-thymus attitude. The thymus is controlled by the most powerful positive and negative emotions, the basic emotions from which emanate all the other emotions we discuss in this book.

When the thymus is active, a person will be on the path of health and positive life choices. To keep the thymus active, we should choose to steer a course in life away from fear, hate, and envy, and toward the positive emotions of love, faith, trust, gratitude, and courage.

Do not take my word for this. Test for yourself. Find out how thoughts of love will activate your thymus while thoughts of hate, envy, and fear will deactivate your thymus.[31]

Along these lines, test for the power of the word, the power of thoughts, the power of emotions, to aid you in overcoming daily stresses. Test some of the factors in your physical environment such as fluorescent lights, refined sugar, synthetic fibers, loud noises, exhaust fumes, and the like. Then test them again, but on the second test, have your subject think intently of someone he loves, or of putting out love to someone. You will almost invariably find that his thymus (*thymos*) has been activated to the point that now none of these negative factors makes him weak. Of course, it would be far better if we did not have these factors around us draining our energy and adding to our stress, but we can often rise above them, become invulnerable to them.

The power of love is incredible. And now you can actually demonstrate this for yourself. For years my internist colleagues have chided me by saying, in effect, that *they* can measure what they do; *they* can look at laboratory reports and congratulate themselves on biochemical changes that they have brought about, whereas I have no measuring system. Psychiatrists simply could not measure love. They could see and sense changes in their patients as their lives changed and as they became more loving, but they had no scale on which to measure it. This was considered a shortcoming on the part of the profession. Now we can demonstrate the power of love on our bodies.

Through a change of attitude, through a desire or a will to be well, the negative emotions we have discussed can be abolished. We could call this will to be well one of the most important thymus qualities, a basic and fundamental attitude toward oneself and others. What do we mean by the will to be well? How is it manifest? Let me give you a few examples.

When I lecture to doctors practicing preventive medicine, I ask,

"How many of your patients do everything that you suggest to them to improve their health?" Regardless of the group or the location, the answer is fairly consistent. Some will say 10 percent, others 5 percent. It is rare for a doctor to say that more than 10 percent of his or her patients do everything—often very simple things that he or she thinks will help—that is suggested. I find that this lack of forwardness on the part of patients is the greatest professional disappointment that most doctors feel. They spend years at school learning, and then they attend many postgraduate courses learning new techniques to help their patients, and yet the patients apparently do not want to carry out their suggestions. Many doctors try to advise their patients to give up refined sugar. Many dentists advise their patients to floss their teeth, or to come in for regular checkups, or whatever it may be. Yet it seems that only 5 percent to 10 percent actually carry out the suggestions. There are even courses designed to teach the doctor and his staff how to "sell" health care to his patients. Dentists are taught how to motivate their patients to floss, or to brush regularly, and so forth. Even so the patients do not do these simple, inexpensive, non-time-consuming procedures that would not only improve their health and appearance but would even save them money in the long run!

The doctor is put into a very difficult situation, called a double-bind, in which the patient says he wants to get better (and he will quickly volunteer the information that he is in the doctor's office for that very reason) but yet he doesn't carry out simple procedures that the doctor suggests. He continues to smoke, he neglects his teeth, he doesn't bother to avoid refined sugar, he does not exercise, or whatever.

This is what I mean by the absence or the diminution of the will to be well. My friend and colleague Dr. Jerome Mittelman says people like this just do not have a "positive get-well attitude." Many doctors call them low-thymus patients. They go through the ritual, they have the appearance of wanting to be well, they may even have themselves convinced that they want to be well, but they do not follow through. Deep down inside them, perhaps they feel it's hopeless, so they don't even bother to try. They will go through the perfunctory motions of coming to a doctor, but when he makes suggestions they just cannot be bothered to try them. They do not listen, and they do not act upon his advice. Let me repeat the finding: only 5 percent to 10 percent of the patients will do everything that the doctor suggests to help them. So it is not a question of the doctor learning new methods, better techniques to treat patients. It is not a question of his learning more pathology, better injection techniques, or improved diagnostic techniques. What is the point of all the magnificent, million-dollar diagnostic apparatuses that we now have, if when it comes down to the bottom line of advising the patient to change his lifestyle, to stop smoking, to exercise, or whatever, only 5 percent to 10 percent are going to do it? All the billions of dollars that we spend on diagnosing the most esoteric of diseases matters little if the patient will not carry out our advice.

What is required is a *fundamental change in the overall attitude of the patient toward himself.* The patient has to *want* to be well. Then the healing process can commence and our marvelous new remedies can be of value to the patient. The incredibly efficient diagnoses that we can make today can be of benefit. But there is no point in diagnosing the patient if he is not going to do what it takes to get better. Thymus activation can reverse this trend.

Let me give you an example of what I mean by the absence of the will to be well. Some years ago I was consulted by a woman in her mid-twenties who was carried into my office by her husband. She had been diagnosed a few years previously as having multiple sclerosis and since that time had been immobile and had to be carried around by her husband. She had been to many doctors and had many forms of treatment to no avail. She asked me pleadingly if I could help her. She and her husband had now exhausted their funds from previous futile attempts to treat her, so I offered to see her twice a week at no charge. She came regularly, being brought by her husband each time. I was very surprised by how much her muscle strength improved over a relatively short period of time in treatment—about six weeks. (The particular type of treatment I gave is not relevant here. However, this patient came to me before I began working with the importance of activating the thymus gland as the initial part of treatment.) At the end of this six-week period, she asked me how she was progressing. I told her I felt she had improved so greatly that I was beginning to doubt that she really had a disease as serious as multiple sclerosis—her improvement had been that good. She asked me what I would suggest for continuing her treatment. I replied, "In view of the remarkable progress you have made with two visits per week, I would suggest that you come five times a week, again at no charge, so that we can maximize this improvement and really get you healthy again." She never came back. She did not, deep down, have the will to be well. Although she had improved physically to a great extent, we had not activated her will to be well. Apparently paradoxically, as she started to improve, she was almost forced by her unconscious desires, by her will to stay sick, to break off treatment.

In contrast to this, let me tell you of Betty Cuthbert, an Australian Olympic gold medalist. Some years ago she was also diagnosed as having multiple sclerosis. She described to me how she went through the usual initial stage of fear and depression. But then while on a vacation in Scotland, she went to the top of a mountain and had a profound experience in which she prayed and in fact composed a hymn which she sang while there. She said that suddenly she understood why she, a runner, was becoming paralyzed from multiple sclerosis. She said that she realized it was her God-given duty to overcome the disease and to use her public position in order to help others to overcome it. At almost that instant, her will to be well was motivated, and since then she has made a most dramatic and satisfying recovery.

I had this experience in mind when I was called by a man who had a severe paralysis of neurological origin. He told me he was too far away to travel to me, but asked if there were anything I could do over the telephone to help him. I said I did not know if I could help him and that I had never treated a case such as his. He then asked me if I had known of any similar cases in which the patient had made a recovery. I said, "I know of a case where a woman made what appeared to be a spontaneous improvement following a profound religious experience." At that point he exclaimed into the phone, "Well, that's certainly not going to happen to me!"

Later, I did see him—he *consented* to come for one visit. He stayed all day and had a great deal of intensive therapy on many levels. At that time I discovered that he had already instructed his oldest daughter as to the contents of his will and what was to be done with the family possessions and with his body when he died. He had even picked out his own grave site and made all the arrangements for his death. There was no desire to be well here. This was a man who had only the will to die. I worked all day to soften his hardness of heart. We did concentrated physical work with his body and actually did make some progress there. But his heart would not soften. I was unable to help him in the one visit which he allowed me.

Frequently doctors see patients who are on what I call a "medical odyssey." They have been to many, many doctors all over the country. They tell how Doctor A couldn't help them, neither could Doctor B nor Doctor C, and so on. They usually have spent thousands of dollars, and yet have not seen any improvement.

I have had my share of patients like this, too. I often tell them early in the first meeting that there is really nothing that I can do that the other doctors haven't already done. I try to explain to them that there must be some basic problem that the previous doctors haven't yet uncovered which is not the illness, but the patient's attitude to life and to his illness. With these patients we find that if we can help them activate their thymus glands, stimulate their will to be well, then they will improve. And their medical odyssey can stop there. If we are unable to activate the thymus, the life energy, the will to be well, then the odyssey continues, sometimes forever.

The great medical breakthrough, the great advance that we are all seeking, is not going to come from a test tube, a laboratory, a drug company, or even from high-powered hospital medical research. It is going to come from where the Greeks knew it would, just as Hippocrates always taught. It is going to come from an activation of the healing power of nature within each of us, through the activation of the patient's *thymos*, his life energy, the activation of his will to be well. When we return to the basic medical truths and the truths of living that were known thousands of years ago, we shall have a breakthrough for today.

I recall a lady who was brought to my office by her two daughters. She had severe diabetic gangrene and one foot had been amputated. Amputation of the toes on the other foot had been recommended by her surgeon. The family pleaded with me, asking that I do something less radical than surgery to help her. I told them that first she must adhere very strictly to a specific nutritional program and should eliminate all refined sugars in particular. This she refused to do. Shortly afterward she had the surgery. Her last words to me were, "I would rather give up my legs than have to give up sugar."

I recall a man who had an amputation for Buerger's disease, which is a type of gangrene of the extremities directly caused by a response to smoking. Even after the amputation he refused to stop smoking.

Contrast these cases of low-thymus activity, no will to be well, with an eighteen-year-old woman I saw only once. She had severe anorexia nervosa, a disease in which for various deep psychological reasons she was refusing to eat, and her weight had dropped to some eighty pounds. This is a very frightening disease, frightening to the family, to the patient, and to the doctor, particularly as it is recognized that severe anorexia nervosa can have a 20 percent mortality rate. I saw her only once because she was moving to another part of the country. But in that one session I talked to her about basic fears, particularly the fear of dying, and I contrasted this with love and explained to her the functions of the thymus gland. We talked about the will to be well. I showed her several ways in which to activate her thymus gland—to activate her life energy. When she left she thanked me. (It is always a good sign when a patient thanks you and means it, because if he or she is truly grateful you know that the thymus has indeed been activated.) She said that she would carry out the programs that I had suggested to her because she wanted to be well. She has kept in touch with us over the years. She has continued to do well, has finished her studies, and is now a mature and healthy adult. This is how much can be accomplished when the will to be well is activated. This is the power of the thymus, life energy.

Just this morning my secretary telephoned a patient I had seen only once. He had been diagnosed as having what is probably a fatal disease, and in desperation he asked me if there were anything I could possibly do that might in any way alter the outcome. On that first visit I suggested a treatment program to him. I pointed out that I could not see him often due to travel and lecture commitments, but that whenever I had an opening I would call him and he could come in. He and I both recognized that if any results were going to be achieved it would be through very intensive work. So my secretary called him to tell him that I had an opening. He replied, "Well, if the doctor thinks it is an emergency, I could come, but I really had planned to spend the day tidying up my apartment."

In this case the will to be well simply was not there. This poor man was still, in addition to the actual sickness, so overcome by the fear that took over when the doctor gave him his diagnosis—his thymus was so underactive—that the thought that he could improve was actually beyond his comprehension. So he came to see me that first time, but he didn't really think we would accomplish anything. He didn't really think that the healing powers of his body could help him. He is back in that state of fear in which he sees nothing but death ahead of him, and he cannot be motivated to roll up his sleeves and get on with the job as best he can, and as best I can advise him. But if he comes back, and as he starts to implement procedures such as those we are suggesting in this book, then he will activate his will to be well and then he can work *with* me. He will then do everything he can to help himself, and I hope to reverse the disease process with which he is now afflicted.

Let us consider another case. Just recently I was talking to a man in his early fifties. Four of his siblings had died from diabetes at early ages. This man had been a large consumer of sugar, despite his family's entreaties to reduce his intake because of the relationship between sugar and diabetes. But he had always refused and laughed it off lightheartedly, as if he couldn't care less. Underneath you could see that he was deeply troubled about it.

Suddenly, on this occasion he said, "You know, I'm pretty fatalistic about my life. I suppose it's pretty definite that I'm going to get diabetes and die young like my brothers and sister." I pointed out to him that nothing was inevitable, that I had seen people with tendencies toward diabetes correct them through a change in their diet, by making a decision to reform their nutrition. And he asked, "Do you think it could happen to me?" I said, "There's no reason why it couldn't, because it has happened to others. What is required is that you make a decision to be really well now and roll up your sleeves and work toward it." He replied, "I'm ready. I'm going to do it." There was enormous relief in his tear-filled eyes and in the eyes of his family. For the first time since the death of his first brother, he had made a decision to be well. It was really a rebirth.

Within the framework of modern medical practices, it becomes very difficult to activate the patient's will to be well. Consider the following: I received a copy of a letter concerning a mutual patient from one of the best-known specialists in the country at one of the very biggest medical centers. The patient had a severe neurological disease—so-called Lou Gehrig's disease—which is thought to be 100 percent fatal. The letter listed several pages of test results and then on the bottom line made the diagnosis and said that the future arrangement was for "clinical follow-up, physiotherapy, and a multivitamin and two Vitamin B tablets daily." I suppose the vitamins were given because "they can't do him any harm anyway and we have to give him something." The physiotherapy is known to be of absolutely no benefit in such a case and was obviously being suggested as some form of pretense that something was being done to help the patient. I suspect that it was being given as much to help the doctor as to help the patient, who was well aware that physiotherapy wouldn't help. Now what of the clinical follow-up? What was that to accomplish? To watch him gradually merge into death?

What was really being done for this poor man? While I was not taught at medical school that the disease is curable, I have heard of a person who had a miraculous cure from it. Certainly the outlook is very, very bleak, but we are all going to die. For all we know, that doctor and I may both die before this patient. When we give someone a label, a diagnosis of a fatal disease, it does not mean that he will die and we will live forever. It means that it is now more apparent that he is going to die, and we probably know when that will occur. This is often put in some enigmatic way that the doctor had *given* the patient x years to live. The doctor does not give the patient life. When a diagnosis of a fatal disease is made, then the patient can no longer pretend he is immortal. He can no longer push the fear of death beneath his conscious level. The person who does not have the burden of a diagnosis of a fatal disease upon him may still pretend to be immortal and thereby deny his fear of death. So there is really little difference between this man and us, except that his fate is a little more clearly outlined and he has the added fear of "certain and imminent" death.

What was being done to relieve this fear? What was being done to help him deal with his tragedy? What was being done to help his family deal with this? Where, in point of fact, from this important doctor from this prestigious center was there any humanity? All I read in the extensive reports were clinical words, and coldness. I sensed no love for the man, no concern for him and his family. Where is the doctor's compassion? Where is his heart? Where is the concern for the suffering? After all, these are the reasons for going into medicine. What has happened?

Summary

The will to be well is of vital importance to optimum health. This is one of the positive qualities of the thymus gland. It is hampered by negative emotions of any sort, and particularly by those of hate, envy, and extreme fear. It can be mobilized in a matter of moments by simple attitudinal changes, and once this will to be well is stimulated, then it becomes easier to do the things that keep the thymus gland active and balanced and functioning properly. When this change of spirit occurs, eliminating negativity, we are on the road to positive health and positive choices through the activation of the life energy.

How To Solve Your Problems

Making the Best Choices

"Problem solving is largely, perhaps entirely, a matter of appropriate selection."

—W. Ross Ashby

The thymus controls our life energy. Positive thoughts activate the thymus while negative thoughts inhibit it. Thus, the thymus test is a valuable tool in finding out what our problems really are and solving them.

Whenever you say something that activates your life energy, your thymus will test strong.[1] When you say anything that is contrary to your body energy, your thymus will test weak. This is not "lie detection" in any way, but it may be considered a form of "truth detection."[2] The thymus test enables you to make the best selection, the correct choice. Let's take a simple everyday example. I recently saw in a craft shop a beautiful hand-loomed rug. The price was very reasonable and I was on the point of buying it. My wife and I then did the thymus test. I test-touched my thymus and it was strong. Then I said, "I want to buy this rug." Surprisingly, I tested weak. This statement had somehow gone against my deep wishes. It was interfering with my life energy. On testing my wife, we found the same results. Naturally I did not buy the rug. Perhaps it did not fit into our home decor. Perhaps unconsciously I knew it was too expensive for us. Or perhaps, and most likely, there was something about the design which lowered my life energy, something of which I was not aware at a conscious level.[3] When I was tested I found out what I really thought, what my unconscious mind knew.

We must remember that we are ruled by our unconscious. Our decisions, large and small, are made by our unconscious.[4]

Theodor Reik, one of Freud's early disciples, used to tell the story of how he was walking with Freud in Vienna one afternoon and was discussing how difficult he was finding it to make a decision regarding whether he should go to America to practice as the first lay analyst. Freud said to him, "This is how I solve a problem. If it's a little problem, I add up the pros and cons and go with the highest number. But if it is a big problem, I go with what my unconscious thinks, because ultimately my unconscious desires will determine the success or failure of my decision." They walked on awhile in silence and then Reik said, "But I don't know whether this is a little problem or a big problem." To which Freud replied, "*That* is your problem."

I agree with Freud that in problem solving we must act in accordance with our unconscious desires. But we must find out what our unconscious desires really are. Perhaps Freud knew after many years of self-analysis. But this is not an option for most of us, and when most of us think we are making logical decisions, we are not; we are actually being ruled by our unconscious. So, let us find out through our simple test what our unconscious really thinks and go in accordance with the motivating powers within us. Then the decisions we make will be harmonious with all of us and much more likely to be successful.

The test reveals your wishes only at the specific point in time when you perform it. It may be that later, perhaps even the next day, you have changed your mind. But the test does tell you what your unconscious desires really are at the moment. This simple thymus test is a way of tapping your unconscious, and you can use it as many times as you like, in whatever ways you wish.

There is inside each of us the basic answer for every decision we are required to make each day of our lives, from superficial to very deep matters, at all levels of our existence, including our very survival. All these decisions are in some way already "known" to us. In a situation of choice, the "right" one is that which has been called *ego-syntonic*. It goes with the basic nature of our egos, that part of ourselves which deals with all of reality. In a mode of ego-syntonicity, our life energy is high and we test strong. In a mode of action which is ego-alien, that is against our deep wishes, then the stress causes a diminution of life energy as demonstrated by the test.

The answers range over all levels. Those that are very deep do not change throughout life and are ethologically-based. That is, they are not specific to any individual and are universally true, for example, a choice for love over hate. At the other extreme, some are very superficial and very individual and may relate to events of yesterday, like testing differently in regard to a boyfriend because of the events of the previous evening.

Most of our problems we create ourselves. A person who is not sure of his goals is likely to overreach or buy or do something that, in his heart, he really doesn't want to do. He wasn't really sure of what was in his heart, and now he is stuck with a house he can't afford or didn't really want, or a swimming pool he doesn't use, and so forth.

By the same token, all our unconscious attitudes, which by their very nature are not perceptible, may cause us, for example, to enter into a marital relationship that we would have found was not the right thing for us if we had monitored the unconscious beforehand. If we had tested the thought of being married to that person beforehand, a bad marriage may not have been contracted.

So, there are two points here. First, if we are aware of our real goals, we are unlikely to make a big mistake—whether it be buying a car or marrying a spouse. Second, if we know and can balance any negative emotional attitudes that are operating on us at any given time, we may not enter into inappropriate relationships or business deals.

For example, suppose a woman is suffering from a state of depression. In that state, she may contract a marriage, or be motivated to buy or to do something that she would not have done if she were not depressed. If she could instantly recognize and correct her energy imbalance, she would make another decision that would be much more in harmony with her unconscious.

What is necessary for avoiding problems is being able to test for the problem before we get involved in it—and now this can easily be done.

Think of a problem that has been nagging you, or, if you are not particularly troubled at this moment, just imagine that you are. Now, let us look at the ways in which we can bring this problem, which is beyond your reach, back within your reach so that you can do your best to solve it.

First of all, we know that when you are in a state of stress, you are using predominantly one brain hemisphere.[5] Unless a person is well into a state of positive health, every time he or she is confronted with a stressful situation, he will respond by using either the right or left hemisphere of his brain. Thus, immediately upon being confronted with a problem, you become less capable of solving it. People are either predominantly right-brain or left-brain dominant under stress. If they predominantly use the left hemisphere, they are applying all of their logical and mathematical powers to the problem, but have ceased using their intuitive faculties, which is right-brain activity, in solving it. They are stewing over the mathematical figures involved, so to speak, but then failing to apply the other attitudes of the personality in the situation.

Conversely, if the response to stress is to use predominantly the right hemisphere, they are more likely to want to escape, and may tend to run away and forget about it. The debts mount up, or the marital situation worsens. In short, the problems become insoluble.

When both hemispheres are operating, we are creative. We are able to apply all of our intuitive faculties, as well as our more logical ones, to solving the problem.

Obviously, if we can reduce the stress to the point where both hemispheres operate equally, we can apply our whole-brain creativity to solving the problem. And we can get both hemispheres operating by activating the thymus. As long as we are centered, as long as our hemispheres are balanced, we are less likely to be further uncentered by such things as more legal notices, and so on. We can now manage more energy-draining problems, and prevent any snowball effects.

Most problems can be solved once we increase our life energy and find out what our unconscious really desires, and then move in accordance with those wishes. We can even look back on these difficult problem periods and see that we actually progressed and matured as a result of the experience.

I was consulted some years ago by a middle-aged accountant who was very tense and had many symptoms of anxiety. He was unhappy with his present work situation, although he had built up a good practice in his accounting firm. In his teens he had wanted to be a free-lance writer, but his parents had dismissed the idea as impractical, and he had followed his father's footsteps and become an accountant. He said he had always liked California but had only toyed with the idea of living there. I then tested his thymus. It tested strong. Since he wanted to find out if the major cause of his anxieties was in his domestic life or in his work life, I asked him to say, "I am happy with my domestic life," and he tested strong. I then asked him to say, "I am happy with my professional life." Instantly he tested weak. He looked at me in amazement. I asked him to say, "I want to continue my career as an accountant," and again he tested weak. I then asked him to say, "I want to become a free-lance writer." I asked him to visualize it in his mind as strongly as he could and he then tested strong. He looked even more amazed than before. Next, I asked him to say, "I want to become a writer in New York City," where he lived at the time, and again he tested weak. When he said, "I want to move to California, give up accounting, and become a free-lance writer," he tested strong.

Of course, I did not recommend to him on the strength of this one test that he should throw away his whole career and move across the country. He continued to get the same results each time he was tested during the next several weeks. One afternoon he said, "I get the message that my unconscious is giving me," and he decided to move with his family to California. In a short time, he became a highly successful writer. He calls me from time to time to tell me how happy he has been with the change that he made.

Remember, in the testing situation, if the subject's thymus tests weak on initial testing, then positive thoughts will activate the thymus. For example, if the man in the example above had tested weak at the thymus point initially, then when he said, "I wish to move to California," his thymus would have then tested strong. The test procedure would be the same, only now you would be testing to see what strengthened the life energy; whereas, when the thymus was strong initially, we tested to find what would weaken the life energy.

A friend of mine is a highly respected member of the business community. His thymus has nearly always tested weak. When he says, "I want to leave the business world and become a lay minister," he tests strong. He recognizes that this is what he really wants to do, and he says that although he cannot make the change now for financial reasons, this is what he is planning to do in the near future. He knows how he can correct his life energy weaknesses.

Recently I was talking to Dr. H., a very dedicated and responsible doctor. He told me how tired he had been feeling of late, and how he really did not know what to do about his ever-increasing patient load. He said he was getting worried about himself and his responsibility to his patients, and about how he could best help them while looking after himself at the same time.

The first thing I asked Dr. H. was, "How many days a week do you actively work in the practice now?" "Five," he answered. I then asked him, "And do you feel happy working five days?" He answered that he wasn't sure whether he was or was not happy with this.

Next we tested him. We asked him to say (and notice how exact and unambiguous we are in what we ask him to say), "I want to work four days a week in my practice." His thymus tested strong now—but only with four days, not with three, not with two, and not with six. His life energy was enhanced by the thought of working four days a week.

Dr. H. smiled, looked obviously relieved, and said, "That makes sense." But I was not convinced that this was his entire problem, so I asked him to say, "I am content that the only change I need to make in my practice is to work four days a week instead of five." As I had suspected, he tested weak.

I asked him what kind of practice he had in terms of patients. Did he follow strict appointments, or did he take a patient for as long as he felt that the patient needed to be seen? He told me that he kept to a strict twenty-minute appointment schedule. So I had him say, "I want to continue to see my patients for twenty-minute sessions." He tested weak. When I had him say, "I want to treat each of my patients for however long is necessary in each session," he tested strong.

Next, I had him combine the two strengthening statements and say, "I am content to change my practice to work four days a week, and to see my patients for as long as necessary in each session." He still tested weak when he said both of these, and the new problem was not hard to guess. He would be working one less day a week, he would obviously be spending more time with each patient, and, clearly, his income would drop. Each patient was now going to be getting more of his time while paying the same fee as before. No doubt, we had a fee issue to discuss.

The final step in solving this problem was to settle this fee matter. He said, "When I restructure my practice, I will continue to charge my present fee," and his thymus tested weak. I asked him to say it again, this time raising his fee by five dollars. Dr. H. now tested strong. He knew, saw demonstrated, and was convinced that the answer to his problem was to implement the following statement: "I will work in my practice four days a week. I will see my patients on an open-ended basis and will charge five dollars more per visit." He was greatly relieved, and I am sure he is now a more effective doctor because he is far less stressed—in other words, far more centered—when he is treating his patients.

This year, I was consulted by Peter, a young man who was having great difficulty pursuing his academic courses at college. He said that he really wanted to graduate from a particular college, but was totally unable to bring himself to complete any of the required term papers. If he did not complete them, of course, there was no way he could graduate from the school. As a result he had—as he well recognized—a gross disharmony and stress.

On the one hand, he said and felt that he wanted to finish his courses; on the other hand, his actions were those of a person who did not want to complete his studies. Which revealed the truth, his statements or his actions? Did he really want to complete college and simply need help to do his papers, or was the inability to do his papers an indication that he really didn't want to complete his course?

The answer was easy to find through testing. We had him say and visualize as clearly as he could, "I want to finish my present college course," and his thymus gland, which had been testing weak, remained weak. As soon as he said, "I want to give up college," instantly he tested strong.

Peter was a big man, weighing about 240 pounds. The difference in muscle strength was indeed amazing. He looked at me with a broad smile on his face and said, "There's something to this. I can't believe what happened, but something sure happened!" And he said, "I don't know whether what the test indicates is my true feeling, but I am now prepared to consider it." I could have spent weeks, or possibly longer, in psychotherapy with him to achieve what he arrived at instantly, what his true unconscious wishes were. Peter saw the results physically demonstrated to him. Even if he was not prepared to accept the findings of the test, he was certain of the change in his life energy which he felt when he made various statements.

This is what we call "instant psychotherapy," because we quickly uncover what the person really feels and believes. It is reinforced through the demonstration and experience of the test.

No patient in psychotherapy is ever given a chance to experience the difference for himself, to witness a physical demonstration of the effects of various thoughts on his body.

Peter now knows his unconscious desires regarding one very important area of his life—he does not want to continue at college. But we have to go further, to other areas of his life. If he does not want to continue at college, the presumption is that he wants to return to living at home. So we ask him to say, "I want to live at home," but he tests weak again. No, he does not want to live at home.

Well, where does he want to live? We pick the nearest city to his hometown. We ask him to say, "I want to live in Chicago." Now he tests strong, and he smiles. Going further, we ask him to say, "I want to *work* in Chicago." He tests strong again.

We know that he wants to work and live in Chicago, and that he wants to give up his college course. But what sort of job does he want?

Well, he had previously listed as some of his interests music, psychology, the study of languages (he is fluent in Spanish), and religion, adding that he is very religious-minded. So we had him say, "I want to work in Chicago in a religiously oriented psychological counseling service," and he tested strong. The smile on his face got broader, but he asked, "Could it be that I am so interested in languages that I really want to work with psychology clients who are of Spanish origin?" We had him repeat his question as a statement, and he tested strong. Then, we asked him to say the full sentence, "I want to leave college and move to Chicago, where I will work in a religious-based, psychological counseling service, dealing at least in part with clients of Spanish descent." He said all this, and he tested strong.

Finally, he knows what he wants to do. It has not taken months. It has not even taken hours. It has taken a very few minutes. The job may not work out. He may never find one that fits his specifications, but at this moment, he is in touch with the very core of his self, and he knows the occupation and the life he would like to have.

I wanted to take it even one step further with him, and so I asked him, "What is it that you would *really* most like to be in life? Not what you want to *do* right now, not where you want to live right now, but what you would ultimately like to be." He said, "I don't know. I think it's something to do with music." Peter is a very competent amateur pianist and singer. I asked him to say, "One of my ultimate goals is to be a really fine pianist." He did not test strong, but when he said, "I want to be a really fine singer," then he did. Next I tested him after he said, "I want to go to Chicago to live, where I intend to pursue serious study ultimately to become a professional singer." He tested strong. I then said to him, "Most people really like to refine their images to one major area. With you we know it has to do with singing or with psychological counseling." He said, picturing it in his own mind, "In the future, I want to be a professional singer, making records of religious music in a church setting," and he tested strong. The smile on his face was now as broad as could be. He was happy and at peace with himself, knowing his immediate goals in life and his deeper purpose in life. This last image, this clear picture of what ultimately he would like to achieve and what he was really striving for, was possible to discover through our new testing techniques. He has discovered this great vision for his future, which we call the homing thought (see next chapter).[6]

I rely on this thymus testing technique for making *all* major decisions in my life. For example, some time ago, I was to have an operation. I had arrived in the city where the hospital was located, and I was within one day of undergoing surgery when I suddenly realized that I had not been tested to see whether I felt that I should have the operation under these particular circumstances. And so, I had myself tested. Test-touching my thymus, I said, "I want to have my operation in the very near future," and I remained strong. But when I added the name of the hospital to which I was to be admitted, I tested weak.

Now I was in a quandary. I had no idea what to do. By coincidence, I was informed at that time of a different type of operative technique performed in another country. I contacted the surgeon, Dr. X, immediately and learned all I could about his procedure, read what I could find that day about it in journals and magazines, and then consulted some of his former patients. The next day I was tested again, then saying, "I want to have the operation in the near future," and I tested strong. When I said, "And I want to have the surgery performed by Dr. X in Hospital Y," and again I tested strong. Now, with confidence in my unconscious, I made a decision to have this operation. I knew that my unconscious had picked up clues from my conversations with the surgeon and from my research about both operative techniques. In terms of my understanding of myself and the procedure, at an unconscious level, this was the right thing to do. With little apprehension I submitted myself to surgery.

You can use this test in your life, too. We have taught this method to patients and students for quite some time. I have had many years of working with this technique, and I put a great deal of trust and faith into what I learn when I have my life energy tested for alternatives. I do not expect you to have this trust and faith in the technique initially, but I do expect that as you continue to work with it, you will become increasingly confident, and rely on your unconscious more and more. Yes, the unconscious will out. I am not advocating that you go blindly along with anything the testing indicates. I am suggesting that this test is a new way of discovering what we really believe.

You might want to use this technique to find out whether or not you really like your job. Maybe you will think, "Oh, sure I like it. It's okay." But how do you *really* feel about your work? What do you *really* want to be doing with your life? Or, you could use this technique when you want to decide with whom to go out, or which school to attend, or to answer any of the questions that are constantly being heaped upon you in life.

This technique is not like a Ouija board, and there is nothing "psychic" about it. We are simply using it to tap that vast pool of knowledge that is in your unconscious, to your real desires and deep feelings about the specific question. If we were in tune with our unconscious and preconscious, as a person who has been in long-term psychoanalysis usually is, this process would not be necessary. But most of us are not in touch with our unconscious—and we need to put ourselves in touch.

I am frequently consulted in such decisions as, "I don't really know whether I should marry so and so. I know I like so and so, but I am just not sure how much." This person is "in two minds" and is not in touch with his basic mind, his unconscious—which ultimately will out and dictate the relationship with the other person. Suppose for the sake of an example we are dealing with Tom who wants to know about Mary. All Tom has to do to solve his dilemma is to visualize and say, "I want to marry Mary," and then to say, "I do not want to marry Mary," and see which statement strengthens and which one weakens. This does not mean that he will have a happy marriage if they wed, but it tells us that this is what his body and unconscious really believe at the time. The method is a powerful aid to him. It is now much easier for him to make up his mind.

It is absolutely essential that the statement you make to test be very precise. Do not make the statements too long, and make them very exact. If the statement is long and rambling you will not be able to zero in on the thought and visualize it as clearly as possible in your mind. You will not be able to focus on your test image. Use simple, direct statements with no ambiguity. As an example of the accuracy of the test and how it reflects what a person really knows about himself (and as an example of how explicit the question must be), consider the following case. A friend has had a very unhappy marriage for many years, and, although I do not like to take sides in such matters, it is quite obvious that her husband, Jonathan, has been a very difficult and unloving man. Now, after all these years, she has found someone who has caused her to question her commitment to her husband. I asked her to say, "I want to leave Jonathan." She tested strong. She tested weak for, "I want to stay with Jonathan." The next step seemed quite clear. I asked her to say, "I want to live with Raymond," (her new friend) and she tested strong. For, "I do not want to live with Raymond," she tested weak.

But did she want to marry Raymond? Yes, she did and this was confirmed on testing. Thus, she obviously wanted to divorce Jonathan. But when she said, "I want to divorce Jonathan," she tested weak! I said to her, "Jean, this is not logical. How can you marry Raymond unless you divorce Jonathan? Let's test again." And we did, with the same results. Had something gone wrong with the testing? Jean blushed, swallowed, and said, "Well, let me tell you the truth. Jonathan and I have never really been married. We have lived together all these years, and everyone, including our children, thinks we are married, but we are not. That's why I test weak for wanting to divorce him, because how can you divorce someone to whom you are not married?"

This is an example of the surprises that you can find when testing. The answer is there, and it is found through asking the correct question. It is the unexpected answers, the ones that make you doubt the testing, that often lead you to learn much more than you would have anticipated—and to help the person much more than you had expected.

With this technique not only are we arriving at quick and easy answers, which in analysis might otherwise take a very long time to determine, but we are physically experiencing and seeing the difference in our muscle strength. The power of the word is amazing, and the power of the body to crystallize these words and feelings into an instant response is absolutely marvelous.

Almost invariably, after I have used this method with one of my patients or students, he or she will remark on how much tension has been relieved. Nearly everyone reports that a load has been taken off his or her mind.

We have used this method with thousands of patients and students over a long period of time, and of course, not all the resulting decisions worked out. The test is not 100 percent foolproof. *There are many variables, and the test is accurate only when they are all controlled.* Remember that the test indicates your present attitude, not necessarily what will ultimately be the right decision, but in every case, the subjects have felt much happier with the results. They recognized that they were, as one patient said, "going with the flow," going with what the body and mind really believe. There was a harmony about their decisions. If for reasons outside the patient's control the situation did not work out, he didn't blame the experience. Instead, he recognized that at the time, he felt it to be absolutely correct. Perhaps he was not fully aware of all the factors involved when he visualized his test image and then made the decision, but still his decision was in harmony with his wishes at the time.

When you have problems that are holding back your progress through tension and stress, and if you want to know what your instincts are, you don't necessarily have to undergo deep probing. Just test. It is remarkably quick and inexpensive.

Furthermore, we find out what *you* think, we know that you have not been influenced by anyone else. You can see the results on your own body. The energy in the unconscious thought, when expressed, now has the power to strengthen the weak muscle, or conversely, to weaken the strong muscle. It is an exceptionally powerful tool.

So, if you have a problem, if you are in two minds about something, have a friend test your thymus. Say the two alternatives, testing after each. See which makes you weak and which makes you strong. You now have your answer, and you know how to solve your problems instantly—how to make positive choices.

Note: If you test weak when you say, for example, "I want to continue to live with my wife," or, "I like my present job," this does not mean that you necessarily should rush out and divorce your wife or leave your job, nor should any major decisions be made as a result of isolated testing. Such extreme action may not be required to solve the problem; however, testing weak for one of the examples stated above means that you should individually evaluate experiences related to the broader concept. For example, test to find out just what it is about living with your wife that makes you test weak. Or find out what aspect(s) of your job specifically cause a diminution of life energy. Try to alleviate these smaller problems one by one. You probably acted in accord with your unconscious when you made the decision to marry your wife, or to take your job, for example. Of course your wishes may have changed, but often there will be just a factor or two in the situation that affects you and weakens your life energy, and you may find that by examining and correcting these factors, the major "problem" is solved automatically.

Let's take the marriage example one step further. One man tested weak when he said, "I want to stay married to my wife." I said to him, "We now recognize that your body is saying that there is something in your relationship with your wife that is devitalizing you, that goes against your high-thymus activity." I asked him for some suggestions. We tested a number of them, but did not find the problem area. For example, when he said, "I still love my wife when she is extravagant with the finances," he tested strong. But then I asked him to say, "I still love my wife when she pesters me for sex." He tested weak. He told me then that he was very happy with his sexual relationship with his wife and enjoyed having sex with her, but then he said that he did not like the way that she was so forthright in asking him for it, which he was beginning to interpret as demands. He said, "Before we were married I was delighted with her sexual forthrightness. But now it somehow grates against me." He went home and talked about this with his wife, and she said she could understand his point of view and modified her behavior. The sexual relationship itself did not change, but he was less pressured, no longer feeling that he had to perform. He now tests strong when he says, "I am happy with my marriage." He says that he is very happy with his marriage, and his wife says the same thing. They have both told me that this simple test and her willingness to act on the results had really saved their marriage.

Another man tested weak, as is frequently the case, when he said, "I enjoy my work"—some 90 percent of workers test weak when they say they enjoy what they do. What does this tell us about our society and what work has become? Most workers can see and are prepared to admit that they really do not like their jobs, but say, "Well, it's a way of making money so that I can enjoy myself on the weekend or when I retire." Or, "I have to do it for the children's education." But the frightening fact still exists that 90 percent of people lose their life energy just thinking about their jobs. Imagine what it is like for them when they are actually on the job. This does not mean necessarily that they should change their employment situation. But again we go through, one by one, all the aspects of the work situation, and we often find that when a particular factor for which they tested weak is changed, they are happier with the job. There are usually strong, unconscious, positive reasons for engaging in a particular form of employment, and the decision to change should be thoroughly considered over a period of time.

For example, one man tested weak when he said, "I like reporting to Mr. X," who was his superior. Strangely enough to him, he did not test weak for any other aspects of his job. He liked the work he was doing, he enjoyed his job, but this one aspect, having to report to this particular man, really upset him. So I asked him if it were possible to change his reporting procedure so that he could report to someone else for whom he tested strong. He was able to arrange this at work, and he has told me that ever since that one change, he has felt much happier at work. His wife has remarked upon how much more contented and peaceful he seems when he returns home in the evening. In most situations, it is the "little things" which cause the problems, and these can generally be corrected. It usually comes down to minor aspects, such as in our examples above, the spouse unknowingly pressuring for sex, or personality differences with a certain superior. And when these little things are resolved, the apparently big problem seems to disappear. To discover what these little things are, you need to use the testing technique described in this chapter.

With this tool you can find out for yourself if you are really happy in a given life situation, such as your marriage, your job, your friends, where you live, your choice of educational pursuits, or whatever. You have a way of making them all high-thymus activities, ones which increase your creativity and your life energy.

The noted English scientist Sir Fred Hoyle has said that we are all "choice machines."[7] There is some function inside our brains as yet barely recognized which determines whether we make the right choices in our lives so as to achieve health and happiness. By the exercise of these correct choices, by embracing what is good for us, we can achieve health and happiness for ourselves and for others. And these choices may be made many, many times each day. As H. S. Jennings stated, "Life is a continuous process of selecting one line of action and rejecting another." When we have to make a decision about any aspect of our lives, we may believe that we have a wide range of choices. Actually this is not the case. There will be one choice for which we test strong, which activates our life energy and is in keeping with our deepest desires for life and health. Then there are all the other choices—but they are against our grain. We might call our options "bioethical choices." Through the tool of testing, we can find the correct choice for the individual—the choice that is pro-life, pro-evolution, and which ensures survival of the individual and the species.

The test that you have now learned can help you make the right choices, those which are in keeping with your deepest desires for health and life, harmony and peace. Whenever you need to make a choice, about any aspect of your life, you can now find out what is right for you at the moment. Through the utilization of this apparently simple test, you now have the option of choosing the path of your personal growth and evolution. Some of the answers that you find may not change throughout many years, or at all. Other answers may change very rapidly. These tend to be the more superficial ones, decisions that you only recently arrived at in your unconscious and preconscious, or else choices which are easily altered by external data. Thus it is always advisable in the case of something as important as a choice of career, for example, to test over a period of time for consistency. Particularly with new ideas the decision may change with additional information or a more refined definition.

A new future is yours—but you must at all times invoke your will. The testing will show you what is right for you, but it cannot make you do it. You must want to be healthy, want to be well, want to be balanced and creative. Your task in life is to aspire for what is right and healthy and uplifting for you. Now as never before you can see the road to health and fulfillment in front of you. This is your goal, and this you can now achieve—psychobiological harmony, optimum life energy.

The Homing Thought

"God has given to each man the light that was his due; so that he need not go astray."

—Paracelsus

When I was a youngster growing up in Australia, I often went surfing at the Sydney beaches. Whenever there was a big wave coming, my friends and I would dive for the sand at the bottom of the water and hold on to that sand with our fingertips. The wave would pass over, and we would come up to the surface. The water would now be perfectly calm, but on all sides there would be scattered surfboards and people sputtering for breath and spitting out water. We had learned that as soon as we were faced with this situation of stress, we could dive down, grab our securing, and hold onto our "rock" until our stress passed. There is a rock that each of us can have all the time, throughout our lives. That rock is the homing thought.[1]

In the previous chapter I told you about Peter, whose homing thought was that he would someday become a recording star singing religious hymns in church. I demonstrated to him that if I pushed him, shook him, threatened him, or made sudden noises, he would lose life energy and his indicator muscle would test weak. But as long as he held on to his homing thought, no stress could weaken him.

Peter learned to keep this thought in his mind as often as possible. This homing thought was more complex than his immediate goal of obtaining a psychological counseling job. His homing thought was his purpose in life. As long as he held on to that purpose—and this is greater than a goal—he could be severely stressed and yet remain strong.

I call it the homing thought because I am reminded of an airplane pilot who is lost in the storm. He turns on his direction finder and tunes into his homing beacon which guides him safely to home. We each can have this homing beacon for our lives, and this is the homing thought. It holds us steadfast.

Herbert Read's "Unamuno's Comment on Don Quixote" is one of the best descriptions I have encountered of the homing thought:

> In saying, "I know who I am," Don Quixote said only, "I know what I will be!" That is the hinge of all human life: to know what one wills to be. Little ought you to care who you are; the urgent thing is what you will be. The being that you are is but an unstable, perishable being, which eats of the earth and which the earth some day will eat; what you will to be is the idea of you in God, the Consciousness of the universe; it is the divine idea of which you are the manifestation in time and space. And your longing impulse toward the one you will to be, is only homesickness drawing you toward your divine home. Man is complete and upstanding only when he would be more than man.[2]

We can all develop our homing thoughts. To begin to find yours, sit down and list some of the things that you would really like to be. Of course these will differ from individual to individual. You may wish to be a priest, a horticulturalist, a seamstress. You may see yourself walking through life in a monk's habit, like Saint Francis of Assisi. In your mind, you may be conducting music or playing the piano. It need not matter to anyone else—it is *your* homing thought. Just sit down and write some of the possibilities to which you aspire.

As we go through life, our thinking, our desires, our aspirations, and our sense of purpose will evolve and change. That is to be expected. But write down what you think are some of the most likely choices that you would work for at the moment. And then, one by one, test them. Think each one very clearly in your mind to yourself. Picture it as vividly as you can. Then, have someone test you. If you next ask him to shake you, or shout "Boo!" at you, or otherwise introduce a sudden stress and then immediately test you again, you should test strong if your homing thought is "right" for you. When you keep your homing thought in your mind, you will be much less vulnerable to the effects of stress.

Let's find out just how vulnerable you are to stress at the moment. Start by testing your friend, your "subject." When you test the indicator muscle it should be strong. (For this test you do not need to touch the thymus gland test point as this is a less refined, or grosser, test.)

Now that you have tested the indicator muscle and found it strong in the clear, shout "Boo!" at your friend rather suddenly. Test again, and he will most likely test weak.

When I lecture to doctors, I often invite them to come up and be tested for their vulnerability to stress. I test the doctor in the clear and find his indicator muscle is strong. Then I ask his receptionist or assistant to say to him, in a normal voice, "Doctor, Mr. X is on the telephone." (The receptionist has been asked beforehand to name a "difficult" patient.) Even though there is no telephone in the lecture hall, and even though the doctor knows that there has been no call from the patient, *the thought is enough* to make the indicator test weak, revealing a distinct loss of the doctor's vital life energy.

Whenever a stimulus such as described above causes a reduction of life energy, then we know that the individual affected is uncentered. Any sudden environmental stress, even something as simple as the example above or even *thinking* of an environmental stress, will deplete the life energy if the subject is uncentered. For example, you could try the following with your test subject. Say, "This is just a joke, but your car has a flat tire." Watch him test weak, and then watch the startled look on his face. He was certainly not consciously aware that a joke could arouse such a reaction in his mind and body. This weakness, this vulnerability to stress, can be overcome through use of the homing thought.

One of the most advantageous applications of the homing thought is its use for someone who is sick. The homing thought gives the patient a purpose. If someone you know is sick, ask him to create an image of himself being really, really well—no longer in pain, no longer bleeding, no longer disabled, or whatever the problem may be. Ask him to visualize himself as vital, upright, full of energy, perhaps running on the beach, basking in the sunlight, running a marathon, riding a horse, planting a garden, and so on. The imagery and the aspiration are his and his alone. We as outsiders can only offer some suggestions. Let him choose the one that feels best for him. It is his picture, his fantasy, his desire. Then show him how his life energy is increased when he has this image in mind.

The first step in being well is to picture yourself well, to have a goal, a purpose. If you don't see the purpose, it is hard to activate the healing energies. But if you have the homing thought well in mind, then you have activated your own positive get-well attitude.

I was once asked to go to a hospital to see an elderly man with a very serious disease. It was expected that he would die very soon. I was aghast when I saw him, as he looked so gravely ill. He was pale, emaciated, nearly lifeless. There was a fetid smell coming from his mouth and body.

There was so little I could do to help him. I wasn't even one of his doctors. But I said to him, "Can you imagine yourself as being really, truly well? I don't mean just free of the intravenous fluids, or free of all your symptoms, but truly well? With a spring in your step and a glimmer in your eye? Can you visualize yourself in a state of positive health, upright, active, in touch with nature?"

After a little while, he said that he thought he could. I demonstrated to him how when he thought this his thymus gland, which had previously tested weak, suddenly tested strong, and that even in his debilitated condition if I introduced the shock of a minor stress, he continued to stay strong when he had his homing thought in mind. He was convinced of the power of his own positive thoughts to make a difference in his body energy.

I next suggested to him that by mobilizing his life energy he could start to get well from inside, which is the only way to achieve positive health. I attached a piece of white paper to the television set at the foot of his bed and I said, "Whenever you can, I want you to look at this piece of paper and visualize your homing thought." Then I asked him, "What is the absolute minimum time in which you could possibly leave this hospital?" He thought about it. He knew the state of his body, he knew he could barely sit up. But he said, "Ten days." Although I thought his answer was extremely optimistic, if not unrealistic, I said, "Fine. I want you to look at this white paper whenever you can, and visualize yourself leaving the hospital ten days from today, in a state of glowing health."

In exactly ten days he went home and has remained in good health since. The doctors attending him were astounded by his recovery. The man has since informed me that he has left instructions that his piece of white paper be buried with him, as he says it saved his life. Of course, it was not the piece of paper that saved his life, but what it symbolized. He saved his own life through the vital healing energy within his own body that he mobilized himself with the power of his homing thought.

I recently saw a middle-aged man who has done very well for himself in life. He has a happy home life, loving wife and children, a successful career, and all that he can possibly want in the way of material possessions. He is secure against any potential financial problems and has been able to prove to himself some of his inner strengths. He had previously been on the point of bankruptcy, but repaid all his loans and accumulated a large sum of money. He plays sports, exercises strenuously and regularly, eats judiciously, and is generally pretty satisfied, it would seem, with his lot. When I asked him, "Well, what do you plan to do now that you have achieved all these wonderful things? What do you want to do next with your life? What is your life for?" He looked at me with a very puzzled expression. He said, "That's exactly the problem. None of what I have done, none of what I have achieved, not even my dear wife and wonderful children, and certainly not my business accomplishments or my cars or my house or my boat, really means anything. I know the importance of your question. I somehow feel the same question from inside me, but I don't know how to answer it. I certainly do not know what to do."

He is not alone with this problem. I cannot tell you how many times a middle-aged female patient has said to me, "Well, my husband is at work all day, the children have left home, now what will I do? Will I take up some social activities, will I get a job? I somehow feel that at the age of forty-five my life is over. What will I do?"

Now the question to me is not "What will I do," but "Who will I become?" This is the time not to think in terms of employment, but to think in terms of personal development. To me, the greatest task that we have in our passage through life is to evolve, so that when we finish our lives, we have matured more than just through passing the years. We have had tasks, goals, problems, and as we have coped with these we have grown and learned and earned and enjoyed and experienced life. But more than this, somehow there has been a personal unfolding, some personal evolution. We have reached, or at least attempted to reach, our true home—that personalized image of a fully evolved individual.

I do not know yet what that state is for me, and I certainly do not know what it is for anyone else. But I have managed to find a way whereby we can take steps to achieve this. That is by finding our homing thoughts. Let me give you a very personal example. Some time ago, I sat down quietly and meditated on a mental picture of myself as the person I would have been had I developed more nearly into the potential that was mine. I saw myself sitting on the sand in front of a calm ocean, playing the recorder. The morning sun was streaming down on me, and I could feel its heat and life coming into me. I could feel and smell the breeze coming from the sea. I was erect, with my chest, my heart, open to receive all the goodness from the sea and the sun. I felt warm and full of vitality and energy. I knew that in this state I was perfectly healthy and totally loving.

I was surprised at the image of playing the recorder. Some years earlier I had played it; I had taken a few lessons sporadically and with no real enthusiasm, and then quickly let my interest drop without any feeling of loss. Now this image came back to me very clearly. I asked someone to test me for it, and it was right. Yet, I had not been happy with my previous experience with the instrument in terms of the lessons. (In fact, I am rarely happy with any form of musical tuition in the usual sense of the word.) Then we did the thymus test and when I said, "I want to play the recorder and have instruction in it," I tested weak. When I said I wanted to play the recorder but not have any "lessons" I tested strong. Now I play the recorder and other instruments and have encouraged many of my patients and students to do the same when their homing image has been along the same lines. I have found great satisfaction in this and through it have experienced a personal evolution. I have perhaps learned more about myself from this glimpse of my homing thought than through any other insight in the recent past.

Of course, this is not all there is to the homing thought. This is just one part of it—a beginning. Through a simple situation such as this, you can initiate your own self-discovery as you seek your homing thought.

Remember that each of us is unique, although our present society tends to at best minimize and often destroy this uniqueness. We all must have the same houses as the others in our neighborhood. We all must mow our lawns, we all will plant the same trees in our yards, we all will eat the same food, we all will read the same books, we all will drive the same cars, we all will take the same sort of vacations. Modern civilization is not favorable to the unique development that is within each individual. But through your homing thought you can discover your own uniqueness and reveal your own inner kernel which is you and no one else.

Stop for a moment now. Sit quietly and try to picture yourself as perfect as you can imagine being. (Let me make two remarks upon this image. First, always see yourself in the positive. Rather than picture yourself as "not fat," see yourself as slender. Rather than thinking of yourself as "without pain" see yourself as being free and mobile in your movements. Second, refrain from comparing yourself with another. Avoid such thoughts as "I see myself playing the violin like Yehudi Menuhin," or "I am playing golf as well as Arnold Palmer," for example. This is your specific and personal uniqueness; it is not to be compared in any way to anyone else. This is you.) Choose your own area of concentration for beginning your definition of your homing thought. It need not be all-encompassing. Think now, for a moment, and try to discover your homing thought.

When I first discuss finding the homing thought with my students, they often remark that it reminds them of prayer, or of meditation or reflection. Of course it is all these things. Prayer is not asking God for favors on a day-to-day basis, but rather a request for assistance in achieving and refining our homing thought and in following the path that will help us to attain it.

Thinking about your homing thought, your thymus will test strong and you will be centered, your vulnerability to stress will be reduced, your life energy will be raised so much that factors that earlier might have stressed you now will not. When you are in touch with your true self through your homing thought, you are above being affected by most of the environmental factors that stress us from day to day. Your life energy has been dramatically raised. Furthermore, your own life goals will be clearer to you and you will have new confidence in your decisions.

Quite some years ago I met an elderly lady who, late in life, had become a very highly regarded professional photographer. She told me her story. She had been in her early sixties and a widow when she was diagnosed as having breast cancer. She had surgery, and her doctor told her, "I don't think you have long to live. If there is anything you would really like to do, now is the time to do it." Now I don't know what he had in mind, but I doubt if he could have ever dreamed what she did. She sat down and thought about it. Finally she said to herself, "I've always secretly wanted to be a professional photographer." She knew absolutely nothing about cameras. She went into a store in Sydney and asked what was the best camera made. She was told it was a Leica. She asked where it was made and found that the factory was in Germany. So with this clear image in her mind of what she wanted to achieve in life, of what she wanted to become, of how she could best fulfill herself, she flew to Germany. She arrived at the Leica factory and announced that she wanted to learn how to become a photographer. She was told that they did offer classes, but only to advanced professional photographers. But in her case they finally relented and permitted her to enroll in the professional class. While she was there, she saw her own camera being made and saw each of the lenses that she planned to purchase being specially hand-ground just for her. She returned to Australia as a fledgling, fully equipped professional photographer, and she continued to pursue her goal and became highly respected for her work. She is still living a very happy, fulfilling, and evolved life now, many years after she was first told of her illness.

I was told of a woman whose experience was similar to this. A friend of mine was put up overnight at a house with an elderly lady who took in boarders to help meet expenses. When my friend came down for breakfast the next morning, this elderly lady offered him a beautiful, healthy breakfast. She quickly said, "I hope you don't find it too peculiar for your tastes. I eat only health foods. Let me tell you the reason." She went over to her fireplace and from the mantelpiece took down a framed letter. This letter had been sent to her some forty-five years previously by her doctor. It stated that she had advanced cancer of the bowel and unless she had surgery within the very near future, it would prove fatal. She waited for my friend to finish reading it and then said, "When that diagnosis was made forty-five years ago, I asked the doctor to give me this letter. I took it and framed it and put it where it was today. Then I prayed. I prayed to be perfectly well. I decided to do everything I could to become perfectly well and wholesome and an example to my community. Ever since that day I have been careful to eat only healthy food, and each time I have a meal I visualize myself as being perfectly well. I have never been sick since."

In fact, many of the present techniques that have been taught for the meditational cure of serious illnesses really involve the invocation of the homing thought. Every day and for quite prolonged periods, the person imagines himself as being perfectly well in every possible way. This is the power of the homing thought. It can activate our life energy so greatly that the thymus can then go about its immunological task of defeating the cancer.

Yehudi Menuhin once wrote, "It has been my good fortune to spend my life doing the thing I love most, being a musician. To be in tune with oneself, with one's environment, with the music one plays and with those who listen, sounds almost pagan in its wholeness, in its total unity with nature."[3] Early in life Menuhin discovered a major portion of his homing thought and has been able to focus on it more and more clearly; hence his great satisfaction with himself and his life. The wholeness that he talks of—how many of us have experienced this? How many of us are doing what we love most, and how many of us even know what we love and want to do most?

I recently tested a professional football team and discovered that nearly all the players tested weak when they were charged by an opponent; in fact they also tested weak when they were about to catch the football. Both of these situations were putting the players under stress to which they were vulnerable and thus their capabilities were reduced. They were less able to resist the charge and were less likely to catch the ball cleanly because of this vulnerability. When we combined the two activities—that is, when they were charged as they were about to catch the ball (which is, after all, one of the most common experiences on the football field) they also tested weak. Most of the team members were shocked and disheartened by this finding, and didn't know what to do about it. They became disillusioned with their playing technique. Suddenly one of them said, with a light shining from his face as if struck with a ray of illumination, "Now I see what makes a great football player great! He is the one who can keep his energy up under this sort of pressure!" The greats in the various sports, as well as the greats in other aspects of life, are those who hold their energy when most others would lose it. I have tested many "greats" and find this to be a nearly universal factor.

The same applies, for example, to a long-distance runner training for an event. For two or three or even more years he trains with that solitary goal in mind, that one event. Of course these two examples, the runner and the football player, are illustrations of what we might call mini-homing thoughts. As regards that aspect of his life, the football player puts all his energy into only one thing, catching the ball. When he is running for it, that is 100 percent his goal. He gives no regard to the fact that he might be hit by a defensive player. He operates totally with the one goal in mind. Over a longer period of time, that is what the distance runner is doing—training with that one event in mind.

On a broader scale, this is what we need to achieve in terms of our homing thoughts. To use a familiar analogy, we need the homing thought to help us achieve our goals in the game of life. It applies to the daily tasks such as catching the ball, and the short-term goals such as winning the race, and to the ultimate goal, the race of life.

The homing thought is not constant. It will continually change or be enlarged as we contemplate it more and more. For example, my own personal homing thought has expanded well beyond that first day when I saw myself playing the recorder. I have worked and refined my image considerably since then. While fixed in its more abstract aspects, it is constantly changing on a more concrete level as my own life is changing.

Of course, this change applies to us all. That is part of growth, of evolution. It has been said by some that Leonardo's *Mona Lisa* was constantly with him for years after the major work had been completed. He carried it around with him, refining it, making minute changes as he saw fit. It has been said that the *Mona Lisa* represents his female self. As his ideal of himself changed and evolved over the years, so he continued to make subtle but definite changes in the painting.

As we go through life, our thinking, our desires, our aspirations, and our sense of purpose will of course change and evolve. This is to be expected. As you refine your own homing thought, you will begin to find that it is difficult to tell anyone else what it is. It is partly visual, partly a feeling, an experience, and you cannot really tell anyone else about it because you cannot find words to express your inner self. This is your private, innermost self, your own personal goal and image, and there should be no need for you to try to explain it to anyone. It is your personal aspiration.

We can imagine that each of us starts off as a seed. In that seed is all that is required for perfect development into a majestic, fully proportioned, beautiful individual. Of course, perfect development rarely happens. Even a tree, which has no conscious mind as we define it nor an advanced physiology as we have, has hindrances to its perfect development. The soil is often inadequate. The winds may distort it. Yet we know what that tree could have evolved into —the shape it should have assumed, the height and girth it would have attained had it grown perfectly. So it is with us.

Imagine that when you were conceived you were a perfect seed. When we plant a flower seed from a packet that we have purchased, we see on the packet a picture of what the seed is supposed to grow into, what we should expect it to become. Each of us must find out what was on our own individual "packet"—what we were supposed to grow into. Then we must look at ourselves with courage and insight and realize how far we have deviated from this. Through the exigencies of life, we have wandered far from the ideal. We are lost in the fog. Now by picking up this homing thought again we can redirect our energies, we can work to develop into the perfect creations that we were meant to be. "Thou shalt be perfect with the Lord thy God." (Deuteronomy 18:13)

Your homing thought becomes your touchstone; it becomes the final arbiter of many decisions that you will make throughout your day. Suppose that you are saving for the down payment on a house, and you see an expensive piece of clothing in a shop window. You may be tempted, but you will say, "No, I cannot buy it because I'm saving to get my house." That is the same as with the homing thought. Suppose that your homing thought includes the image of yourself as being upright and active with good posture. Suppose now you have the choice of sitting in a chair which will support your spine or a deep, soft, so-called comfortable chair that will collapse your spine. The choice of one will be consistent with your homing thought; the other will not. In the same way, if your homing thought includes the concept of being healthy, you will tend to reject foods that may be tempting but which you know will take you from your homing thought. Instead you choose those that will bring you closer to home.[4]

These findings are of vital importance clinically. I have used these techniques to help people with many serious illnesses. You can find out for yourself, by testing, just how valuable the homing thought is.

Remember Peter, when he had his homing thought clearly in mind (and he has told me that since our early meetings he has elaborated and crystallized this thought), if he is presented with stress he will not test weak. Some of the simplest stresses to test are, for example, fluorescent lights (have your subject stare at the fluorescent light), artificial fibers (put an artificial fiber hat on your subject's head), refined sugar (have him eat a small amount of it), or just say "Boo!" to him.

There is no universal answer for stress. We each respond to it in our own individual manner. But if we have the homing thought clearly in mind, stressful stimuli will have much less detrimental effects on our life energy. I suggest to my students that they combine this homing thought concept with the meditation they practice each day. They work on building this positive image, and they carry it with them when they leave their symbolic or physical meditation rooms. Then whenever they are faced with stress and feel vulnerable, they hold on to their homing thought just as we held on to the sand as children surfing on the beach. This homing thought becomes your rock, your home base, your center. It is *you*, as you believe you were created to be. In Psalm 31 we read, "Be thou my strong rock. . . ." Our homing thought can do that for us. My students usually begin with the thought of positive health and gradually refine it. The important thing is to have your homing thought constantly in your mind. It will color your actions and change your life. For your homing thought not only gives you a goal and an aspiration in life, but it also helps you to follow the guidelines for reaching that goal. It helps you to make decisions and to reject roadblocks or detours on the road. The homing thought is an invaluable tool to aid in reducing stress, mobilizing our life energy, and achieving a glowing state of positive, vibrant health.

The Cerebral Hemispheres

Whenever there is stress, not only will there be thymus under-activity, there will also be an imbalance between the two cerebral hemispheres which prevents us from arriving at a creative solution to the problem causing the stress.

To be oversimple, the left hemisphere in a right-handed person has the function of dealing with the everyday situations of reality with which we are confronted. By contrast, the right hemisphere has mainly to do with fantasy. A businessman who is wrestling with his tax forms, deadlines, and inventory problems is using his left brain; when he stares out the window and begins to daydream, he is using his right brain. He uses his right hemisphere in an attempt to correct what we call the hemisphere imbalance created by the overactivity of his left hemisphere.

The functions of the left cerebral hemisphere include everyday reality, ordered "logical" relationships, semantics, and arithmetic. Those of the right hemisphere include fantasy, imagination, intuition, dreams, visual imagery, rhythm, rhyme, spatial relationships, humor, syntax, and music.

Normal *creative* activity involves the equal participation of both hemispheres.[1] Creativity is the ability to make something new. When you are creative you can come up with a new solution to your problems, not just the same old stereotyped responses as before. Every new problem requires a new solution, and to find the right solution, you must be creative. This you can accomplish only when your life energy is high and when your hemispheres are balanced—when you have psychobiological harmony.

On testing we find, unfortunately, that approximately 95 percent

83

of those tested are not in a creative mode. One hemisphere, usually the left, is dominant or overactive. This occurs for a number of reasons. The left hemisphere is related to activity on the right side of the body. Since most people are right-handed, it is not surprising that most people tend to activate the left hemisphere with the physical activity of writing, painting, and so forth. Furthermore, as mentioned previously, the left hemisphere is concerned with day-to-day reality. John Gardner referred to it as "the lobe that calculates and squints."[2]

By contrast, the right hemisphere is concerned more with fantasy and dreams, intuition and imaginativeness. Associated with the right-brain musical activities we find rhythm and rhyme. As I speak, the logic and semantics and "cold, hard reality" of what I say are determined by my left-brain functioning, but the rhythms, flows, syntax, and rhyming—in other words, the "music" of my speech—are a right-brain function.[3] A good communicator will use both hemispheres as he gives his presentation.

Curt Sachs has stated that the most primitive musical instruments were purely rhythm-oriented.[4] Melody then evolved through the repetition of rhythm. The same process is found in language as reduplication. The speech of children has a tendency toward combinations such as poppa, momma, ding-dong, singsong, and ticktock.

Humor is also a function of the right cerebral hemisphere. The lack of a sense of humor always indicates cerebral imbalance and diminished life energy. When a speaker is under stress and left-hemisphere-dominant, the right hemisphere may manifest itself in a humorous fashion. The resulting laughter aids in restoring cerebral balance. Bloopers such as those below are an example of this type of humor:

> "Try our delicious-tasting cough syrup. We guarantee you'll never get any better."

> "Mayor Richard Daley of Chicago says, 'The police in Chicago are not here to create disorder, they are here to preserve it.' "

> "The topic of tonight's 'Sermonette' is 'Cast Thy Bread upon the Water.' This is the National Breadcasting Company."[5]

Bloopers and slips of the tongue are examples of right-brain attempts to balance left-brain overactivity.[6] The right-hemisphere component will frequently have rhyme, rhythm, and humor which bears unconscious relationships to the left-brain activity. The fact that so many of these slips have an obvious sexual basis further substantiates Freud's work. Consider the following examples:

> Announcer says, "And Dad will love this delicious flavor, too. So remember, it's Wonder Bread for the Breast in Bed."

> Radio announcer: "It's a hot night at the Garden, folks, and at ringside I see several ladies in gownless evening straps."[7]

The sudden humor and subsequent laughter occasioned by a slip afford what Freud referred to as "the yield of humorous pleasure." While the slip itself is an indication of stress, the resulting humor is a powerful therapeutic agent.

Let me give you an example in a related sphere, that concerning nicknames. I was once present at the birth of a nickname which stuck on a particular person for quite some time, proving its basic truth. (If a nickname is unattributable, it is quickly discarded. But if it fits, then it stays.) When I was at grammar school we had a very kindly old headmaster. One year he was replaced, causing much sorrow for the students, by a much younger man with a reputation for being the "new broom." He was going to sweep everything clean, and clear up all the sloppiness and lack of discipline that were allegedly our school's major sins. His name was Mr. Healy. When Mr. Healy first arrived we were all very apprehensive. No one knew what to make of him, or what to do. But we knew that he was probably going to be punitive. And we feared him. On his second day as headmaster, he arrived at school driving a very small and rather battered old car which he ostentatiously parked in the playground, which was not the place where the schoolmasters usually parked their cars. There were about three hundred of us watching him. None of us knew what to think when a very attractive young woman got out with him. (We never discovered who she was.) Within half an hour of this event, he was nicknamed "Hot Rod Healy."

Let us examine this nickname and see if we can point out the right brain component and then recreate the final act which brought all the words and imagery together into a name which was both consciously and unconsciously fitting. First, this new headmaster drove up in what was anything but a "hot rod." At that time, "hot rod" was the slang expression for a customized fast sports car. We also knew that he had a reputation for being quick on the draw with the cane—a hot rod. And when we saw him with the attractive young woman, sexual fantasies came to mind—the hot rod again. Lastly, the Austin Healy was at that time a very popular sports car.

Out of this came the reduplicative "Hot Rod Healy"—a new creation resulting from left brain stress and right brain humor.

Shakespeare loved wordplay. In fact, an entire book has been written on this subject.[8] For example, in *Richard II*, when Richard, having lost his crown, is asked by Bolingbroke, "Are you contented to resigne the Crowne?" he replies:

> I, no; no, I: for I must nothing bee:
> Therefore no, no, for I resigne to thee,   (IV, i. 201-2)

As Mahood says, "Besides suggesting in one meaning (Aye, no; no, aye) his tormenting indecision, and in another (Aye—no; no I) the overwrought mind that finds an outlet in punning, [it] also represents in the meaning 'I know no I' " his worry, "Can he exist if he no longer bears his right name of King?"

This wordplay is so much a part of Shakespeare's genius. It involves creativity, the full and harmonious functioning of the two cerebral hemispheres—unstressed, balanced, rich communication.

Humor and rhyming are basic to another type of wordplay, Cockney slang. It has associations that are invoked between the slang expression and the original subject. For example, the Cockney "wife" becomes "fork and knife." "Stew" is "garlic and glue." "Miss" is "cuddle and kiss." And "boy" is "pride and joy."[9]

Let us take an example from Freud's *Jokes and their Relationship to the Unconscious*,[10] where there is a leap of meaning from concrete to abstract. Again, what seems to be left-hemisphere activity suddenly has a right-hemisphere component and there is an immediate, often surprising, burst of humor. In this case, the marriage-maker has told the suitor that the girl's father is no longer living. After the marriage it became known that her father was indeed still alive and was serving a prison sentence. The suitor complained to the marriage-maker, who replied, "Well, what did I tell you? You surely don't call that living!"

Visual imagery is also a right-brain activity. Thus, when we say to someone, "Do you see what I mean?" we are really asking him, "Do you understand me, not just with your logical left brain, but with your whole brain? Do you visualize, do you *see*, what I am talking about?" In psychotherapy we have learned that it does little good simply to state an observation, such as, "You really don't like your wife," or, "You are intolerant," or the like. The patient cannot act on the suggestion implied unless he is in harmonious balance, unless he is creative. The whole person must be receptive to what the therapist has to say. One way to assist him to "see" what you mean is through the test procedure itself, and this is one of its most beautiful applications. The individual can actually see what is true for him and what is not. His body will tell him, and he will experience the understanding for himself.

The word *imagination* comes from a Greek word meaning to become visible, implying a visual component to thought. In early childhood much of our imagining is visual. As we develop and get more involved in left-brain functioning, visual imagery, except in daydreams and in dreams, begins to diminish until by adulthood, for most people, a left-brain dominance has developed. Yet, it is the synthesis of the functions of the hemispheres that leads to true understanding. This is what great poetry, great music, all great art forms, through the use of metaphor, can initiate for us—true comprehension, perception, knowing. The whole of "logic" and "intuition" is so much more than merely the sum of its parts. The two streams of the brain meet in a tremendous outburst of creativity. It can be said that there are three stages in the creation of a new idea. First, there is actually surveying the problem—that is, left-brain activity; then there is incubation, sleeping on it, letting it hatch (right-brain activity); and last, there is the sudden inspiration, with both brains coalescing.

Now we can appreciate the power of poetry—combining rhythm, rhyme, and visual imagery with logic—to form a new creation.

The left and right hemispheres have other separate functions. For example, the left hemisphere is concerned with one aspect of the autonomic nervous system, the parasympathetic, that part of the nervous system controlling our daily functions—breathing, heart rate, digestion, etc. The right hemisphere is involved with the sympathetic nervous system.[11] The left hemisphere relates to six of the twelve acupuncture meridians while the right relates to the other six.

For full harmonious functioning, psychobiological harmony, we require coordinated balance between the two hemispheres so that every activity has the appropriate input from each. We can then enjoy totally integrated activity, and consequently, enhanced life energy.

The test for cerebral dominance is as follows:

First, have your partner test you in the clear. You should be strong. Now place the palm of your *right* hand approximately two to four inches away from the *left* side of your head, opposite the ear. Have your partner test you again. If you test weak, we say you are "left-hemisphere dominant." If you test weak when you place the palm of your *right* hand off the *right* side of your head, in the same position as before, then you are "right-hemisphere dominant." If you did not test weak for either position, you were balanced at the time of testing. This is the normal, but unfortunately not the common, test result.

If you want to find out what your reaction would be in a problem situation, introduce stress and test again. For example, hold your right palm near the left side of your head, opposite the ear, as before. Then think of a fairly difficult arithmetic problem, such as dividing 950 by 25. If you are "borderline balanced," your indicator muscle will test weak. This will not happen when you place the palm of your right hand near the right side of your head while thinking of the same division problem.

Most people will initially test weak for either the left or the right hemisphere, which we term the *dominant hemisphere.*[12] As I have previously mentioned, most people test as left-hemisphere dominant. They are caught in a verbal and intellectual struggle with their environment, and have sacrificed the aesthetic and intuitive aspects of the right hemisphere.

It is important to remember that this test is standardized by using the *left* deltoid muscle and holding the *right* palm off the head (not touching the hair) in line with the ear. What we are actually doing is applying the magnetic energy of the hand to each side of the head. This phenomenon could be duplicated using magnets, but the technique as we have outlined it requires no special equipment.

Of course, being either right- or left-hemisphere dominant is not a desirable condition. We should not be working under such stress, nor should we be so vulnerable to it, that this results. The ideal is for both hemispheres to be active and symmetrical at all times— this is true cerebral balance.

Obviously, if we can reduce the stress to the point where both hemispheres are active, there will be increased life energy. There are many activation techniques, including thumping the thymus, concentrating on the homing thought, listening to certain music, reading certain poetry, alternating the ear used in telephone con-

Testing for right-hemisphere dominance.

Testing for left-hemisphere dominance.

versations, good posture, shaving with the other hand, and the following reading exercise. Obtain a storybook for children—one which contains simple words in large type. Hold the book so that it faces away from you and toward a mirror, and read the mirror image. Additional balancing techniques have been explained in *Your Body Doesn't Lie.*

When the two hemispheres are working together throughout the day, we find that there is a flow and a grace to all our activities: walking has new rhythm; there is a cadence to our voices; when we think, the logic of our thoughts does not overpower intuition and spatial perception. This harmony of brain functioning leads to creativity, the fully active and integrated state, man's highest functioning.

We should strive at all times to keep our life energy as high as possible so that we will not be affected by everyday stresses. Thus we can concentrate on achieving our highest goals. We are now going to examine the more specific ramifications of life energy. This involves understanding the role of the acupuncture system.

Part III

The Acupuncture Meridians

William Furtwangler is one of the great high-life energy conductors of all time. His music activates life energy and so do his musical gestures. Most people will test strong when looking at this photo.

Introduction to Acupuncture

Have you ever been curious about acupuncture? Have you ever wanted to explore it but were frightened by its complexities, its mystique—and by the needles? Remember that acupuncture does not require needles. This concept was begun by a mistranslation of the Chinese word by one of the first Western observers of the technique. The treatment is frequently carried out with needles, but they are not essential.

Acupuncture is the science and art of rebalancing the life energy (which the Chinese call the Chi) throughout the body—and now you can do it.

Acupuncture energy, the Chi, is probably electromagnetic in origin just as the life force itself probably is, although we cannot, of course, be sure of this. When the acupuncture energy is flowing strongly and freely throughout the body, we will find that the cerebral hemispheres will be balanced. Also we will find that the thymus will test strong because the thymus test is basically a test of how much acupuncture energy is coursing through the body at that time. This energy flows through the body in a definite pattern, entering through the lung meridian. The Chinese said that the Chi comes into the body as the breath. It then flows through the twelve paired channels called meridians and is, in a sense, collected in two midline meridians, one at the back and one at the front. That at the back is called the governing vessel and that at the front is called the conception vessel. The two meet when the lips touch.

The acupuncture meridians are named after the various organs of the body, which the Chinese recognized some thousands of years ago were energized by specific meridians.[1] If there is an en-

93

ergy problem or a physical problem with the stomach, for example, there will be an impairment of energy in the stomach meridian. The acupuncturist's task, in this case, whether he uses needles or other means, is to rebalance the energy in the stomach meridian so that the healing energy of the body can correct the problem and then, by continually supplying energy as needed to the area, enable the stomach to go about performing its everyday task of digestion. Whenever there is an energy imbalance in the meridian serving an organ, it means that the organ's physiological function is impaired, which may ultimately lead to physical disease in the specific organ.

Through our research we have discovered that each meridian also has *a specific emotional attitude, positive and negative, related to it.* For example, in the case of the stomach meridian, the negative emotional attitudes, those that can reduce the energy in the meridian and therefore in the organ and tend to lead to the organ's impaired functioning, are those of disappointment, disgust, and greed. Later, when we come to consider the stomach meridian in more detail, you will learn exactly what these emotional states are and why it is so appropriate and inevitable that they relate to the stomach and to the stomach meridian. The positive emotional state that optimizes the performance of the stomach meridian, that maximizes the positive energy in that meridian and therefore the functioning of the organ, is the state of contentment.

Just as we have twelve sets of organ meridians, we have twelve psychological meridian types, positive and negative. And as I have stated previously, each is basically controlled by the deep feelings of love or fear and hate that are the properties of the controller of all the acupuncture energy, the thymus gland.

Further, six of the sets of meridians, and therefore six personality types, are related to the left cerebral hemisphere, and six to the right cerebral hemisphere. A person who has, say, left-hemisphere dominance, will have energy impairment in the group of meridians related to the left hemisphere. So, to arrive at an understanding of the personality types we will now discuss at length, we first needed to understand the thymus gland, the master controller of all our emotions and all our acupuncture energy, as well as the functions of the hemispheres. To understand the functions of each cerebral hemisphere was also essential because each hemisphere regulates and is regulated by six sets of meridians and six sets of emotional states.

Psychosomatic Illness and Health

We are beginning to understand the origin of psychosomatic illness. Suppose we are subjected to a specific negative emotional state. This will cause a weakening of thymus activity, a general impairment of life energy, as well as a specific impairment of energy in the particular meridian relating to that specific emotional state. If that emotional state persists long enough, the associated meridian will remain impaired and the impaired physiology of the organ could lead to disease. Thus, to continue with our example of stomach-meridian energy imbalance, we could say that should the negative emotional attitudes of disappointment or disgust persist long enough, it could lead to gastritis or perhaps to a gastric ulcer. This would be the specific emotional state that relates to these stomach-meridian energy problems. We could likewise say that if the person always was contented, he should be almost invulnerable to gastritis or a gastric ulcer.

What about somato-psychic illness? What about the emotional state induced by a physical illness? For example, suppose someone has suffered a trauma to the stomach. The stomach meridian will be impaired, and this will then provoke the specific emotional state of disappointment, greed, or disgust. The way to overcome this somato-psychic component of the physical illness would be to encourage the person to feel contented. All this will become more obvious in the section devoted to the stomach meridian.

If we can determine which meridian is impaired, we will know the particular negative emotional attitude operant at that moment. How do we test the meridians? In the chart, we have designated the meridian test points. These points have been used for several thousand years in acupuncture treatments. In order to test the meridian for an energy imbalance, first test the indicator muscle in the clear. Then while test-touching a point and retesting the indicator muscle, you may detect a meridian energy imbalance.

If your subject's thymus tests weak, then you will almost always find a meridian imbalance. For example, if the subject places one or two fingers midway between his umbilicus and the point where the ribs come together in the midline at the front of the body and his indicator muscle tests weak, this indicates a stomach meridian imbalance, and it gives us the indication that the predominant emotional state affecting him at that moment is one of disappointment, disgust, or greed.

Can we prove this? Yes, and very simply. If your subject tested weak at the stomach meridian test point as described above, ask him to say, preferably aloud, "I am content." He will test strong.[2] To look at this from the other direction, suppose your subject's stomach meridian test point does not test weak. Ask him to say, while continuing to touch the test point, "I am greedy, I am disappointed, I am disgusted." Now you will find that these, and only these, statements will cause his stomach meridian point to test weak. The remarkable power of these precise affirmations cannot be overemphasized.

This test is simple to perform and it can be done by anyone. However, it requires experience and practice to do the testing reliably and accurately, and variables must be controlled. Through its use, we can discover which of our body organs are functioning under stress, the particular emotional attitudes affecting us at the time, and how to correct them. In the process of learning this test technique, we have discovered more than anyone practicing psychosomatic medicine has been able to determine with the myriad of complicated laboratory procedures at his disposal—that is, specifically which emotional states are related to which organic diseases.

Let me give you an example. The other day, I had a severe headache. I had no idea why I had it, but it was so severe that I decided to cancel my appointments for the day to stay in bed. Before doing that I had my wife test my meridians. We discovered that my thyroid meridian was testing weak. I then recognized that, although I didn't actually feel it, I was depressed. So I said the positive affirmations for the thyroid meridian, thinking clearly about what the words meant as I said them several times: "I am light and buoyant." My headache vanished instantly, and I got up and completed a full day's work without any recurrence. I could mention hundreds of examples such as this, and in the following chapter we will discuss a few more in detail.

Another common example occurs in the late afternoon when many people start to feel tired. This time is when their blood sugar drops—what we call the "hypoglycemia hour."[3] On testing at this time we often find that the spleen meridian controlling the pancreas, which regulates blood sugar, tests weak. If the subject says the positive affirmation for the spleen meridian, "I have faith and

confidence in my future," the spleen meridian weakness disap-
pears. Often these people report that they no longer feel tired. In
fact, after using this affirmation, most feel energized.

Through the use of this simple test, *you can demonstrate to
yourself the power of thought and the power of the word to create
great energy changes throughout the body.* You have already
learned that, in extreme, thoughts can cure us and thoughts can kill
us. You have learned what we have tried so hard to teach in psychiatry and what now is so easy to demonstrate. Thoughts have
power. Hence good psychiatry, and all techniques that reduce
stress, overcome negative emotional attitudes, really can save our
lives. This is the ultimate working point. Our positive thoughts are
our greatest form of prevention.

As you examine the diagram of the acupuncture test points, you
will see that six of the test points are represented just once and are
in the midline of the body, whereas six of the test points are on
each side and thus are represented twice. These we call, respectively, the "midline" and the "bilateral" test points.[4]

When your subject is left-hemisphere dominant, one of the midline meridians will test weak, but none of the bilateral points will
test weak. Conversely, if the subject tests right-hemisphere dominant, then one of the bilateral points will test weak, but none of the
midline meridian test points will be weak. This is because each
hemisphere controls six sets of meridians.

To review: Whenever we are subjected to any form of stress,
there will be a disturbance of the life energy such that the thymus
will be deactivated and one hemisphere will become dominant. A
specific meridian that is controlled by the dominant hemisphere
will also be affected. This meridian will have specific negative and
positive personality characteristics. We can overcome the effect of
the stress by balancing the hemispheres or by activating the thymus, or by saying or thinking the specific positive emotional attitude affirmations for the involved meridian. *This is the wonder of
the human mind and body.*

This is the manner in which the surging forces, the waves, of
Chi, of life energy, flow through us. And this is the way we can at
all times attempt to rise above the stresses to which we are constantly subjected, which threaten to weaken us and lead to disease.
This is our way of prevention. And it can be done with our thoughts
and our words. This is the power of the mind to control the energy
of the body. This is the greatest form of psychological care, and

each of us can do it for ourselves. This, as I promised at the outset, is the emancipation of the psychiatry patient. This is what you can do for yourself.

Psychiatry, unfortunately, has become obsessed with determining *why* we are troubled in the ways that we are. Here we don't need to concern ourselves with the *why*. All we need to do is find out *what* is the negative emotional attitude affecting us and then to transmute it instantly through our will to be well into its positive opposite. This is instant transmutational psychiatry—the way that you can, day by day, keep yourself well, mentally and physically. This is the way to psychosomatic health.

The Meridians and Their Emotions

In this chapter our goal is to arrive at the true meaning of the positive and negative emotional states associated with each meridian. It is very important for several reasons that we be specific about these emotional states. The first reason is so that we will be talking about the same quality. One of the biggest problems in any discussion of the emotional states is that frequently everyone does not mean the same thing when they talk about depression, for example, or frustration, gratitude, or contentment. We all think we mean the same thing, but we may not.[1]

Then, too, we have discovered that the better we know the word and its history and its usages throughout time, the better we understand the emotional state that accompanies it. The better we know the emotional states, the better we will be able to correct our negative attitudes and to balance our meridian energy.

In addition, it is important that we be specific so that we can differentiate between apparently similar emotions, such as depression and unhappiness. Although these are often used interchangeably in describing how we feel, they do in fact affect different meridians, and it is important to distinguish between them. An examination of their origin and meaning helps make all this clearer. (Incidentally, this is the first time, to my knowledge, that all these common positive and negative emotional states have been so discussed—not only in terms of the meridians, but also in terms of their etymology and usage over the years.)

In the course of our investigation, we frequently go back to the hypothetical Indo-European roots of the words (referred to as the I-E root). It is believed that most words in the English language have come from such an origin, of which Sanskrit is a late form, and the only form of which we have much knowledge. By getting back to these root words, we can often understand a great deal more about the words and thus the emotional states.[2]

History in a sense persists in our unconscious. The historical origin of the word in the past lives on in our unconscious as our deep understanding, our gestalt of the word. The history of the word is thus deeply rooted and embedded in our present-day unconscious.

As you read these etymologies, keep in mind that they are physical interpretations of the words. In the primitive word the physical and the abstract were combined as they are in a primitive language today. Over the years we have, with our reasoning intelligence, tended to remove the right-brain poetic qualities of the words, while concentrating on the more physical characteristics. Owen Barfield has pointed out that the earliest elementary meanings carried the poetic, metaphorical qualities along with the physical, and that later these qualities became separated.[3] How this happened will be apparent as we examine the specific emotional states that follow.

For each meridian I will delineate the predominant negative and positive emotions. As you will see, there will be many apparently separate emotional states connected with each meridian. We know that all these apparently different emotional states are in fact related because they involve the same meridian on testing.

With each meridian type, a photographic representation will be given. You will find that when you look at the picture and test the appropriate meridian, it will test weak, demonstrating that it is the meridian that is being affected. But if at the same time you say the specific positive affirmation for that meridian, the negative effect will be overcome.[4]

It is important that the positive affirmation always be stated positively. You do not say, for example, "I am not depressed," but rather, "I am light and buoyant." It is not the *absence* of the negative that we want, but the *presence* of the positive.

I am not in any way advocating the techniques in this book as the primary treatment of any severe physical illness. But I am suggesting that there is usually an emotional component in serious physical illness that can be specifically helped by these techniques. Especially when the illness is minor, or when it still exists as an energy problem before there is grossly disturbed physiology in any way, then what I am advocating can be truly preventive and can then lead to positive health.

"Bilateral" Meridians

The meridians whose test points are bilaterally represented:

Lung
Liver
Gall Bladder
Spleen
Kidney
Large Intestine

One of these meridians will test weak when the subject is right-hemisphere dominant.

Lung Meridian

The meridian of humility

Tolerance	Lung
Intolerance	

Negative Emotions:	Disdain
	Scorn
	Contempt
	Haughtiness
	False Pride
	Intolerance
	Prejudice
Positive Affirmations:	I am humble.
	I am tolerant.
	I am modest.

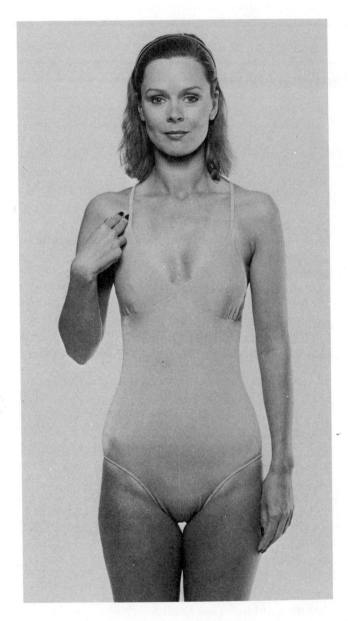

The test point for the lung meridian. In the first intercostal space on the anterior paraxillary line.

Test Image: You are with someone who you feel is very
               silly or ignorant. You feel much smarter
               and you are very aware of the contrast be-
               tween your genius and his or her stupidity,
               and you feel superior.

"Blessed are the meek: for they shall inherit the earth."

Matthew 5:5

We will commence with the lung meridian because, as previously mentioned, the Chinese regarded the life energy, the Chi, as
being derived from the breath and entering the body through the
lung meridian and then passing into the other meridians. They
regarded the lung meridian as the prime meridian. The lung meridian is that which is most involved in normal and abnormal early
childhood development.

With each meridian personality type, I will give you an instance
(test image) to think on which will activate the associated negative
emotional attitude. Then you can prove for yourself that these emotional states do indeed relate to these specific meridians. For example, test your subject's lung meridian test point and it should be
strong. Now have your subject think of and strongly visualize being
with someone who he feels is silly and ignorant. The subject feels
much smarter and is very aware of the contrast between his own
genius and the other person's stupidity. His lung meridian will test
weak. This is the specific negative emotional state associated with
the lung meridian.

The negative words relating to the lung meridian all have to do
with feeling superior to or looking down on another person. In fact,
one of the negative gestures that relates to the lung meridian is a
tilting of the head backward, a "looking down the nose" with a
feeling of scorn, and frequently, a wrinkling up of the nose, as if
one had smelled something bad. The image of this I always have
in mind is of the English upper-class snob.

The negative emotional attitudes associated with the lung meridian, then, are disdain, scorn, contempt, haughtiness, false pride,
intolerance, and prejudice. We could say in many cases that people
who have lung-meridian energy problems are those whose chests
are "puffed out with pride." "Haughty" is often applied to those
who imagine themselves as being higher than or superior to others.
We could call the lung meridian "the meridian of judgment of
others in relation to self," or the meridian of humility. Now these

Most people will test weak for the lung meridian when looking at this photo. Saying the positive affirmation for the lung meridian will overcome the weakness.

are very powerful words, and it may offend you somewhat to find that your lung meridian tests weak. It may seem particularly distasteful to you that anyone, especially you, could be harboring such negative qualities. Rest assured, though, we all do at one time or another. At some point in testing any person, we are going to find these feelings.

Remember, too, we are speaking of degrees. If your lung meridian tests weak, it does not mean that you are contemptuous or scornful. It simply means that you have a tendency to feel this way at the particular time of testing. If we find that we have a lung-meridian weakness on testing, we should acknowledge this, and then turn it around, transmuting it into the positive feeling.

Transmutation is surrendering the negative state and turning it around into the positive—instantly, harmlessly, inexpensively, and without outside intervention. To do this, you do not need a psychiatrist. You just need to have the will and desire to give up the negative and come forward into the positive.

Disdain

Disdain is that "feeling entertained toward that which one thinks unworthy of notice or beneath one's dignity; scorn, contempt."[5] Lindley Murray wrote, "Haughtiness is founded on the high opinion we entertain of ourselves; disdain, on the low opinion we have of others."

Each meridian's related positive and negative emotional states are like a continuum, going from one extreme to the other. We can see in Murray the idea of highness and lowness in our opinion of others in relationship to ourselves. This highness and lowness is the continuum of the emotional state of the lung meridian. The lung meridian is a continuum of what we might call superiority/inferiority.

(Dis)dain is derived from the primitive root *dek*, which meant to take or accept. It is also related to several Latin roots, *decere*, from which we get the word *decent; dignus*, which gave rise to the word *deign*, meaning to think worthy; and *dedignore*, which meant to think unworthy.

Scorn

Scorn comes from the Latin *cornu*, a horn, and it means literally to deprive of one's horns, and thus to mock, to humiliate. The horns have long been a symbol of power and fertility. To be dehorned, to be scorned, is to suffer gross humiliation. Thus we get the saying, "To scorn a thing, as a dog scorns tripe."

Shakespeare in *Twelfth Night* wrote,

> Oh, what a deal of scorn looks beautiful
> In the contempt and anger of his lip!

Contempt

Contempt has been defined as "the holding or treating as of a little account, or as vile and worthless." Thus Thomas Hobbes said, "Contempt, is when a man thinks another of little worth in comparison to himself." Contempt has also been called bitter scorn. It comes from the Latin *cum*, meaning wholly, and *temnere*, to despise, and so means to wholly despise. It is probably related to the Greek *temnein*, to cut, and perhaps has a similar unconscious meaning as scorn. Indeed, Johnson defined contempt as "the act of despising others; slight regard; scorn."

The idea of the attacking, cutting, destructive quality of contempt is well shown in the expression, "Contempt pierces even through the shell of the tortoise."

Haughtiness

"Before destruction the heart of man is haughty, and before honor is humility." Proverbs 18:12

Haughtiness obviously relates to highness, again with the idea of being superior, of having one's nose in the air. When Richard II was deposed, Northumberland contemptuously addressed him as "Lord." Richard angrily replied, "No Lord of thine, thou haught insulting man."

Haughty is derived from the French *haut*, meaning high, which is derived from the Latin *altum*, from which we get *altitude*. Haughty means to be high in one's own estimation; lofty and disdainful in feeling or demeanor; proud, arrogant, supercilious, elevated.

Haughtiness beautifully describes the idea of the lung meridian characteristic of "nose up in the air," rising up above others, feeling oneself to be higher and superior to others. (Hence Crashaw's, "Down, down, proud sense."[6]) Interestingly, the origin of *altus* is from the Latin *alere*, meaning to nourish—and well-nourished implies growing, becoming tall. This is the origin of *alimentary*.

False Pride

Buck notes that in many Indo-European languages, several of the words for *pride* imply over or high, "thus connoting superiority of spirit or mind."[7] In Shakespeare's *Henry VIII* we read "my high-blown pride." True pride, the true feeling of one's own self-worth and accomplishment, is a very valuable and essential state, as we shall see when we come to consider the large-intestine meridian and associated emotional states. But false and overbearing pride is a negative emotion weakening the lung meridian. (Isaiah 2:11—"The lofty looks of man shall be humbled, and the haughtiness of men shall be bowed down.")

Hubris is "overbearing pride; arrogance," and interestingly was derived from the hypothetical Indo-European root *ud*, meaning "up," which is most apt when we think of the proud person with his nose up in the air. The *New Encyclopedia Britannica* speaks of "impious disregard of the limits governing men's actions in an orderly universe . . . and in Greek tragedy it is usually the basic flaw of the tragic hero."[8] The heart of the traditional Greek religion and Greek tragedy, Gilbert Murray suggests, is "the story of *Pride and Punishment*."[9] Melanie Klein refers to Murray's definition, "the typical sin which all things, so far as they have life, commit is in poetry *Hubris*, a word generally translated 'insolence' or 'pride' . . . Hubris grasps at more, bursts bounds and breaks the order; it is followed by *Dike*, Justice, which re-establishes them. This rhythm —*Hubris–Dike*, Pride and its fall, Sin and Chastisement—is the commonest burden of those philosophical lyrics which are characteristic of Greek tragedy."[10]

The Greek scholar, E. R. Dodds, defines hubris as "arrogance in word or deed or even thought . . . the 'primal evil,' the sin whose wages is death."[11] Adrian Stokes defines hubris as "the great sin of pride, which comes about by believing oneself to be the god, by scorning the laws of gods and men." [12]

The primary meridian is the lung meridian, and it is here that we will find the most deeply rooted disturbances—those present in our earliest days and the most all-prevading influences throughout our lives. The Greek religion was based on the overcoming of pride, a problem of the primary meridian, the lung meridian. This also became the basis of Greek tragedy. Perhaps the Greeks understood human nature even better than Shakespeare.

Intolerance

"Judge not that ye be not judged." Matthew 7:1

From the I-E root *tel*, meaning to lift or support and to weigh, we get the idea of measuring weights, thus implying money and payment, hence the related English word *toll*.

The verb from which *intolerance* was derived was *tolerare*, meaning to bear or to endure. We speak today of being able to tolerate the pain, for example.

We say a tolerant person is one who bears with our imperfections and hopes that we will bear with his. On the other hand, an intolerant person is one who feels that he has no imperfections and cannot bear those of others. Again, the basic attitude of intolerance is one of superiority, or what has been called hateful superiority.

I recall a patient who suffered from severe asthma for many years. He was a very small man who always seemed to have his nose up in the air, looking down at people. He had what was described as a "Napoleon complex." He was blustery and intolerant of anyone's mistakes, and for this reason his secretaries were continually resigning. He was argumentative and tolerated imperfection very badly indeed. He continually tested weak at the lung meridian test point. It was a difficult task to gently point out to him what this meridian weakness implied. Eventually he got the message and he began saying the appropriate affirmation regularly. Surprisingly for him and for me, his asthma attacks stopped. He changed; he stopped looking down his nose at people, both physically and metaphorically. He became a pleasant, tolerant, and much more likable person.

Read how the Psalmist has summed up the negative emotional states related to the lung meridian: "Our soul is exceedingly filled with the scorning of those that are at ease, and with the contempt of the proud." Psalm 123:4

Prejudice

Prejudice is a prejudgment, a preconceived opinion. It is a bias usually, although not necessarily, against a person or thing. Prejudice means that one's mind is made up beforehand. Rather than judging an individual truly on his own merits and then reaching a decision, someone who is prejudiced makes a decision based on race or religion or education, or the like. The decision is made before the faculties of reason are invoked. The *Oxford English Dictionary* defines it as a "preconceived, unreasonable opinion, bias, or leaning; a judgment formed before due examination or consideration" of the facts. We might call prejudice a mental set, a rigid attitude which exists before enough data are available to exercise reason and arrive at a considered opinion.

It will be found that when there is prejudice there will be a weakness of the lung meridian on testing. In fact, it is possible to use this test to find out a person's potential for prejudice. For example, print on a plain piece of paper a neutral name such as "Robert Jones." (If your subject happens to know someone by that name, then use a similar name which he does not associate with a particular person.) Have the subject look at the name on the piece of paper and he should test strong. Now, under "Robert Jones," write the word, "Banker." Your subject will most likely test strong. If your subject has a potential lung meridian weakness, he may test weak for "Roberta Jones, Banker."

Your subject may test weak in the clear or just at the lung meridian test point. In either case the basic meridian involved is the lung meridian. By reinforcing the meridian with the positive affirmation, "I am humble," he will now test strong when he looks at the sign, "Roberta Jones, Banker," and he is on the way to overcoming his prejudice.

There are many other prejudices for which you can test. Of course, not all prejudices are gender-oriented. For example, most people test weak when looking at the name, "Robert Jones, Psychiatrist." Even other psychiatrists often test weak, indicating the widespread prejudice involved. Many people have unconscious prejudices against the handicapped, for example. Test for yourself and discover your own prejudices. In every case, the weakness found on testing will be overcome by the affirmation, "I am humble."

The positive emotional attributes of the lung meridian are tolerance, humility, and modesty. Perhaps the "best," and the one that has been found most effective in clinical practice besides tolerance, is humility.

Humility

> *"Better it is to be of an humble spirit with the lowly, than to divide the spoil with the proud." Proverbs 16:19*

Humility has been defined as meekness, the opposite of pride or haughtiness. The primitive Sanskrit word from which *humble* is derived means earth, and this gives rise to the Old English word *guma,* meaning a man. In Latin, the word for earth is *humus*—an expression we use in gardening even today. Hence humility reminds us of our origins from the earth. We recognize and accept these origins and we are humble. It is difficult to feel superior to others if we recognize that we are all from the earth.

Whateley said, "That is true humility, to have a meane esteeme of himselfe out of a true apprehension of God's greatnesse." [13]

There is a bird called "the Humility," so named because "it seldom mounts high in the air." Perhaps this best sums it up. The negative attributes of the lung meridian arise when we "mount high in the air," our noses up in the air, when we feel proud and superior and contemptuous of those whom we judge to be below us. But the positive attributes of humility and tolerance come with our recognition of our imperfections, the realization that we are not to judge others by our own standards, and an understanding of our own places in life.

Modesty

Another positive affirmation for the lung meridian is, "I am modest." Modesty is "having or showing a moderate estimation of one's own talents, abilities, and value." It comes from the I-E root *med* which means to take measures. This became in Latin *modus,* a measure, from which was derived in Latin *modestus,* meaning modest, within bounds or measure.

Thus Samuel Butler wrote, "Nothing renders Men modest, but a just Knowledge how to compare themselves with others." Modesty illustrates and embodies the positive qualities of the lung meridian, neither undervaluing ourselves nor overvaluing ourselves or our attributes in relationship to others—seeing ourselves fairly and justly and seeing our own abilities within bounds, having a reasonable comprehension of our own worth and value. Modesty is the opposite of false pride.

Liver Meridian

The meridian of happiness

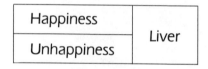

Happiness	Liver
Unhappiness	

Negative Emotion: Unhappiness
Positive Affirmations: I am happy.
                        I have good fortune.
                        I am cheerful.
Test Image: You are very unhappy because your lover has left you. Everything would be perfect if only he would come back to you.

Happiness and Unhappiness

The predominant emotions for the liver meridian are happiness and unhappiness.

Let us examine some of the expressions and origins of the word *happy*. You will be reminded, as I was when I first came across them, of the successful gambler. For example, happiness is defined as luck, or good fortune, or the state of prosperity. The original root meant to succeed. This gave rise to the word in Old Norse, *happ*, which was chance or good luck. From this we got our English word *happy*, via the Old English word *hap*, which in its original sense meant good luck. Johnson defines happiness as "Good luck, good fortune, lucky, successful, fortunate." Hence the phrase *happy-go-*

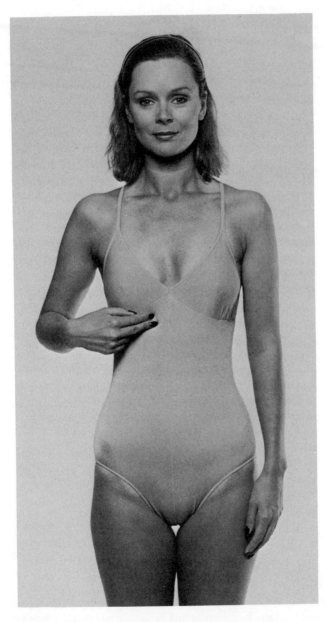

The test point for the liver meridian when looking at this photograph. In line with the nipple at about the costal border, usually just above it.

Most people will test weak for the liver meridian when looking at this photo. Saying the positive affirmation for the liver meridian will overcome the weakness.

lucky. We feel happy when fortune has smiled on us—when the gods smile on us, when those who control our destiny, be it good fortune, the gods, our parents, lady luck, or the government, are benevolent. When these external benefactors smile on us, we feel happy. Conversely, when we feel that those who are in a position to give to us withhold from us instead, then we feel *unhappy.*

We read in Psalm 144:15, "Happy is that people, that is in such a case: yea, happy is that people, whose God is the Lord."

And in the context of happiness as feeling smiled upon by the gods, Catullus wrote, "What is given by the gods more desirable than a happy hour."

It is important that we distinguish between depression and un-happiness. There is considerable confusion in psychiatry regarding the state of depression. Depression has now become quite accept-able because we have antidepressant drugs. On the other hand unhappiness is not acceptable and even has a rather childish or epithetical connotation about it that depression does not have. Thus a great many people who are called "depressed" are really not depressed at all—they are unhappy. The depressed person feels that he is heavy, he is down, he is literally de-pressed. He also feels that it is his fault and his responsibility to get himself out of this situation, if it can be done, which he usually doubts. "Gen-uine" suicide attempts usually come out of depression, but the attempt that is not "genuine" is usually a product of unhappiness and a wish to have others do more for him.

The unhappy person feels that the fault always lies with someone else: if only his wife had done such and such, then he would not be bankrupt. If only the government would do more for him, then he would be a success. If only lady luck had smiled on him, he would have made a fortune at gambling. If only God had answered his prayers. With the state of unhappiness there is always the feel-ing that if only the powers that be (which in our psyche always comes down to our parents) had given me more, I would now be perfect, I would now be happy. Joseph Ratner wrote, "If we are born under a lucky star, and are fortunate and happy lovers of the ideal, the ecstasy of the mystic's beatific vision is ours." [14]

Those who continually complain that they are not given enough are unhappy. You constantly hear that everything would be fine *if only* they were given more. These are the unhappy people. They are not depressed. It is in this state that an alcoholic will turn to the bottle, feeling that his happiness can be given to him through the bottle.[15] But he is not a baby any more. He must find his own goals in life, he must find his own homing thought. He must activate his will to be well, roll up his sleeves and find what he needs for himself. He will not gain if he stays back in a state of unhappiness and expects to have "it" given to him.

So much of our present-day social and political thinking and advertising plays into the state of unhappiness. We have been led to believe that the government will provide us with all we need, or that the corporation for which we work will assume this responsibility to provide, or that big business itself will take care of us. So we abdicate our responsibility for our own fulfillment and expect these external, godlike, fortune-distributing institutions to supply our needs. And we become unhappy when this does not occur. When the next election comes we turn to another candidate. We reject the previous candidate and elect a new one, who again has promised to do everything he can for us, and whom we know we will reject in a few years' time—because he has no more satisfied our unhappiness than the previous elected official.

Advertising plays into our unhappiness almost constantly, making us aware of what we do not have and implying that the institution, the company, the advertiser, will supply us with happiness with their largess. All we have to do is pay for it. The implication is that we are gaining more than just goods in exchange for our money. We believe the answer lies in possessing the product—an external solution to an internal problem. Thus we find, for example, that when a shopping mall is built, part of the basic design, part of its gestalt, is that it was not created to be a place where you will exchange money for goods but rather is a place of fun, of happiness.

Yet honorable advertising can actually strengthen, and raise your life energy. Unfortunately, most advertising weakens us. It is quite possible for advertising to be honorable and to work to the advantage of society while at the same time encouraging the usage of the product being advertised. Wholesome advertising could actually energize us.

Perhaps it is significant that the liver is called just that. Many physicians have stated that the proper functioning of the liver is absolutely essential for good health, bearing in mind the multiple functions that the liver performs. I think the quotation of Spencer is appropriate here: "Happiness is added Life, and the giver of Life!" As the founder of the International Academy of Preventive Medicine, Dr. R. O. Brennan, has remarked many times, "To have a long life, you must be a liver lover." To this I would add, "And you must be happy."

At the beginning of this book I said that the fact that my patients did not get better made me unhappy. This was because I recognized that they were not doing as well as they should, and I felt I had done everything I possibly could do to help them be completely well. If only I had been given more assistance; if only I had been taught better. If only the hospital had done a better job; if only the medical insurance agencies would leave the patients alone; if only the relatives would leave the patient alone. I kept looking for that extra source, that smiling of fortune from outside that was going to help me to achieve what I felt was beyond me to achieve.

Happiness goes with coming to grips with the fact that we must not rely on other people—that we are masters of our own fates. Only this way can we mature and develop from our position of dependence on our parents and others in society, particularly its institutions. Ultimately, through overcoming our unhappiness it is possible that we can develop our own correct relationship with fortune, with the gods, and with God. The concept of prayer today seems to be, "If only God would do more for me, if only He would provide more, than I would be happy. Therefore I will pray to Him that He will give me these things." The "if only someone would . . ." is the complaint of the unhappy, dependent child, not of the independent, self-contained adult, striving toward his goal of personal evolution. An independent, self-sufficient course through life is what we require.

Cheer

Another emotional state closely related to happiness and thus to the liver meridian is cheerfulness, which has been defined as "gaiety; animation; happiness." Its origin is very interesting. The I-E root is *ker*, which the American Heritage Dictionary states is "horn, head; with derivatives referring to horned animals, horn-shaped objects, and projecting parts," from which we get such words as *unicorn, cornet, horn.* The extended root *keras* gives rise to such words as cervix (related to neck) and words to do with the head itself—cerebrum, cerebellum, and cranium. It also gives rise to the word *carrot,* which is derived from its horn shape. In Greek the word *keres* means horn. The Greek *kare* means head, from which our word cheer is derived. An obsolete definition of cheer is the face; for example, Shakespeare, in A *Midsummer Night's Dream*, wrote, "all fancy sike she is, and pale of cheere." It also came to mean the look or expression of the face, and from this to mean someone's state of mind as reflected in the face. And the smile we see on the face leads us to believe that the person is cheerful.

Gall Bladder Meridian

The meridian of adoration

Love	Gall Bladder
Rage	

Negative Emotions:	Rage Fury Wrath
Positive Affirmations:	I reach out with love. I reach out with forgiveness.
Test Image:	Someone has just done something very infuriating. He has just read your most personal letters and your private diary without your permission. You are shouting at him. You want to hit him.

Rage and Fury

The gall bladder meridian's negative emotional state is that of *rage*. Rage comes from the Latin *rabere*, which means to be furiously angry. From the Latin, we get not only the word *rage* itself, but also such words as *rave* and the *rabid*, "mad dog."

Rage is defined as "violent anger, furious passion, usually manifested in looks, words or action." In Buck's survey of many European languages, he states that the words for *rage* and *fury* "are specialized from 'mental excitement,' based in part upon notions of violent physical action."

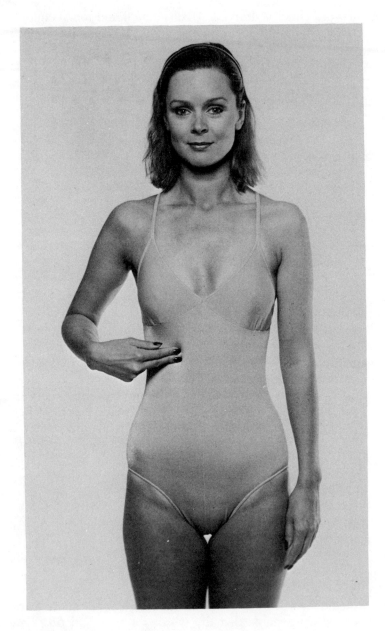

The test point for the gall bladder meridian. At or just below the junction of the ninth rib and the costal border.

Most people will test weak for the gall bladder meridian when looking at this photo. Saying the positive affirmation for the gall bladder meridian will overcome the weakness.

Another dictionary states, "Rage and fury are closely related in the sense of intense, uncontained, explosive emotion." The close relationship between rage and fury is perhaps best exemplified in Johnson's dictionary, where he calls rage "violent anger; vehement fury." It is the combination of the anger with the violence, the acting out of the anger. Shakespeare in *Coriolanus* referred to it as "this tiger footed rage."

The difference between rage and anger is that rage carries a sense of doing something about one's anger. Rage is in a sense the physical manifestation of anger. It is the act or the strong wish to act on the anger. Anger does not specify the manner of expression, but rage implies that something will be done.

Not surprisingly, the positive transmutation is not just the thinking of love, but the conceptualizing of love in an active form. Instead of reaching out to strike the object of the rage, think of reaching out to love him or her. The affirmation we use here is, "I reach out with love."

The emotional continuum for the gall bladder meridian is not merely ranging from anger to love or forgiveness, as it is for the heart meridian (see page 150), but rather it is from violent, active anger to love and forgiveness, with the added concept of movement toward the other person with that particular emotion. We say in the positive, "I reach out with love. I come forward with love and forgiveness." When we turn to the positive, we find as in Ezekiel 21:17, "I will cause my fury to rest."

Wrath

Another negative emotional attribute of the gall bladder meridian is *wrath*, which has been defined as violent, resentful anger; rage; fury. Again, we can see that it is more than anger, it is the acting on the anger; the violence; the violent act associated with the anger. Wordsworth wrote, "On he drives with cheeks that burn/ In downright fury and in wrath." "In wrath remember mercy." (Habakkuk 3:2)

Choler

Choler was one of the four humors of medieval medicine, denoting bitter anger and wrath. It comes from the Latin *cholera*, which meant bile or wrath, as well as the disease. *Chol* (see *melancholy* page 171) refers to the bile in the gall bladder, from which we get *cholecystectomy,* the removal of the gall bladder. Gower wrote in 1390 (*Confessio Amantis* III), "The drie coler with his hete, By wey of kinde his propre sete Hath in the galle, where he dwelleth," illustrating the relationship between gall and hate—which we have corroborated six hundred years later through our research.

Who else but Shakespeare, in *The Taming of the Shrew*, could so beautifully play on the relationship between anger and bile. In Act IV, Petruchio throws some meat which he has been served about the stage. Katharine says, "I pray you, husband, be not so disquiet: The meat was well, if you were so contented." Petruchio replies, "I tell thee, Kate, 'twas burnt and dried away; And I expressly am forbid to touch it, For it engenders choler, planteth anger; And better 'twere that both of us did fast, Since, of ourselves, ourselves are choleric, Than feed it with such over-roasted flesh." He is alluding to the belief that it was the excess bile that led to the humor of choler, wrath to excess.

I was once visiting the office of a friend of mine who is a doctor of osteopathy. A woman was brought in who during the previous night had suddenly developed a wrist drop due to a muscular paralysis. She lay down on his treatment table and he spent the next hour manipulating her hand and neck. Although he had made quite definite changes in the structural balance, the wrist drop persisted, unchanged. He then told me that he did not know what else to do to take the pressure off the involved nerve and relieve the paralysis. He asked me for a suggestion, but I had none, as I had never worked with such a case. I decided to check her meridians. I found that she had an energy imbalance in the gall bladder meridian. For the duration of her treatment she had been lying passively on the table, but when I asked her, "Are you really angry about something? Is there something or someone making you furious?" she immediately sat bolt upright and said, "Yes, there certainly is!" Then she launched into a tirade of anger and rage about the hospital in which her mother had died only a few days earlier. Every muscle of her body was contracted into a gesture of total rage—every muscle except the paralyzed one in her right hand. The rage subsided and she lay down again. My friend then re-examined her neck and reported that there had been a great change—all the muscles were loose and free, and there was greater mobility in the neck and shoulder. He felt something had been unlocked. The muscle was still paralyzed, but he was confident enough to advise her to go home and rest and call the next day.

I was alarmed. My medical training said that this was a severe condition. I thought, "She needs cervical X rays. She needs myelograms. She may need a spinal tap. This could be a serious condition. She needs hospitalization!" But she called the next morning to report that she was cured. That was a year ago, and there has been no recurrence.

This was not a hysterical episode. She had a definite paralysis in the muscles of her hand, as confirmed by neurological testing. What had happened, I presume, was that the rage she was feeling toward the hospital had caused a distinct pattern of severe contraction of certain muscles which had then pulled the bony structures of the neck and shoulder. This had caused an interference with the nerve supply from the neck to the muscles of the wrist. She needed the osteopathic treatment to release the musculature, as my friend had attempted. But she also required correction of the rage which, after all, was the primary problem in this case. When both the physical and psychological procedures were carried out, her symptoms were relieved and she was spared what could have been prolonged and traumatic medical and neurological investigation. The osteopath acknowledged the importance of the psychological work. Yet all I had done was check the meridians, a simple procedure, and ask her one question. It took less than a minute. Certainly it would not have succeeded without the osteopathic intervention, but just as certainly, the osteopathic treatment was greatly enhanced by this simple, yet valuable, procedure.

Adoration

The best word for the process of overcoming rage is *adoration*. It is defined as "the act of worshipping, or paying divine honours," and "the exhibition of profound regard and love." It is from the Latin *ad*—to—and *orare*—to pray. This adoration overcomes rage. Rage is anger in action; adoration is love in action, a reaching out with love.

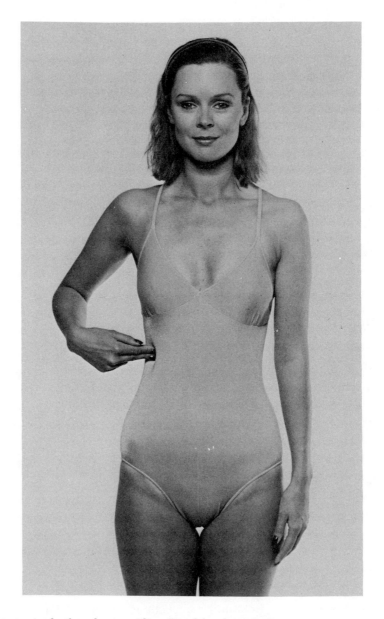

The test point for the spleen meridian. Tip of the eleventh rib.

Spleen Meridian

The meridian of confidence

Faith in Future	Spleen
Anxiety About Future	

Negative Emotion:	Realistic anxieties about the future
Positive Affirmations:	I have faith and confidence in my future. I am secure. My future is secure.
Test Image:	Next month's bills are before you. You do not have the money to pay them, and you can see no way of coming up with it.

Realistic Anxieties About the Future

The spleen meridian supplies energy to both the spleen and the pancreas, and we find that it is frequently involved in patients who have hypoglycemia (low blood sugar). This condition is a very common problem today. The test point for this meridian is the tip of the eleventh rib on each side.

The specific state involved in spleen meridian problems is one of worry and anxiety about the future, about real problems in the relatively immediate future. "Where is next month's rent coming from?" "Will I be able to go back to college next year?" "How can I pay my wife's medical bills?" "Am I going to be fired from my job? If I am fired, what other work can I do?" These very real practical problems seem to affect the spleen meridian.[16]

The positive affirmation here is, "I have faith and confidence in my future." I recognize that I have a path in life, and to the best of my abilities, I am trying to determine my true goals, and I am trying to act accordingly. I recognize that if I try to do what is right, I have no need to feel anxiety and worry about the future. Or, if my motives are clean and good, good will come to me. I have faith. I have

Most people will test weak for the spleen meridian when looking at this photograph. The positive affirmation for the spleen meridian will overcome the weakness.

confidence. I can advance forward, knowing that what is right for me will come to me.

The state of faith and confidence brought about by these affirmations overcomes spleen meridian problems. This affirmation is used a great deal, because so many people have a spleen-meridian energy problem. We live in an age of anxiety about the future. Furthermore, the refined foods we eat predispose us to blood sugar disturbance, which also affects the energy in the spleen meridian.

In Johnson's dictionary we find that confidence means "assured beyond doubt." We also find confidence meaning "secure of success; without fear of miscarriage."

Secure

Someone who is "confident in expectation" is secure. To be secure means to be "free from fear or doubt; not anxious or unsure," and "not likely to fail." The word derives from the Latin *se*, without, and *cura*, care, attention (hence *cure*). The literal meaning is thus without care or anxiety, but the virtual meaning is "without cause for anxiety, safe." And *security* is "freedom from care, anxiety or apprehension."

Imagine that you are swinging on a trapeze bar high above the ground. You are about to let go and sail through the air, your arms outstretched to grab the other bar coming toward you. How fearful you would be in this situation depends on whether there is a safety net. If a safety net is there, it does not matter if you fall. You will not be hurt, and all you have to do is climb up the ladder and try again. But if there is no safety net, you may die.

Every day of our lives we are being invited to release one bar and fly to another one. Every day we are being given a chance to let go of what we have and, with faith and confidence in our future, to reach out for a better way, a better life. Often, rather than welcoming the situation, we are fearful. We hold back because we do not believe there is a safety net. We believe that if we miss we will die, and thus it is better to hold back, even better not to develop, than to run the risk of dying. But if you feel that the new bar will come, and you have the deep and secure knowledge that there is a safety net, then you will take the risk.

I have observed many small babies being swept up into the air and even momentarily let go and then caught again in their mother's arms. Some will laugh with glee and others will exhibit a startled reaction of fear. Already some of them know that they have a safety net they can trust—the foundation of which is the mother's love. If we are secure in our mother's love we are free to fly anywhere. We are free to take giant leaps, free to explore, free to let go and await the right way. We are secure. This safety net not only provides the freedom to explore in the world, it also gives a freedom to explore inside ourselves. It gives us the courage to have insight, to look at ourselves as we truly are.[17]

When faced with realistic concerns about the future, it is helpful to affirm "I am secure. My future is secure." With this secure confidence, your spleen meridian energy will be positive and you will be in a better position to make constructive decisions and find a creative solution.

It is not uncommon to find the safety net syndrome in people who have blood sugar disturbances. Often they seem overburdened with realistic anxieties about the future. Many of my hypoglycemic or diabetic patients push themselves beyond their limits in an attempt to obtain material security. This pattern usually long predates their physical symptoms. They fear that if something goes wrong, there will be no one there to catch them, no support. They have no trust in the future. They struggle hard to build security through possessions, money, position, and so forth, in order to protect themselves from the feared fall. It is as if Mother has not provided them with a safety net, so they are going to make their own.

Consider Brenda, a twenty-three-year-old woman who suddenly developed diabetes last month. I discussed the safety net syndrome with her and she saw many similarities with her life. Ever since she was very young she had feared for the future. She worried that something would go wrong, that she would never have enough money, food, or clothes. As soon as she was old enough, she found part-time jobs to make sure she had enough for "a rainy day."

Yet only a few years earlier she had made a very brave decision. She left her native Greece and moved to America, even though she had only one relative in the country. She initially stayed with him and his family in Syracuse. He looked after her and protected her as she adjusted to the new country. His family became her safety net. Then she decided to move to New York City with her new boyfriend. They found a small apartment and settled down, but soon she became very apprehensive. He could not find steady employment, and she had no special skills. She managed to find a job, but the salary was very low. There was a constant nagging fear in her mind that she wouldn't be able to make the rent. She saved as much as possible from each week's pay to make sure there would be enough when the rent was due. The financial burden became hers completely, as her boyfriend still had not found a steady job. She became preoccupied with the thought, "What if something goes wrong and I'm fired, or get sick. Then there won't be enough money to pay the rent. We will be put out in the street."

Her anxieties were compounded by the fact that she had not yet obtained her immigration papers, and she was worried that she could be deported. The crowning worry was the fear that her boyfriend would fall out of love with her and kick her out of the apartment, leaving her stranded, completely alone, and virtually broke. Then one evening a woman called and asked to speak to him. Brenda suspected this was one of his old girlfriends. Suddenly her safety net, thin as it was, disappeared altogether. A month later she developed diabetes.

Of course, many other people survive similar circumstances without developing diabetes. But in Brenda's case, due to her particular makeup, physically and psychologically, this was the result. Her medical treatments will be supplemented with the specific affirmations for the spleen meridian, "I have faith and confidence in my future. I am secure. My future is secure."

Kidney Meridian

The meridian of sexual assuredness

Sexual Security	Kidney
Sexual Indecision	

Negative Emotion:	Sexual Indecision
Positive Affirmations:	I am sexually secure.
	My sexual energies are balanced.
Test Image:	You are having sex with an acquaintance— someone you are not particularly attracted to, yet are not totally turned off by.

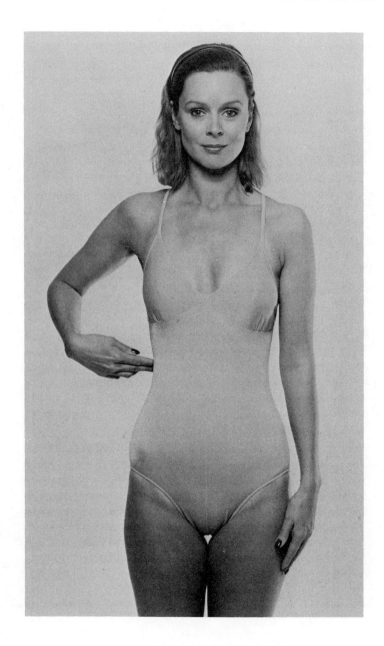

The test point for the kidney meridian. Tip of the twelfth rib.

Most people will test weak for the kidney meridian when looking at this photo. Saying the positive affirmation for the kidney meridian will overcome the weakness.

Sexual Indecision

The kidney meridian's negative emotional states are related to *sexual indecision*. The test point for this meridian is the tip of the twelfth rib. We frequently find kidney meridian problems in people who cannot make up their minds about a sexual problem. "Should I sleep with this man?" "Do I really want to?" "Am I ready for this sort of involvement?" These types of problems tend to affect the kidney meridian.

The problems here can be very subtle. For example, I have frequently found weaknesses on testing men who are having problems with their wives, and are even possibly contemplating having affairs. It will show up with anyone who is experiencing not so much sexual dissatisfaction as sexual indecision.

The transmutation of sexual indecision is the positive affirmation, "My sexual energies are balanced." I encourage my patients with this problem to state this affirmation as part of their daily program. I tell them, "There is some sort of sexual indecision troubling you. What I suggest is that you try to make a decision, even if you make the positive decision not to make a decision until some point in the future. Stop letting the problem drain your kidney meridian energy. Make a decision about what is bothering you, and then file it away. Don't let it take up all your time, attention, and energy." Usually patients are eager to correct the problem, and follow my advice. I do not know what they are thinking or doing privately, but when they come back, they usually test strong. We have had fine changes in people's personalities and often in their kidney problems when they have made this sexual decision. The patient is further strengthened when he reaffirms his decision with the affirmation, "My sexual energies are balanced."

I remember a man who, on the several occasions when I tested him, had a kidney meridian problem. He was a very strait-laced, proper, religious man who, I thought, was happily married and devoted to his wife. One day I said to him, "You are contemplating having an affair with another woman." He looked at me in amazement and said, "How did you know?" I said, "That's what your body is telling me—that is what a continuous weakness in the kidney-meridian energy supply often indicates." He then told me that he was undecided about having an affair with his secretary. He recognized that he loved his wife but was also infatuated with his secretary; he didn't know what he should do. Hence, the sexual indecision.

I told him, "I'm not your judge. I am not telling you whether you should have an affair or not. But what I am suggesting to you is that your continuing indecision about the affair is interfering with your kidney meridian energy."

When he returned next, I found that his kidney meridian tested strong. I asked if he had made his decision. He said that he had, and that he was going to have the affair with his secretary. Of course I am not advocating this as the solution to kidney meridian problems. It seems to me that he could just as easily have made the decision not to have the sexual encounter with his secretary. The important point here is that ongoing sexual indecision seems to lead to kidney meridian imbalances.

I remember a woman who had had several episodes of renal colic. She also, not surprisingly, had a recurrent kidney-meridian energy weakness. When I questioned her about her sexual indecision, she confided that for quite some time she had been debating whether to encourage one of the tradesmen coming to her house, as she was becoming more and more dissatisfied with her sex life with her husband. Incidentally, she also suffered from bruxism— night grinding (think on that expression for a minute). Both the night grinding and her kidney disturbance disappeared after she made the sexual decision. She decided to give up the thoughts of the other man and instead to concentrate on rekindling her sexual relationship with her husband.

In every case of kidney disease there may not be a state of sexual indecision. But in my practice I have found this to be the case so often that it would surprise me if I did find a case of renal impairment where there was not sexual indecision at some level.

The most characteristic feature of Beethoven's music is its underlying expression of a kidney meridian problem. Not coincidentally, he had a large kidney stone.[18]

Many illustrated advertisements, particularly those for cosmetics and toiletries and certain types of clothing, tend to interfere with the energy flow in the kidney meridian. This effect may well not be accidental.

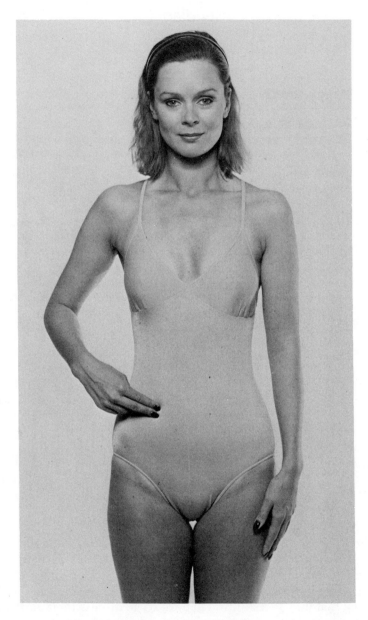

The test point for the large intestine meridian. Approximately six centimeters lateral to the umbilicus and two centimeters below.

Large Intestine Meridian

The meridian of self-worth

Self-Worth	Large Intestine
Guilt	

Negative Emotion:	Guilt
Positive Affirmations:	I am basically clean and good.
	I am worthy of being loved.
Test Image:	You have just done something over which you feel extremely guilty. Use an example from your own life.

Guilt

Melanie Klein found that the origins of guilt lay in what she called the depressive position,[19] the second stage of the psychic development of the child, the depression and consequent guilt being in response to the child's anger, hatred, and envy of the mother. Thus we frequently find that there will be a close relationship between the thyroid meridian, which has to do with depression, and the large intestine meridian. In clinical practice, we frequently hear people who feel depressed say that they feel guilty. In fact, many will say they feel so guilty over what they have done that they should not have their depression treated, that they don't deserve to be treated. Also, very frequently, severe depressives will be constipated. In fact, they will often remark how their bowels are full of evil and badness.

I have seen many patients with ulcerative colitis, a disease of the bowel. Every one of them has had a deep sense of guilt, a punishing conscience. I have had some fortunate successes with these patients, one of the major reasons for which is that I have always, very early in treatment, shown these people how their bodies are saying that they feel guilty. Then we try to discuss their guilt and I ask them to say the positive affirmation, "I am basically clean and good. I am worthy of being loved." Very frequently these people

Most people will test weak for the large intestine meridian when looking at this photo. Saying the positive affirmation for the large intestine meridian will overcome the weakness.

say, "Yes, you're right, my conscience is killing me." Often, an ulcerative colitis patient will call me up and say, "Doctor, my bowel is acting up again. There's something I'm feeling really guilty about." When they say the affirmation it almost invariably leads to a reduction of their colitis symptoms.

At the beginning of this book I stated that in my early days of practice I began to feel that professionally I wasn't good enough. I felt that if I knew more, if I were more conscientious, if I spent longer hours with the patients, if I had taken better histories, if I had attended more conferences to learn more about the various diseases, if I had spent more time talking to the relatives—then perhaps the patients would have improved more. This professional guilt haunted me.

I first became aware of the relationship between guilt and large intestine disease when I was a young resident. A boy of eighteen was admitted to the hospital to have nearly all his large bowel removed for ulcerative colitis. I talked to him at great length because it worried me and puzzled me that he was having this surgery. In fact, I felt terrified and somewhat ashamed that this was all the treatment our profession had to offer—removal of nearly all the large intestine of a young man. The one outstanding characteristic that came through to me in my naive psychological understanding at that time was how very responsible this boy was for his family. His father had died when he was thirteen, and the boy had assumed the entire responsibility for both his family and the farm that they owned. He supervised the education of the other children, insisted on doing all the shopping for his mother, managed the family's finances, and it seemed he put in very nearly a full day's farming, seven days a week, as well as attending school until he became old enough to leave legally. He was already, when I first saw him, in many ways an old family man, weighed down by responsibilities. What I now know, which I did not know then, is that almost invariably when someone takes on such a load as this, it is out of a sense of guilt.

The price he paid for this was great. Soon he was back in the hospital again and this time the colitis had spread from his large intestine up to his small intestine; not long afterward he died, a victim of his overburdening guilt.

Guilt can be an incredibly powerful negative emotion. Conversely, it is rare to find people who, without false pride or conceit, have a sense of their own self-worth and a legitimate and real pride in themselves and their lives. So many of us, it seems, are ridden with guilt—and so many of us have bowel problems.

The next time you have constipation or mild diarrhea, test your large intestine meridian energy. If it tests weak, say the appropriate affirmations repeatedly and see if they assist you. This technique has helped many people.

We see that the negative large intestine meridian emotion of guilt is really a form of self-hatred and low self-esteem. The guilt-ridden person is always blaming himself or herself for what goes wrong in his or her own life and often in the lives of family and friends. According to Johnson, guilt originally signified the fine paid for an offense, and later it came to mean the offense itself. It is not only the offense but also the mental attitude that accompanies the offense, I would say.

Guilt is derived from the Anglo-Saxon word *gylt*, which meant a crime. Guilt is now defined as "the state (meriting condemnation and reproach of conscience) of having willfully committed a crime or heinous moral offence; criminality, great culpability." It has often been said that "a guilty conscience needs no accuser." When we feel guilty, then, we feel like criminals. We feel we should be punished because we are no good.

Thus, the "seat" of our conscience is in the large intestine. This is where all our primitive guilt attacks us. Whenever you hear of someone with bowel problems, whenever you find someone who continually tests weak at the large intestine point—not just occasionally, but continually—you know that this person has a deep sense of guilt, a strong punishing conscience. This is someone who does not love himself.

Psychologically, people who feel guilty tend to be obsessional; they tend to feel they are not clean enough. This heavy burden of guilt (dirt) is why they are, for example, always washing their hands. As you might expect, I always find that they have large intestine meridian energy imbalances. Those who are unfortunate enough to become psychotic or schizophrenic often, when they are severely ill, will scream that they are all dirty inside, they are full of feces, they are full of dirt.

The positive affirmation that counteracts the effects of guilt is, "I am worthy of being loved" and/or "I am basically clean and good."[20]

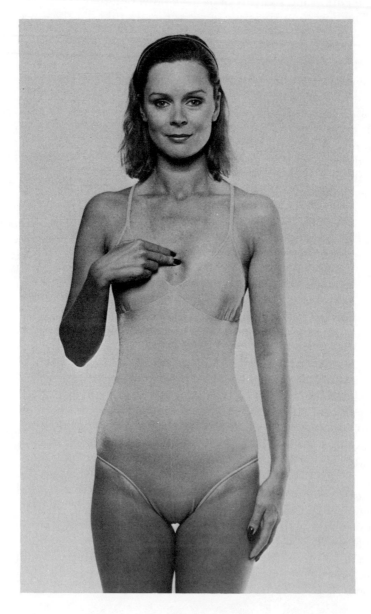

The test point for the circulation sex meridian. Approximately level with nipples.

"Midline" Meridians

Those meridians whose test points are in the midline:

Circulation-Sex
Heart
Stomach
Thyroid
Small Intestine
Bladder

One of these meridians will test weak when the subject is left-hemisphere dominant.

Circulation-Sex Meridian

The meridian of relaxation, generosity, and abjuration

Circulation Sex	Renunciation of Past, Generosity, Relaxation
	Jealousy, Sexual Tension, Regret, Remorse

Negative Emotions:	Regret and Remorse
	Sexual Tension
	Jealousy
	Stubbornness
Positive Affirmations:	I renounce the past.
	I am relaxed. My body is relaxed.
	I am generous.
Test Image:	• You are in the midst of a long project, and it seems that the project will never be completed. You sincerely regret that you ever began it.

- You are thinking of a person who really turns you on, and the more you think about this person, the more excited you become.
- You find your lover with a rival and you are trying to figure a way of getting your lover away from the rival and back for yourself.

The circulation-sex meridian is a very complicated meridian as it supplies energy to two major organs of the body, most of whose functions are quite separate. These are the adrenal glands, which almost as much as the thymus gland determine our responses to physiological stress, and the sexual glands (the ovaries and testes) and the associated sexual organs. The positive and negative emotional states associated with this meridian are of three basic types. Because these types do not seem to bear a great deal of relationship among themselves, I am inclined to think that this may be a complex meridian that has not yet been completely mapped out. There may be some subdivisions of this meridian still to be enumerated. Perhaps the adrenals and the sex glands are subserved by the same meridian because they both secrete sex hormones. Or perhaps at some deep level, somewhere in the realms of the unconscious, the two apparently separate emotions of jealousy and regret are related.

Regret

The first negative emotion of the circulation-sex meridian which we will consider is *regret*. This word is derived from the Old Norse word *grata*, which meant to weep, and in Northern English the word still has this meaning. There is a Scottish song that says, "Around my feet are twenty-one greeting wains." (Wains are children).

Regret has been defined as: "Sorrow or disappointment due to some external circumstance or event"; and "sorrow or pain due to reflection on something one has done or left undone." [21]

Cowper wrote of the "scenes that I love, and with regret perceive Forsaken, or through folly not enjoyed." [22] Shelley wrote that "pining regrets, and vain repentances . . . pervade Their valueless and

Most people will test weak for the circulation-sex meridian when looking at this photo. Saying the positive affirmation for the circulation-sex meridian will overcome the weakness.

miserable lives."[23] Johnson defines regret as "vexation at something past."

As you can see, the basic meaning of the word *regret* seems to be a feeling of particular displeasure on looking back. The English word *grede*, which has the same origin as regret, means to cry or to wail.

Remorse

Remorse has been defined as bitter regret. It comes from the Latin *mordere*, to bite. The idea it gives is to bite again, or to bite afterward; that is, after the traumatic event has passed it is still biting at us, it is still attacking us. The past is still hurting us. We have not let it go.

Nearly every person I test who has been through a divorce will test as having a sense of regret and remorse. There is a holding on to the past, an unwillingness to let it go, to say, "That was my past life. It is no longer me. I am going my way. She is going her way. Our paths are now separate," and to have no hang-ups or ties to this past life. There is a reluctance or an inability to acknowledge the good parts, to forgive the bad, and to move forward into the present, renouncing the past, living life day by day. This ability to release the past is rarely found in people who have been divorced.

Regret and remorse thus both imply a holding on to the past. When I work with people who have a recurrent circulation-sex-meridian energy imbalance I often find it necessary to spend considerable time showing them how it is affecting them and encouraging them to release the past. Tears are often required to accomplish this release or renunciation. The easiest "technique" is to encourage the person to coordinate his breath with saying, "I renounce the past." He or she takes in a big breath and then slowly lets it all out while thinking that as he or she is letting the air out, the past is being released, being let go.

A circulation-sex meridian imbalance is often found in people who experienced a broken love affair from which they have never recovered. I recall a man who came to see me complaining that he had no energy. He was always tired, always run down, he had one cold or sore throat after another, he never seemed to be well, and he had great difficulty in making any form of close contact with women. He recognized that he did want to have a close relationship, but somehow he could not manage to develop it. On testing we found a recurrent circulation-sex-meridian energy imbalance.

I then learned from him that he had once had an affair with one of the women at his office. He was deeply in love with her, and they spent several wonderful months together. However, she started hinting to him that perhaps everything wasn't right between them, and gradually she told him that she felt they should break up their relationship. She did not leave him for someone else, but merely because she found it increasingly difficult to get along with him. He was shattered. For months and months afterward he analyzed their times together and wondered what he had done to "ruin" the relationship. He began to dwell on the past, not just reminiscing over their good times together but also looking for clues as to why they had broken up. They still worked in the same office, and he found it more and more difficult to walk past her desk without feeling very upset.

After discussing this problem with him, I suggested that he recognize that he must release the past and get on with his present life. He did work on this, and he often said the positive affirmation, "I renounce the past," to himself. He realized that his attitude toward this past affair was hampering any possible relationships he might form in the present. Eventually he was able to walk past his ex-girl friend's desk without becoming upset, and he even found it possible to carry on social conversations with her—something he had been unable to do since she suggested that they end their affair.

Within a short period of time his life energy increased, he felt better in general, and he was able to relate to women in a much more satisfactory manner. The continual energy drain associated with his circulation-sex-meridian energy imbalance had been corrected and he was now able to use his energies more creatively and effectively.

We also find this meridian imbalance frequently in adults who complain about the way in which their parents brought them up. They will say, "I regret the fact that my parents didn't treat me better. If they had given me a different type of education, or if they hadn't been so strict, or if they hadn't been so lenient—or whatever." These people are caught in the past and blaming it for their troubles in the present. They must be encouraged to say, "That is done. It is past. I will let it go and move on in the present."

Others who often develop energy imbalances in the circulation-

sex meridian are people who have been involved in serious trage-
dies—accidents and so forth. At some level they will generally test
as undergoing bouts of remorse and regret. When they recognize
that such thoughts are a source of continual energy drain and when
they begin to use the positive affirmations, they gradually renounce
the past and accept it, deciding to move forward. In such a manner
we may even achieve the Zen state of "my mind is wholly discon-
nected with things of the past."

Renunciation of the Past

I have been unable to find one word to describe the precise
positive emotion that is the antonym of regret and remorse.
Through clinical testing, we have found that the affirmation that
corrects these two emotional states is, *"I renounce the past."* What
is necessary to correct these negative emotional states, then, is a
letting go of the past. That way all our life energy may be concentrated upon the present and achieving our true goal.

It may even be tenable to suggest that a definition of psychiatric
normality would be the ability not to bring the past to bear on a
present problem, for example, the ability not to be upset by what a
friend does today when it reminds you of a similar occurrence with
another friend in the past which was unpleasant for you. In love
affairs, we must remember not to carry over problems from previous affairs into the present.

Imagine that you are looking for a hard-to-find item. You may go
from store to store trying to obtain it. After trying several, you get
angry with the sales clerk at the next store—not because he did not
have the item so much as because you had been unable to find it
so many other times previously. You have carried over the resent-
ments from the previous stores. Of course, you should approach
this store as if it were the first. And in a situation involving an
intimate relationship, we should deal with each person as if he or
she were the first.

Thus it is throughout life. Often we attempt to deal with a problem that exists in the present in a manner that is clouded with those
of the past. Instead, we should be able to treat it afresh, not bringing with us the "baggage" from the past. In one sense, this is what
a psychiatrist attempts to do with his patients—getting them to deal
with the present in the present, not with predetermined ideas as to
how the problem will be solved because of patterns that even-

tuated in the past. We must renounce the past and deal with the present as just that. In Genesis 19:17 we read, "Look not behind thee." In Luke 9:62, "No man, having put his hand to the plow, and looking back, is fit for the kingdom of God."

The word I most prefer for the process of overcoming regret is *abjuration,* which is defined as a "solemn or formal renunciation or giving up of anything." It is often used in a legal sense, even as an oath, reinforcing the renunciation process by making it more definite, deliberate and binding. *Jury,* a body of people who swear to hear and give a verdict, is from the same root. *Regret* involves holding on to the past; abjuration is an undertaking to let it go, a foreswearing.

Tension

Another negative emotional attitude of the circulation-sex meridian is that of sexual *tension.* This is a very common finding. You will discover on testing that many advertisements affect this meridian. Present-day clothing often affects this meridian, as do many of the titillating advertisements in newspapers, magazines, and billboards. (Remember the pretty girl in the car ads, for example.) Many of these ads are designed, unconsciously if you will, to make us feel sexually tense. In this state of tension we will act to resolve the aroused meridian imbalance—and this action is often to the benefit of the advertiser or the promoter. One marketing expert told me that in the example of the automobile ads the "pretty girl" was used as the come-on to entice the man to buy, only he was subconsciously not buying the car at all, but the "mistress" who accompanied it in the ads. He said further that in more recent ads for cars a handsome man is often used, because there are more single women out on their own now who are buying cars for themselves and more married women who are now getting their own cars. I would suspect that such advertising expertise is not limited to the marketing of automobiles.

The penalty we pay for the "excitement" introduced by such advertising is a weakening of the energy flow in the circulation-sex meridian. This in turn affects our adrenal glands.

Note here that I am not saying that all tension is of a sexual nature, although it is much more common than we may realize. Remember that whenever there is stress, at some level there will almost invariably be mental and/or physical tension—and there will also be stress effects on the adrenal glands.

We live in a state of stress and therefore one of tension. Added to this is the specific sexual tension that is so prevalent in our present society—the idea that we must constantly be seducing members of the opposite sex. No wonder this very complex meridian often tests as having energy imbalances.

Stubbornness

The emotional quality of *stubbornness* connotes the idea of rigidity, inflexibility, refusing to bend, mold, and adjust. Consider the business executive who has been successful by following one pattern of operation and who, when offered a more efficient method, refuses even to consider it. This rigidity or inflexibility comes from and then adds to tension.

Relaxation

The positive state that is opposite tension is *relaxation.* The word *relaxation* comes from the Latin *laxare,* which means to loosen, slacken, or soften. The word literally means to be lax or soft again. The *Oxford English Dictionary* in part defines relaxation as, "To render [a part of the body] less firm or rigid; to make loose or slack."

Since tension is a state of rigidity, the positive affirmation is a return once again to a lax, softer state. The sexual connotations here are obvious, and it is certainly not by coincidence that these emotional states are related to the meridian that supplies energy to the sex glands. The positive affirmations, "I am relaxed," or "My body is relaxed" have been found to restore the energy balance to the circulation-sex meridian.

Jealousy

Jealousy is derived from the Latin *zelus,* meaning zeal or fervor. The idea behind jealousy is that we act and even fight with zeal to protect and regain what we feel is rightfully ours. The *Oxford English Dictionary* says jealousy is "vigilance in guarding a possession." It involves a state of rivalry. It has been stated, perhaps metaphorically, that rivals may be considered as opponents on opposite river banks facing each other.[24] Thus, jealousy implies that we regard the possession (and a spouse or lover is regarded a possession in this context) as "ours" and one for which we will fight, if necessary, to regain.

Jealousy is always a triangular situation. The husband is jealous of the rival who has "made off" with his wife. So, with all his energy, he fights the rival to regain his wife for himself. Involved in this action is no concept of the wife as a separate person, making her own decision as to what she wants to do with her life and with whom she wants to spend it. In a jealousy situation there is always the feeling that the party fought for, the wife in this case, is seen purely as a possession, something to be regained. Love for the wife is of less importance than the wish on the part of the man to regain what is his. Owen Meredith wrote, "No true love there can be without its dread penalty—jealousy." [25] But jealousy is not love. It arises out of selfishness and a sense of possession of the other person, not out of a true loving relationship with him or her. Robert Louis Stevenson wrote, "Jealousy, at any rate, is one of the consequences of love; you may like it or not, at pleasure; but there it is." I disagree. With true love there is no jealousy. We respect the wishes of the other person and out of love we want what is best for him or her as well as what is best for ourselves. La Rochefoucauld put it very well when he stated, "There is more self-love than love in jealousy."

The little child who refuses to share his toy with his siblings or playmates, defensively shouting, "It's mine, it's mine!" and clutching it with all his might is expressing jealousy, the unwillingness to share, the holding on to the possession at all costs.

Generosity

The positive emotion in this instance is generosity and sharing. Generosity is "the willingness to give or share." Johnson defines generosity as, "magnanimous; open of heart." It is a particularly appropriate word because the I-E root from which it is descended, *gen*,[26] bears such words with a sexual connotation as *generation* and *gender*.

It is not surprising that jealousy is so prevalent today. In our society we have become so attached to our possessions that we guard them jealously. This may be related to an unwillingness to release the past. By contrast, *kindness*, which comes from the same root as generous *(gen)*, means "of a friendly nature; generous or hospitable; warmhearted; good." Kindness is another positive attribute of the circulation-sex meridian.

We recently witnessed an example of jealousy among our cats. We obtained two female kittens from the same litter when they were ten weeks old. They are now over six months old and still play together, sleep together, and groom each other. When one is petted, held, or fed, the other doesn't seem to be upset by this but instead waits her turn. One is not jealous of the attention given to the other. Of course this in part stems from their very early mothering. When we first brought home the new kittens, the cat that had been living with us for some years displayed all the signs which, if he were human, we would interpret as jealousy. He hissed at them and tried to drive them away from his "territory." It was as if he were trying to say to them, "This household is mine. I am going to protect it with all my energy. Go away. This is mine." If he were human we could have encouraged him to share and feel generous by counseling him. Because he is an animal, we simply displayed even more love toward him, spent more time with him, and tried for a gradual and gentle introduction to the kittens. However, he indignantly refused our offers of love and now refuses even to come into the house.

In some cases it is very difficult to overcome feelings of jealousy and stubbornness. With a patient or student, we would be able to counsel and assist him to overcome these negative emotional states through the appropriate affirmations and other work. Furthermore, we would work directly with his overall life energy as governed by his thymus gland, and activate it so that with love he could release his feelings of jealousy.

I once had a patient, a married man, who was having an affair with his secretary. I asked him if he felt that this affair was interfering with his relationship with his wife. He protested loudly, "Not at all, in fact, quite the contrary. My girl friend has so stimulated my feelings of love that my wife is really the beneficiary of this increased love which is now being kindled." Some years later this same man came to me in tears. He had found out that his wife was having an affair and he felt he wanted to kill the man for what he had done to break up his household. He told me that he would fight for his wife with all his might because he simply was not going to lose her.

This story tempts me to repeat La Rochefoucauld's statement that

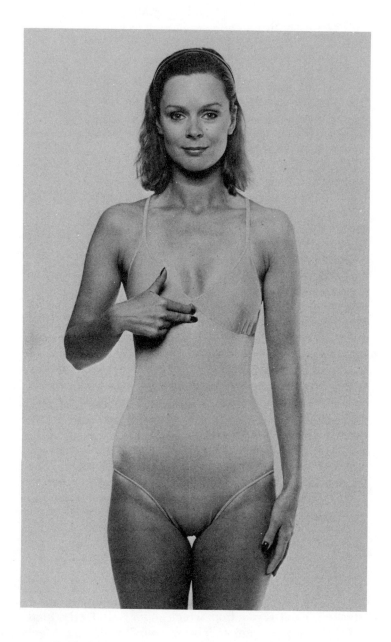

The test point for the heart meridian. Tip of xiphoid process below sternum.

jealousy is more self-love than love. After carefully discussing this man's history with him and explaining to him the negative effects on his own energy that this unbridled jealousy was creating, I was able to suggest that he use the affirmations "I am generous" and "My body is relaxed." He recognized that jealousy and sexual tension were draining his energy and preventing him from arriving at an unstressed solution to the problem at hand. It was not long before he had resolved his problem satisfactorily.

Heart Meridian

The meridian of forgiveness

Heart	Love, Forgiveness
	Anger

Negative Emotion: Anger
Positive Affirmations: I love.
                        I forgive.
                        There is forgiveness in my heart.
Test Image: You come back from a walk in the neighborhood and catch a vandal in the act of letting the air out of the tires of your car.

Anger

As previously discussed, the predominant negative emotion relating to the heart meridian is *anger*. This emotional state, and problems with this meridian, are very prominent in patients who have heart ailments.

Examining the origin of the word *anger*, we can see relationships between the heart and anger which we otherwise would not have suspected. The I-E root from which anger is derived is *angk*, which meant to choke or oppress. This of course is the exact feeling that people have when they suffer from the cardiac condition of *angina*

Most people will test weak for the heart meridian when looking at this photo. Saying the positive affirmation for the heart meridian will overcome the weakness.

pectoris. The word *angina* is derived from this same root. In Latin, the word is *angere,* which means to strangle.

In Middle English, *anger* was more passive than it is now. It meant trouble and affliction, no longer having the more violent connotation of strangling and torture. Now, the word has yet another meaning. It means in a sense a retribution and the feeling provoked against a person who has troubled, afflicted, or tortured us. Perhaps anger was best described by John Locke, "Anger is uneasiness or discomfiture of the mind, upon the receipt of an injury, with a present purpose of revenge."

It is evident from Locke's definition that anger has revenge as its purpose. To stop the negative effects of the anger there must be a counteracting quality of forgiveness. To forgive is to pardon.

South wrote, "Anger is, according to some, a transient hatred, or at least very like it." As we know from our testing, hatred is a basic negative thymus attribute, while anger is associated with the heart meridian.

Forgiveness

Forgive means "to give up resentment or claim to requital for pardon (an offence)." Robert Burns wrote, "Fain would I say, 'Forgive my foul offence!'" It has been said that forgiveness is the renunciation of anger or resentment. It is this renouncing, this giving up of anger and resentment that turns the weakening effect on the heart meridian energy—and therefore on the heart—into a positive energy state. This is a good example of transmutation. We are transmuting anger into love and forgiveness, turning weakening effects into strengthening ones.

Most primitive words for forgiveness involve giving or letting go. We can think of forgiveness as releasing anger and giving love. As the Bible says, "For if ye forgive men their trespasses, your heavenly Father will also forgive you." (Matthew 6:14) Johnson described forgiveness as "tenderness; willingness to pardon." And Dryden wrote:

> Mercy above did hourly plead
> For her resemblance here below;
> And mild forgiveness intercede
> To stop the coming blow.

Anger, of course, is a very common finding. Its cure is forgiveness. Yet often today we seem to have the idea that the cure of anger is what we would call a psychological enema—to get it all out, really tell the object of your anger off, get it out of your system. On testing you will find that this does not cure the anger. Instead you will discover that not only does the angry person still have the heart-meridian energy imbalance, but the person who has been the object of the angry outburst will now also have this meridian imbalance. He or she now has resentment, "feels back," toward you.[27] Thus the "cure" of anger is not to let it all out but instead to transmute it into love, into forgiveness. This can be done instantly when the life energy, the will to be well, is activated.

The next time you are driving and encounter a traffic jam, have someone in the car test you. You will find that being in such a situation usually produces a heart meridian imbalance. "He that is slow to anger is better than the mighty." (Proverbs 16:32)

Stomach Meridian

The meridian of contentment and tranquility

	Contentment
Stomach	Disappointment, Disgust, Greed

Negative Emotions:	Disgust
	Disappointment
	Bitterness
	Greed
	Emptiness
	Deprivation
	Nausea
	Hunger
Positive Affirmations:	I am content.
	I am tranquil.

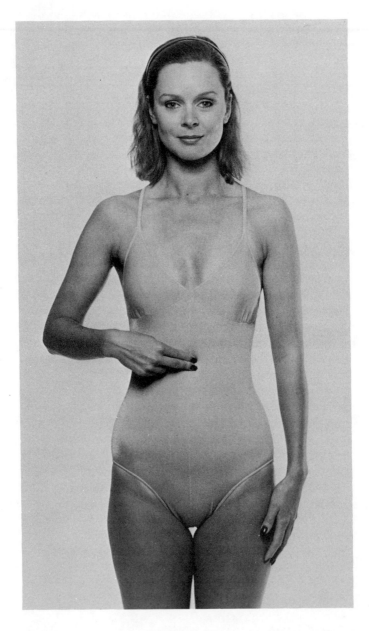

The test point for the stomach meridian. Halfway between xiphoid process and umbilicus.

Test Image:
- You are walking down the street and see your lover strolling arm-in-arm with someone else. You realize that you have been displaced.

- You have been in line for a promotion for some time. When the vacancy occurs, someone else is given the job.

The emotional states associated with the stomach meridian quite obviously relate to stomach functions.

Disgust

Disgust is "strong distaste or disrelish for food; sickening physical disinclination to partake of food, drink, medicine, etc., nausea, loathing." It is also defined as "strong repugnance, aversion or repulsion excited by that which is loathesome or offensive," as a foul smell, disagreeable person or action, disappointed ambition, and so on.

Disgust initially comes from the Latin *gustare,* to taste. The word really means something that tastes bad, that causes us to sicken, even to vomit to expel it. The word *choose* comes from the same root as disgust. Thus we can say that we choose either to keep or to spit out things that are of good taste or bad taste—things we do or do not relish. Johnson defines the verb *to disgust* as "to raise aversion in the stomach; to distaste."

Disappointment

Disappointment is defined as "the frustration or nonfulfillment of expectation, intention, or desire," and as "the anguish of disappointed faith." The word comes from the Latin *puntare,* meaning to fix the points. *Punctum* in Latin means point of agreement. In Middle English disappointment took on the meaning of removing from office and dispossessing.

Today the basic meaning is removal from our appointment, from our relationship with another person. The boyfriend takes a new girl friend, and the first girl friend experiences disappointment. The points of agreement have been broken, and she has been removed from office, so to speak—dispossessed of her particular relationship with her man.

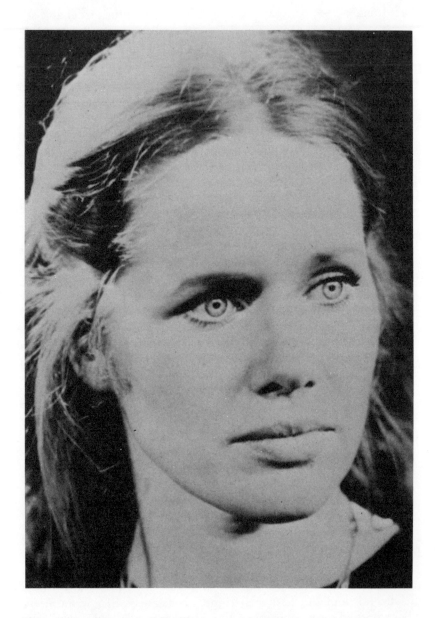

Most people will test weak for the stomach meridian when looking at this photo. Saying the positive affirmation for the stomach meridian will overcome the weakness.

Consider what I meant when I stated that I felt disappointed in my practice. From everything I had been taught I had been led to believe that if I did certain things my patients would be better, and happy, and would go about their lives full and complete and realized. This is what I expected, but it did not materialize. This led to my feelings of disappointment. My disappointment came about because what I had been led to believe would arrive in point of fact did not arrive, in the same way the baby is led to believe that if he is hungry Mommy will provide food. If the food does not arrive, he feels disappointed. The feeling that lies behind that is that he no longer has his favored position with Mommy.

Perhaps now we can understand how a child who wants to put food in his stomach feels when that food does not come. The child feels that he has been removed from his special position with his mother. The food, like the boyfriend, has gone to someone else. But when the food does arrive, we can expect an overreaction—the feeling now becomes one of greed, of devouring everything.

Johnson defines *disappoint* as "to defeat of expectation," and *disappointment* as "miscarriage of expectation." In a situation where disappointment occurs, a state of expectation has existed, and that expectation has not been met.

Many times a woman has told me that she has been jilted, that she feels disappointed, and then begins to overeat because of a gnawing emptiness in the pit of her stomach. She has had, in psychological terms, her love supplies cut off. She turns to a substitute, the food, to provide love just as when she was a baby her mother supplied her with all the food and love that she required.

The prototype of this situation is a mother with her baby at her breast, supplying the baby's needs. (It may be significant in this regard that milk is used for the treatment of so many stomach conditions.)

Disappointment with oneself is also reflected in a stomach-meridian energy imbalance. One may feel that he has let himself and others down, that he deserves to be demoted and has demoted himself in his own eyes.

Bitterness

A related emotional state is that of *bitterness*. The *Oxford English Dictionary* defines *bitter* as unpalatable to the mind; unpleasant and hard to "swallow" or admit. Here the facial expression differs markedly from that of disgust. With disgust, there is a down-turning of the corners of the mouth, as Charles Darwin observed, "as if the child was forming a channel through which the vomit would come up from his stomach to be expelled."[28] With bitterness, the lips are often held tightly together and pursed. As we know, bitterness is the sensation we often experience just before we vomit, before we expel the food that tastes bad or is bad. It may be that this gesture of pursing the lips is an attempt to stop the vomit from coming out. Thus bitterness could be an intermediate stage between disgust and actually vomiting.[29]

In many problems involving a faulty chewing mechanism, the dentist frequently describes the problem as connected with the temporomandibular joint. With such a disturbance, there will be an impairment of the energy flow in the stomach meridian. This is compounded by the fact that the improperly chewed food is not adequately predigested in the mouth and creates difficulties of digestion when in the stomach.

We have also found that most cases of food allergies are related to impaired stomach meridian energy. We have been quite successful over the years in relieving food allergies by activating the stomach meridian using the appropriate affirmations and reinforcing with the thymus affirmations.

In the context of this meridian, how appropriate it is when we speak of "bitter disappointment."

Greed

When we feel we are not receiving enough from others, or when we have been disappointed many times in the past and those same disappointments crop up again, we turn to a source of gratification and try to take all that we can get, or all there is. With the greedy person, it is as if he is never sure the next meal will come, so he overeats at this meal and hoards all he can get.

Hanna Segal states that greed "aims at the possession of all the goodness that can be extracted from the object, regardless of the consequences."[30] Despite the effects of overeating on the greedy person, he will continue to do so. It may even reach the point where he takes what another needs just to satisfy his own desires. The greedy person feels, in essence, "I have been disappointed before. The milk was cut off when I needed it. Now, while it is flowing, I am going to take all I can and store it inside me like a camel, prepared for the next trip in the desert, because I don't know when it may be cut off again." He says this in the same emotional state that we have all experienced when we have hoarded gasoline during acute energy crises. During such times we see motorists stopping to fill up when they need only one or two gallons—they want to be safe, to have a full tank when the crunch comes.

The word *greed* comes from the root *gher,* meaning to like and to want. This became in Old English *graedig,* hungry, from which we derive our present word *greedy.* Remember that greed is not hunger. There is a cartoon in an early *Punch* of a lord seated at his dining table while his butler is bringing in a very large meal. He says to the butler, "I'm not hungry, but thank God I'm greedy."

With stomach meridian problems in general, one of the most common attempts to correct the imbalance is the seeking of gratification by food. The individual attempts to overcome his stress by oral gratification. As Theodor Reik wrote, "Excessive intake of food has the function of consolation and compensation for those emotional frustrations." [31] This applies in particular to disappointment or deprivation. Most compulsive overeaters will readily admit that they are not hungry, but that they cannot resist the craving for food. Reik goes on to say that this greed is an exaggerated defense to ward off the anxiety of starving. He says, "that elementary fear can be put into the formula: Eat or you will starve."

Of course, greed need not be expressed in overeating. Any excessive taking in—of food, clothing, objects, any excessive accumulation—is a manifestation of greed and stomach-meridian energy imbalance. Melanie Klein in *Envy and Gratitude* stated that "greed is an impetuous and insatiable craving, exceeding what the subject needs and what the object is able and willing to give. At the unconscious level, greed aims primarily at completely scooping out, sucking dry, and devouring."

There is frequently a considerable hint of aggression in greed. A very greedy baby may almost, it seems, attack the breast to suck as much as it can—to the point where the vigor of the sucking hurts the mother. A greedy person may attempt to satisfy his own desires with little thought of the consequences to others or even to himself.

Nations can be guilty of greed. I read that the Boer War was conducted primarily out of a motive of greed. Over a hundred thousand people were killed to gain possession of the South African gold mines.

Emptiness

People who have been disappointed will often state that they feel *empty*. Empty has been defined as "needing nourishment; hungry." Hence the baby who needs more from his mother. In the *American Heritage Dictionary* we find empty defined as "void of content." Now the word "content" as a noun means "that which is contained in a receptacle"—and thus when we see empty described as "void of content," it can be taken in both senses—content as the noun and as the adjective.

Deprivation

Deprivation implies a dispossession or a loss. It is defined by one dictionary as "to depose from office." Thus you can see how it relates to disappointment. It is no wonder that both of these emotional states relate to the stomach meridian.

The origin of the word is very interesting. In Latin *de* means completely. *Privus* means private or individual. The Latin *privatus* meant "free from office." I am reminded here of a politician who has been dispossessed of his elected office by the people.

The origin is also of considerable significance. The I-E root *per* had the sense of *forward* and this gave rise to *prei-wo*, which meant forward from the rest—isolated from the others, on one's own, not part of the crowd. We say to ourselves that our private thoughts are those which are not shared with anyone else—they are separate and belong just to us. When we have been dispossessed we have been separated from that involvement and isolated from it.

The word *deprivation* is frequently used in present-day psychology, particularly in the phrase "maternal deprivation," which was coined by John Bowlby, an English psychoanalyst, to describe the psychological trauma that young children went through when separated from their mothers, especially by hospitalization. This he saw had very definite stages and was a clinical syndrome.[32] It is now clear that the symptoms of maternal deprivation can occur apart from the hospital setting and to some extent are contributing factors in most childhood psychological illnesses. They may initiate weaknesses that could affect a person throughout his life.

Thus we see how beautifully and precisely deprivation relates to the stomach meridian—the meridian that is primarily related to receiving love and food from the mother. It is the meridian of sucking, so when we are deprived by the mother it means we are removed from the sucking situation, we are separated from our "love supplies," and we feel a sense of loss, we feel dispossessed, we feel deposed—and disappointed. It is not surprising that the positive emotional attitude for this is one of contentment, of receiving enough from mother. We feel, in essence, that "she has given me enough to sustain me mentally and physically through my activities. Through her love she has nurtured me. I am content."

Nausea

People who often suffer from nausea and stomach meridian problems may describe themselves as feeling psychologically nauseated by something. The origin of *nausea* is very interesting. It comes from the Greek *naus*, from which we get, among other words, *nautical* and *nausea,* in its original meaning referring to seasickness. The *Oxford English Dictionary* describes nausea as a feeling of sickness, with loathing of food and an inclination to vomit. It also is a strong feeling of disgust. What we do not like the taste of tends to nauseate us—physiologically and psychologically.

Hunger

Perhaps the best definition of *hunger* is a "strong desire, or craving." Initially, in both the history of the word and our own individual development, hunger applied to a need for nourishment and the uneasy or painful sensation caused by the want of food. Later it became more generalized in its use and was applied to any strong desire or craving.

Initially our hungers were physical hungers for our mothers' milk, to satisfy the unpleasant physical sensations in the stomach, to quiet the stomach meridian. But then this also became associated with the love of the mother. We hungered not just for the food or the milk but the sensation of warmth and love that we felt when she gave it to us. Thus those who hunger for food also hunger for love and contentment. Milton, in *Paradise Lost,* put it this way:

> I content me,
> and from the sling of famine fear no harm,
> nor mind it, fed with better thoughts that feed
> my hung'ring more to do my father's will.

You will often find with those who have this hunger for love that if they say at the end of a meal, "I feel satisfied and content," they will test weak, but if they say, "I could go on eating and eating," they will test strong.

In most addicts we will find unrequited hunger and discontent. Then, when the love supplies do not come to ease the hunger and create contentment, unhappiness develops.

Contentment

The positive affirmation that on testing restores balance to the energy supply in the stomach meridian is "I am content." (This seems more effective than "I am contented," perhaps because of the different speech rhythm.)

Contentment is the major positive emotional attitude related to the stomach meridian. Bear in mind that all positive feelings related to the stomach meridian originate in the initial feeding experience at the mother's breast with the first love offerings—the milk —which the baby receives from her. (Perhaps now you realize the genius of the advertisement which depicts a certain brand of milk as coming from *contented* cows.)

The basic feeling behind the affirmation "I am content" is, "I don't have everything I want or everything that could benefit me, but I have enough. What I have is sufficient." Sir Edward Dyer said,

> Content to live, this is my stay;
> I seek no more than may suffice.

Thus the person who overeats, the person who is not satisfied, is not *contented* with what he has. He is always trying for more.

When saying the positive affirmation "I am content," we might be reminded of the saying, "A contented mind is a continual feast." Here again we see the relationship between contentment and eating. In fact the word *contentment* comes from the Latin *continere*, which means to contain. We may think of the stomach itself as a container.

In the Bible we read, "I have learned, in whatsoever state I am, therewith to be content." (Philippians 4:11) Contentment is a state of oral satisfaction, of having received enough—enough love from the mother, enough love from the significant people around us. It is accepting that even though we would like to have more, we have enough now, and for that we are thankful. The writer to the Hebrews (13:5) suggested "Let your conversation be without covetousness; and be content with such things as ye have."

As we mentioned previously, food allergies are a very common clinical finding. It will be found on simple testing that certain foods deplete the life energy, and it has been my experience that in nearly every case of food allergy the meridian involved is the stomach meridian. If the positive affirmation is stated while eating, the effects of the food allergy will usually be reduced.

A great deal of modern advertising affects individuals through the stomach meridian. When we view ads we often become discontented with our lot. We don't think we have enough, so we will attempt to have more and more. Study advertisements for yourself and have someone test their effects on you. Check whether you feel disappointed with your lot, or discontent because your life is not like the life depicted in the ad. You may find that you will become more and more provoked, discontented, as you continue to examine these ads.

An article entitled "The Me Degeneration" begins with the following:

> Maurice Sendak once wrote a story of a pampered dog who had her own pillows, comb and brush, a red wool sweater, two windows to look out of, two bowls to eat from, and a master who loved her. Despite this she left home, explaining, "I am discontented. I want something I do not have. There must be more to life than having everything!"[33]

Tranquil

Another interesting finding in our research is that the stress induced in an individual by noise affects the stomach meridian. The noise of city traffic or general unnecessary clatter will often upset the energy balance in the stomach meridian. The positive affirmation, "I am tranquil," often causes a weak stomach meridian test point to test strong. *Tranquil* comes from the same source as *quiet*. Shakespeare (in *Othello*) recognized the relationship between contentment and tranquility when he wrote, "Farewell the Tranquill minde; farewell Content."

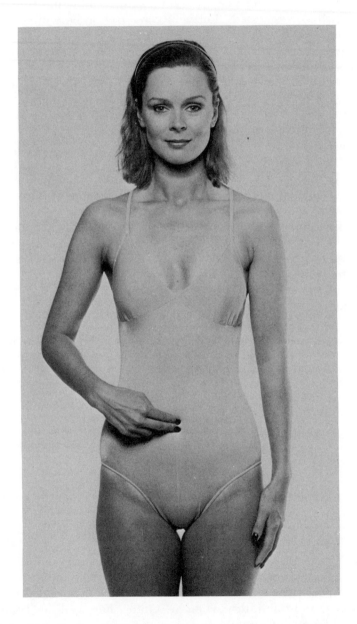

The test point for the thyroid meridian. One-third down an imaginary line between the umbilicus and symphysis pubis.

Thyroid Meridian*

The meridian of hope

Thyroid	Lightness, Buoyancy
	Heaviness, Depression

Negative Emotions: Depression
                                  Despair
                                  Grief
                                  Hopelessness
                                  Despondency
                                  Loneliness
                                  Solitude

Positive Affirmations: I am light and buoyant.
                                  I am buoyed up with hope.

Test Image: You are at home, you have no energy, and you have nothing to do worth doing. You feel heavy and weighed down. Everything is just too much.

Depression

Depression is the predominant negative emotion related to the thyroid meridian. There is a great deal of argument and controversy regarding what is actually meant by depression, and many learned psychiatric tomes have been written on this subject. To me it is quite simple.

For many years I compiled a list of the symptoms reported to me by patients when they felt depressed. All of them seemed to imply that they were literally being pushed or pressed or sometimes pulled down—de-pressed. For example, they would describe themselves as being low or flat, as if there were a weight on their backs. They would sometimes say that they just felt too heavy to move, they just did not have enough energy to raise themselves out

* Classically called the Triple Heater meridian

Most people will test weak for the thyroid meridian when looking at this photo.
Saying the positive affirmation for the thyroid meridian will overcome the weakness.

of a chair. This is what we mean by depression. Of course, it can be very mild. We often feel "depressed" on those days when everything is just too much—just too much effort to get up and begin the day. Our load seems too heavy for us to carry.

Stokes refers to "a fit of the blues" as "a depression over loss." Indeed, many depressed patients report that they seem to be "in a blue funk" or "crying the blues" or "down in the dumps."

The writer of Psalm 69:20 referred to depression when he wrote,

> Reproach hath broken my heart;
> And I am full of heaviness:

The positive affirmation for this feeling is the sensation of being light, buoyant, and floating. The psychiatric opposite state of depression is that of elation, "being lifted up out of." Thus we find that when the thyroid meridian tests weak, if the person says, "I am light and buoyant," and imagines himself as being light and buoyant, then he will test strong.

The thyroid meridian is the continuum of mass—it relates to our self-concept of our own mass. In clinical practice, mild cases of underactivity of the thyroid gland are very, very common. I would estimate that at least 70 percent of the patients I see in my practice have some evidence of underactive thyroid. One of the more subtle tests, and one you can perform yourself, is to take your temperature every morning before rising. The thermometer should be used under the arm and kept there for ten minutes. A normal reading is between 97.6°F. and 98.2°F. If it is generally lower than this, it usually indicates low thyroid activity. It will be found that as the thyroid activity increases to normal, the morning temperature will rise. It is no wonder that most hypothyroid people describe themselves as being most tired and heavy in the morning, because this is when their temperature is at its lowest. The thyroid gland may be seen, in a way, as the body's thermostat. If the temperature is turned down, there will be underactivity.

Frequently it will be found that people whose thyroid meridian tests weak generally tilt their heads to the side. A classic example is that of the Botticelli *Venus*. Often you will find that as the person corrects his head and neck posture, the thyroid meridian will test strong. You may recall that this gesture of tilting the head is often employed, as in the *Venus*, by artists when they wish to transmit the message that the female in the portrait is a dependent waif who requires our nurturing to survive. When a woman tilts her head to the side in this manner it often brings out maternal or paternal feelings in us. We wish to be her protector.

Thyroid meridian weakness often occurs when there is a double-bind.[34] Whenever you find that you or your friend have an underactive thyroid meridian, think "I am in two minds at the moment about the most important person or thing in my life. I predominantly like the situation but I am in two minds about it." (You are one step away from the basic positive thymus attitude.)

The double-bind situation may be related to the fact that very often we find that people whose thyroid meridian tests weak wear glasses. This may be because their refractive errors and often their central problems with reading, which are more basic than the refractive errors (by this I mean the subtle dyslexias that so many of these people have), are from the same source. When they are reading, they are not quite sure what they are reading. It is as if they are in two minds about what they have read. They have a central processing problem and in this state they often tilt their heads so as to try to read or see better. Although it is not invariably the case, you will more likely than not find that people who tend to tilt their heads and people who wear glasses will, at some level, have a thyroid meridian problem and also at some level, either conscious or unconscious, they are depressed.

We often find that men whose thyroid meridian test point tests weak on a long-term basis tend toward loss of hair and baldness, apparently related to underactivity of the thyroid gland.

Let me give you an example to bring these various concepts into focus. A male patient, although only in his early thirties, was suffering from quite severe hair loss. Each morning there would be masses of hair on his pillow, and he would lose more in the shower. His early-morning temperature was very low, about 96°F., and of numerous medications and supplements used to activate his thyroid gland, none had been successful. Of course, I asked him about his depression. He said that at times he in fact did feel very low and depressed over his relationship with his girl friend. She was keeping him constantly in two minds. She would wax hot and then she would wane cold. Sometimes she said how much she loved him and desired him and how much she wanted to marry him, and the next time he saw her, she would say she had decided not to get married and that she did not know whether she should even see him again. This went on and on. Many evenings would be spent arguing about this, and after such an evening, he would test weak.

Eventually I said to him, "Look, this has to stop. Either she is going to continue to have a positive relationship with you or not. This 'on-again, off-again' relationship is affecting you." He exclaimed, "You're right. I'm going to explain this situation to her, and then she's going to have to make a decision and stick to it!" He telephoned me the next day and said, "I don't understand what happened. I haven't even spoken to her yet, but having made this decision I feel so much better! I am no longer depressed!" Then he said, "Miraculously, for the first time this morning, my temperature was normal and even more incredibly I didn't lose any hair last night." Since that day he has suffered no further hair loss! And the relationship is slowly but surely resolving itself to their mutual satisfaction.

I recall another patient, a woman who had been widowed for some twenty years and who suffered from a chronic, clincial low-thyroid condition. She stated that she had been depressed for many years, ever since her husband had died. I asked her when she had started to tilt her head (it was now permanently tilted, it seemed, at quite a severe angle). She said she couldn't remember, but when I asked her daughter, her daughter readily volunteered, "She started that almost the day after my father died." As she underwent treatment, I noticed that as her depression lifted and her thyroid functioning improved, she no longer tilted her head as she had previously.

Incidentally, most flute players tilt their heads. It has been my finding that nearly all of them have some degree of thyroid underactivity, and they also tend to be depressed.

You will find, not surprisingly, that when you look at the Botticelli *Venus* your thyroid meridian will test weak. But if you move the page around such that although the head remains tilted in relationship to the body, it is angled so that the eyes are parallel to your line of vision, you will perceive that the head is no longer tilted, at least in relationship to yourself, and your thyroid meridian will test strong.

In the late 1950s, antidepressant medications were first on the market, and very good results were obtained in clinical cases of severe depression. The cases with which we worked in the early days of antidepressants were those who were called psychotic depressives, those who would otherwise have had electroshock therapy and almost invariably were confined to the hospital. However, not that high a percentage of any psychiatrist's practice, and certainly not a very high percentage of the general population, may be classified as severely depressed.

When antidepressant medications appeared, suddenly depression became respectable. Many patients who were suffering from all manner of nonpsychotic illnesses were suddenly being called "depressed." They were said to be suffering from the disease of "depression" for a number of reasons. One was that we began to recognize depression in milder forms than had been customary, which was a very valuable "preventive" measure. Second, we now had a nice clinical label we could put on all these poor miserable people who had no "diagnosis" before. Furthermore, we had something that we could *give* them. They had never responded to barbiturates nor to tranquilizers (because they basically were neither anxious nor schizophrenic). The psychiatrists were always looking for the magic pill. And so, through subtle reorientation of thoughts based both on the general trends of their own professional societies and the drug house advertising, gradually the antidepressant drugs were dispensed to people who were not clinically depressed. The sales of antidepressant medication skyrocketed, a trend that has continued. More importantly, more and more people were being called "depressed." Depression was "in." It was suddenly not an epithet to be depressed. It was an accepted clinical state.

It is important to realize that the vast majority of people who feel depressed and test weak at the thyroid meridian are *not* suffering from clinical depression. Certainly not everyone who has a thyroid meridian weakness should take an antidepressant drug.

We see, then, that depression became acceptable, but other emotional states did not. For example, if I were writing a letter back to a patient's general practitioner, I could say, "Mr. Smith has the following symptoms. . . . He is suffering from depression for which I have prescribed an antidepressant." Everyone would be satisfied, except the patient. If I had written back to the referring doctor and said, "Mr. Smith is suffering from unhappiness," the doctor would have said two things: (1) that I was not a proper doctor because unhappiness was not a medical disease, and (2) what was the good of diagnosing unhappiness anyhow, as there are no pills to cure unhappiness. For over twenty years I have watched as depression became a loosely used word, and the vast quantities of antidepressant drugs being used came about through this mechanism.

Melanie Klein describes the first stage of the psychic development of the child as the paranoid-schizoid position, and the second stage as the depressive position. The paranoid-schizoid position corresponds to the lung meridian, and the depressive position corresponds in part to the thyroid meridian. As you will see later, there is a direct relationship between the lung meridian and the thyroid meridian. Further, the lung meridian is the primary meridian, the major source through which energy enters the body—the breath. There is a development from predominantly lung meridian problems in the earliest days of life to thyroid meridian problems later. Additionally, lung meridian problems relate to the right hemisphere and thyroid meridian problems relate to the left hemisphere. Thus, there is a progression from predominantly right-hemisphere activity to predominantly left-hemisphere activity. It is only after the child has passed through the positions described by Klein that he is, in a sense, integrated, capable of seeing people as whole objects and relating to them person-to-person and really loving them. This loving state corresponds to high thymus activity, which is achieved only when there is a balance between the cerebral hemispheres, such as is achieved when the lung and thyroid meridians are balanced. Hence these findings are in essential agreement and in fact corroborate the deepest tenets of child psychoanalysis.

Melancholy

Melancholy is the state of depression.[35] In Latin, *melancholia* means literally "the condition of having black bile." The *Oxford English Dictionary* points out that "In early references its prominent symptoms are . . . propensity to causeless and violent anger [that is, wrath]" and in later references mental gloom and sadness. In the ligher sense, it is used as tender or pensive sadness, for example, as in the song, "Come to me, my melancholy baby"— "baby" being tearful and in need of cuddling, hardly the state of a true melancholic.

As early as 1485, melancholy was defined as depression of spirits, a condition of gloom or dejection. In "Mourning and Melancholia," Freud wrote that the first distinguishing mental feature of melancholia was a profoundly painful dejection. The "propensity to causeless and violent anger" is more in keeping with the choleric (see page 120-122) state, that of yellow bile; whereas the state of depression is in keeping with the black bile, melancholia.

Both *choler* and *gall* are derived from the Indo-European root *ghel.* Its original meaning was "to shine" and referred to bright materials, for example, "yellow metal," from which we get *gold* and yellow liquid, the *bile.* (Other words from this root include *glimmer, glisten, glitter, glee, glad,* and *glow.*)

Despair

Despair means the loss of all hope. The Latin *sperare* means to hope. It is derived from the Indo-European root *spei,* which meant to thrive or prosper. As it has been said, despair, hopelessness, depression, despondency, and dejection denote "emotional states marked by lowness of spirit." Incidentally, *spirit* is derived from the same root. (See pp. 4-5)

Grief

Another powerful negative emotional state related to the thyroid meridian is that of *grief.* Grief comes from the same word as *grave,* and likewise means heavy. It is not surprising that in psychological literature grief is closely related to depression and the stage of mourning after the loss of a loved one. The Greek word *baros,* means heaviness and comes from the same basic root, and from this we get *barometer*—an instrument that measures the heaviness of the air.

In this context we may find new implications in Job 6:2—"Oh that my grief were thoroughly weighed."

Hopelessness

Another negative emotional attitude associated with the thyroid meridian is *hopelessness.* The positive state, of course, is *hope,* which is thought possibly to have been derived from the same source as *hop*—quoting Eric Partridge, "the basic idea would be a leaping, or to leap, with expectation." [36] With hope you have the feeling of being lifted up, of being light and buoyant, of rising above the burdens that are pushing you down. Hence the best affirmation is "I am buoyed up with hope."

Let me give you an example of how being in two minds affects the thyroid meridian energy and relates to depression. I recently saw a priest who had been suffering from a severe depression for many years. He was very lethargic, very tired, always feeling that he was "down" and "low" and had no energy, no thought for the future, no hope whatsoever; he had frequently contemplated suicide. Upon testing we found thyroid meridian weakness. I explained to him what this meant, and I talked to him about how hope would overcome his feelings of depression. I told him that I had often found that people who tended to have thyroid meridian problems were those who tended to be in two minds about everything.

When he came back a week later he said, "You know, I feel so much better! I have been saying to myself, 'I have hope, I am light and buoyant.' And I think what is helping me most is this idea of being in two minds. For example, every time I meet a woman and talk to her, I seem to be in two minds. Not about sex, but about whether I should be close with a person of the opposite sex." He said, "I can see myself being in two minds about this all the time. I don't know exactly how to handle it completely yet, but you were so right to bring it up. Ever since I recognized it last week, I have felt so much better."

So I said, "Well, let's find out if you really do want to have a relationship with a woman or not." He said, "There have been two women in my life recently. One is Vivienne, and the other is Laura." Then I told him to phrase his question very precisely, which he did, and he said, "I want to see more of Laura." And he tested strong. When he said, "I don't want to see Laura any more," he tested weak. And with Vivienne it was reversed. He said, "I wouldn't have thought that originally, but now that we see it with the test results I can easily understand and accept that that is the case. So what happens now?"

I then showed him that since he had been thinking in terms of hope and had begun to deal with his dilemma regarding the women, his thyroid meridian tested strong. But his kidney meridian tested weak. So I said to him, "Now that you have solved the question about whether or not to see these women, the next question is whether you wish to initiate a sexual relationship." At this point he said, "Obviously I am not ready for that question yet. Why don't we just hold it in abeyance." When he said the positive affirmation for the kidney meridian, "My sexual energies are balanced," he tested strong.

We then discussed the fact that over the next few months we would deal with the macrocosm of his problem. As he overcomes his two-mindedness about intimacy, in the social sense of the word, with women, and as he overcomes his depression, then he is going to have the obvious question: "Will I have a sexual relationship with her or not?" This, too, can be examined and resolved.

Despondency

The *Oxford English Dictionary* calls *despondency* depression or dejection (*dejection* means literally a throwing down) of spirits. It is distinguished from *despair* as not expressing entire hopelessness but a loss of hope. Someone who is despondent may be described as "laboring under mental depression."

While it is tempting to link *despondent* with *ponderous* and thus associate it with the idea of heaviness, which relates to the thyroid meridian, this is not etymologically the case. *Despondent* derives rather from *spondere*, to promise, which also gives rise to *respond*. *De-* is used in the sense of away from; hence in the sense of giving up, losing. The Greek *sponde* was a drink offering, a solemn truce used when making a treaty, for example, to promise. Thus *despond* means to abandon, to lose; to fall away from one's aspirations and hopes and desires, and perhaps then to sink into a depression.

Loneliness

Nancy and Wayne have been married for twenty years. They are deeply devoted to each other and very close, perhaps more so because they have no children. Each day, Nancy can hardly wait for Wayne to come home from work. If he is even a little late, she becomes apprehensive. And every evening she is there to greet him with her broad smile. It seems so very idyllic, but there is another side to it. Nancy feels terribly lonely all day and, in fact, has felt like that ever since the first day after their honeymoon when she found herself alone in their home.

As soon as Wayne leaves in the morning Nancy turns on the radio, not to hear the news or to listen to music but for the people that come into her room through the radio. She says, "I listen to Carlton Fredericks and Joyce Brothers and all the others." These are her company during the day. She says if she ever turns off the radio, she talks to herself. She cannot bear to be alone. She feels lonely all day. She wants Wayne or somebody with her all the time, so in her mind she creates other people. She often imagines that other people are in the room with her. And when she turns on the radio or talks to herself, she is also imagining that there is someone else there.

Sometimes when this loneliness becomes overbearing and pulls her down, Nancy becomes a closet drinker, often making toasts to the guests in her mind whom she believes she is entertaining. So each day, in spite of the beauty and the comfort of her home, is a day of loneliness and dejection. Her need for her husband to come home is not just out of love, but because she knows that this will relieve the terrible loneliness.

I remember once I suggested to the two of them that to ease some of the business pressure on him he should come home for lunch, as his office was not very far away. Nancy jumped to her feet and clapped her hands in joy and giggled like a child. I realized then just how lonely she was and what a lift this would give her.

Now she is a great deal better. In part this is because for the first time she has openly admitted that she is lonely and that this is why she drinks during the day. Whereas Wayne had always thought that Nancy's great need for him and to be with him at all times was out of love, now he sees that it was also out of loneliness. This did not cause him to love her any less, but to be more sympathetic toward her. He calls her up from work several times a day and he comes home for lunch when he can.

One of Nancy's chief aids has been to reaffirm the thyroid affirmation, "I am light and floating," every morning as soon as he leaves. And whenever she feels lonely she affirms, "I am light and floating." Nancy still prefers to have Wayne with her, but now she can be on her own without having to turn on the radio or imagining that other people are with her.

We suffer so much from this fear of being alone. As P. G. Hamerton says, "Woe unto him that is never alone, and cannot bear to be alone. Who must hang on because of the fear of loneliness, of the fear of being by oneself, alone, naked with themselves and with God."

Loneliness comes from the Old English *an*, meaning *one*, which in Middle English becomes *al one*, meaning all (that is, utterly) alone, from which we get *lonely*. The *Oxford English Dictionary* describes *lonely* as being dejected arising from want of company or society; having a feeling of solitariness; being "quite by oneself, unaccompanied."

One can be alone but not lonely. With the latter there is the sense of dejection (literally "thrown down"), but one need not be adversely affected by being alone. In fact, it may be welcome. We can say that the pathological reaction to the state of being on one's own is that particular feeling of dejection from the hurt of separation, and this we call *loneliness*.

Solitude

Solitude comes from the Latin *solus*, meaning alone. It can be seen as a positive or negative state. It is "the state of being or living alone," which in itself does not imply any form of depression or dejection. It is also defined as a state of loneliness. In that sense, Lady Montagu wrote, "your letters . . . are the only pleasures of my solitude."[37]

On the other hand, solitude can be a great virtue, as Aldous Huxley says, "The most powerful and original mind, the more it will incline towards the religion of solitude." And Henry Thoreau says in *Walden*, "I never found a companion that was so companionable as solitude."

The answer to solitude and loneliness is never to feel alone, but to welcome the time of quiet and of aloneness. Epictetus in his *Discourses* says, "When you have closed your doors, and darkened your room, remember never to say you are alone, for you are not alone. God is within." And perhaps Cicero said it best when he said, "I am never less alone than when alone."

Hope

Hope is "the expectation of something desired; desire combined with expectation." The therapeutic powers of hope have long been recognized. For example, Sophocles wrote, "It is hope that maintains most of mankind." Also, Cowley, "Hope! Of all ills that men endure, / The only cheap and universal cure."

In *The Art of Preserving Health,* John Armstrong pointed out the therapeutic advantages of hope but also contrasted them with the basic negative emotion of fear: "Our greatest good, and what we least can spare, Is hope: the last of all our evils, fear."

The idea of hope as being uplifting and helping to overcome our depressed, pushed-down spirits, is best stated simply by Milton: "Hope elevates."

Elation is the opposite of the state of depression. Depression is being pushed down, elation is being lifted up out of (Latin *ē*, out;

and *latus*, carried; hence *elatus*, carried away or lifted up). And so elation is defined as "being uplifted, elevation of spirits, buoyancy."

Small Intestine Meridian

The meridian of joy

Small Intestine	Joy
	Sorrow, Sadness

Negative Emotions:	Sadness
	Sorrow
Positive Affirmations:	I am full of joy.
	I am jumping with joy.
Test Image:	You feel full of tears, as if you could cry.

Sadness

The predominant negative emotional attitude for the small intestine meridian is sadness. It is difficult to describe this word precisely. The root is *sa*, to satisfy, which became in Latin *sat*, meaning enough, from which we derive *sated*, *satisfied*, and *saturate*. In Old English, *sad* meant serious, discreet, sober, heavy, dark, solid. The oldest meaning was that of sated.[38] Sad is often used in the sense of being full: having one's fill. It would suggest that its original meaning was "full of food," which has come to mean "fed up." Stokes says that "sad" once indicated satiety, then resoluteness.

The "fed up" connotation may well be significant in that the small intestine receives all food passed on from the stomach. Perhaps when energy supplied to the small intestine is inadequate, it will remain gorged and full of food, not being able to digest it and pass it on.

My psychiatric experience has led me to feel that sadness means full—of tears. I know that whenever I see someone who seems like

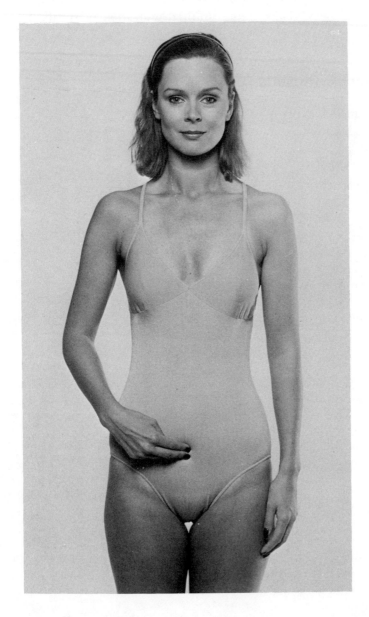

The test point for the small intestine meridian. Two-thirds down an imaginary line between the umbilicus and symphysis pubis.

Most people will test weak for the small intestine meridian when looking at this photo. Saying the positive affirmation for the small intestine meridian will overcome the weakness.

he could cry, and I say to him, "Are you feeling sad?" then he starts
to cry. Sometimes he will say, "I'm glad you said that because I
just couldn't get it out. But I was up to here with tears." And he
will generally point to his cheeks, just below his eyes. So it seems
that sadness may be when we have had enough, when we are fed
up, when we are full of tears, but just unable to express them. The
Psalmist expressed his thanks in Psalm 116:8. "For thou hast deliv-
ered . . . mine eyes from tears."

Milton said, "The Angelic Guards ascended, mute and sad for
Man."

Sorrow

The related negative emotion for the small intestine is *sorrow*.
The roots for sorrow in the Indo-European languages seem to relate
to physical pain and suffering.

The relationship between sorrow and crying is best expressed
by Jean Ingelow: "When sparrows build and the leaves break forth,
My old sorrow wakes and cries." And Thomas Moore, "Weep on!
And as thy sorrows flow, / I'll taste the luxury of woe." Johnson
says, "Sorrow is not commonly understood as the effect of present
evil, but of lost good." In other words, crying over spilt milk.

Through our testing techniques, we can differentiate between
emotional states and consequently the words used to describe
them. Even dictionaries may not be as accurate. For example, sorrow may be "an instance or cause of grief or sadness." We can test
for ourselves and show that sorrow, like sadness, relates to the
small intestine meridian, whereas grief relates to the thyroid
meridian. These emotional states of sorrow and sadness are related
to, but are quite distinct from, grief.

Keats gives us an example of the relationship between sorrow
and tears:

> She nothing said, but, pale and meek,
> And rose and knelt before him,
> Wept a rain of sorrows at his words.

And Pope wrote, "Down his right beard a stream of sorrow flows."
Shakespeare also has the same idea connecting sorrow and tears:

> Where they view'd each others sorrow,
> Sorrow that friendly sighs sought still to dry.

Joy

Both of the negative emotional states related to the small intestine meridian have to do with tears. The positive emotional states that corresponds to the small intestine meridian is joy. The primitive root from which it is derived is *gau*, to rejoice, from which we get in Latin, *gaudium*, which meant gladness or delight. This gave rise in English to *gaudy*, and possibly to the French, *jouer*, to play.

Joy has been thought of as high pleasure or delight. "The joy of the heart makes the face merry." And in Job 41:22 we find a phrase that expresses the continuum of the small intestine meridian: "Sorrow is turned into joy before him."

Note that the *Oxford English Dictionary* calls joy "a vivid emotion of pleasure, arising from a sense of well-being or satisfaction." Here we are reminded of the opposite, sad, which originally meant sated or satisfied.

I remember very clearly a female student who tested weak for this meridian. When I told her what the weakness implied she burst into tears and cried and cried. She eventually was able to compose herself and said that she had been thinking only that morning about how sad she felt because God had not given her a more beautiful body. This, she felt, was the reason that she had never been able to marry. I reminded her of the quotation from Coverdale: "They that sowe in teers, shall reape in joye." She used the positive affirmation for some time and reported a great improvement in her emotional state. She told me that it has really helped her to come to grips with her dissatisfied feelings about her body.

It is wonderful that now we can determine exactly which emotional states are troubling us and then to know exactly, precisely what words and what thoughts can correct them. Before, when a patient cried, or when anyone cried, I did not know the precise emotion that was affecting him. I certainly did not know what would be the most comforting words for me to say or that he could say to help himself. But now I know, for example, that when someone is crying, it would be best for him to think of joy, because joy is the antidote to tears. Now when someone is crying, my thoughts are, "How can I help him turn his tears of sadness to tears of joy?"[39] This is transmutation.

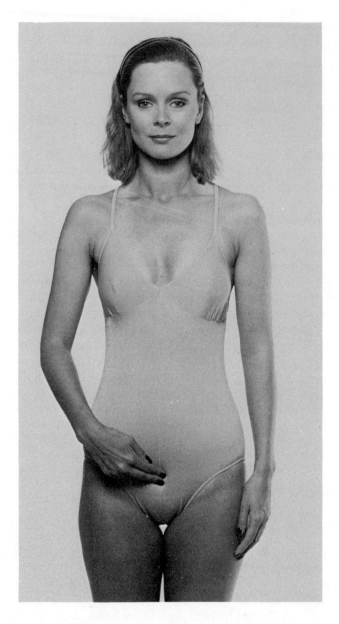

The test point for the bladder meridian. Just above symphysis pubis.

Bladder Meridian

The meridian of peace and harmony

Bladder	Peace, Harmony
	Restlessness, Impatience

Negative Emotions: Restlessness
        Impatience
        Frustration

Positive Affirmations: I am at peace.
        I am in harmony.
        Dissonances and conflicts within me have been resolved. I am balanced.

Test Image: You are caught in a traffic jam. The bus is moving very, very slowly. You are in a great hurry to get home. You are becoming very upset.

Restlessness, Impatience, and Frustration

The predominant emotional states affecting the energy balance in the bladder meridian are *restlessness, impatience,* and *frustration.* Have you ever seen a little boy as he becomes restless and impatient? Sometimes he will hold his genitals as if to prevent himself from urinating. I am sure you know of people who, when they get restless, have to go to the bathroom frequently but they pass only small quantities of urine each time. These are often people who quickly become restless and often shake their legs when they do. They have great difficulty in being settled and at peace. They have in essence what is termed a "nervous bladder."

Johnson defined *restless* as "without peace." His dictionary states that the word was also used in the sense of being "not still."

Frustration comes from the Latin *frustare,* meaning to drag things out. It is related to the Latin adverb, *frustra,* in vain. Again

Most people will test weak for the bladder meridian when looking at this photo. Saying the positive affirmation for the bladder meridian will overcome the weakness.

we have the idea of being held back from achieving our goals. There seems to be a similarity between the quality of patient endurance and frustration as a result of things being dragged out. From the Latin we learn that a thing may be dragged out to the point where the action becomes useless (in vain). In our test image, we can imagine the bus as being jammed in traffic for so long that our purpose has been thwarted.

Patience

Patience has been called the capacity of calm endurance. When on the motionless bus in our test image, this is the very quality we have such difficulty in experiencing.

The primitive root from which patience is derived is *pei,* to hurt, from which we get in Latin *patī,* to suffer. The implication is the ability to suffer something over a period of time. Hence, calm endurance. Impatience, then, is the inability to endure with calm until the goal may be reached: Pepys wrote in his diary that he was "much impatient by these few days sickness." In *Troilus and Cressida* we find the sentence, "There is between my will and all offenses a guard of patience." We also find it said that, "Endurance is nobler than strength, and patience than beauty." Back in 1560 Thomas Wilson wrote, "Patience is a remedy for every disease."

Peace

Shakespeare, in *Henry IV*, beautifully hinted at the basic concept of peace:

> A peace is of the nature of a conquest;
> For then both parties nobly are subdued,
> And neither party loser.

The root from which *peace* comes is *pag,* meaning to fasten or to join. This becomes in Latin, *pace, peace.* This also gives rise to the English word *pact,* meaning an agreement.

We can conceptualize peace as occurring after a pact has been established between the warring parts within ourselves. In our test image, for example, part of us wants to get home as quickly as possible, and nothing else seems to matter at the moment except that. There are desires and wishes within each of us that we are striving to achieve, and yet we are being frustrated in reaching our goals. Inside us there develops a turmoil, with parts fighting other parts. When these internal factions come to an agreement with each other, sign a pact, in effect, then there will be internal peace.

In Job 22:21 we find: "Acquaint now thyself with him, and be at peace; thereby good shall come unto thee."

Harmony

Another positive emotional state related to the bladder meridian is *harmony*, which means "an agreement in feeling." This is when all the separate parts join together for the ultimate good of all. When there is peace and harmony, there can be progress. Harmony has been described as a "combination . . . of parts . . . so as to form a consistent and orderly whole; agreement."

We find that the root behind harmony is *ar*, which means to fit together, to form a cohesive whole—in other words, to be at peace.

In *Henry VI*, Shakespeare wrote:

> How irksome is this music to my heart!
> When such strings jar what hope of harmony?

When there is internal discord and imbalance, there is no internal peace and no harmony.

In musical terms, harmony has been described as the resolution of dissonance. This might apply equally as well to ourselves—mind, body, and spirit.

Byron said, "Where all is harmony, and calm and quiet."

Serenity

Serenity, another positive emotional attribute associated with the bladder meridian, comes from the Latin *serenis*, which usually was used to refer to the sky and the weather. When it was serene, it was clear and peaceful. This is probably related to the word *serus*, meaning "of the evening," from which we get the French word *soir*. From the same source as serenity we also have *serenade*.

Serenity means clear, fine, and calm. The original root was *ksero*, which meant dry—referring to a clear, calm, dry day or evening—a time of serenity, peace, and harmony.

Calm

Calm is another positive emotional attitude related to the bladder meridian. The most pleasing history of the word *calm* is that in the Provençal language the related word *chaume* signifies "the time when the flocks rest." This is a time of peace and harmony. The Greek word from which this comes, *kauma*, refers to "the heat of the day, when beasts are at rest, winds fallen, the fields quiet."

We so often find that restless people have, on testing, an energy imbalance associated with the bladder meridian. We then go over the positive words to be used in their affirmations, and they often state that they think of a serenade, or a peaceful day with the flocks resting in the field, and the like. With this visualization, they test strong.

Conception and Governing Vessels

These two meridians are not primarily organ-related, although it is thought that the governing vessel supplies life energy to the brain. The conception vessel and the governing vessel are more the collectors of energy that has already passed through the organ/ meridian system. The test points are illustrated on pages 188 and 190. For the conception vessel the point is slightly below the midpoint of the lower lip, and for the governing vessel it is in the intermaxillary suture at a point one third of the distance from the anterior nasal spine to the midpoint of the upper lip.

The emotional attitudes associated with these meridians are not in the same category as guilt, for example, nor are they basic emotions such as love and hate. These are more what we might term second-order emotions and, while it is significant to find them on testing, they rarely require specific individual correction. They tend to correct themselves when the associated underlying emotional state is itself corrected.

Governing Vessel

The negative emotional state associated with the governing vessel is *embarrassment*. I have attempted for some time without success to find out how the origin of the word *embarrassment* relates

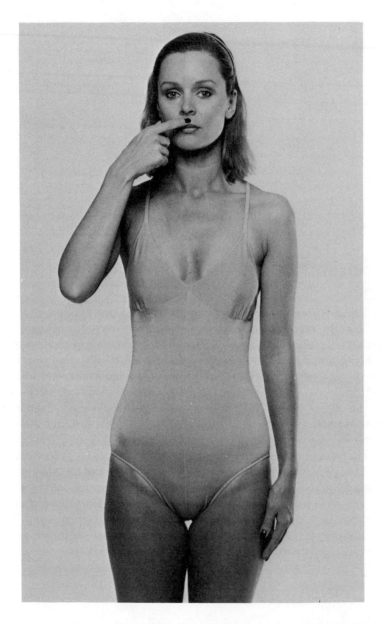

The test point for the governing vessel meridian. Slightly above the midpoint of the upper lip.

to its present usage. It comes from the Latin *barra,* which means a bar, so to embarrass means literally to impede or to put in bars. Perhaps the meaning, although this is merely my own interpretation, implies the situation in which someone is imprisoned and put on display, as in a stockade, for something he has done wrong. The negative visualization, or test image, in everyday life would be something such as to imagine that you are walking down a very busy street and suddenly realize that your fly is undone, or that your wraparound skirt has blown open.

You will find that this meridian's imbalance may transiently appear when another meridian problem is disclosed. For example, a person may reveal a sexual indecision (kidney meridian), and as soon as this is dealt with, he may then show a governing vessel weakness—that is, embarrassment because someone else knows of his sexual indecision.

Conception Vessel

The conception vessel has to do with *shame.* The negative visualization, or test image, would be to imagine that you have just been caught and accused of a crime, such as theft. You may recall that when we discussed the eytmology of the word *hate,* we showed that the root *kar,* which meant to like or desire, also gave rise to *kam,* which meant to cover over, from which we derived in English *chemise* and *shame.* There has long been the idea of covering ourselves in shame, hence the saying "naked and unashamed." We literally use our chemise to cover our shame. When we blush with shame, everyone can see that we have done something wrong. We have been caught in the act. Shame is, in a sense, the public display, the public awareness, of what we feel is our "sin." Shame, like embarrassment, will be cleared up as we overcome our feelings about the "sin." One is reminded here of the expressions "to be shamefaced," and, of course, "Oh shame! Where is thy blush?" In Isaiah 47:3 we read, "Thy nakedness shall be uncovered, yea, thy shame shall be seen."

Johnson defines shame as "the passion felt when reputation is supposed to be lost; the passion expressed sometimes by blushes."

Anthropologists have related that in primitive cultures the time the child learns the word *shame* is when he begins to cover his genitals. One of the beauties of our work with language and psy-

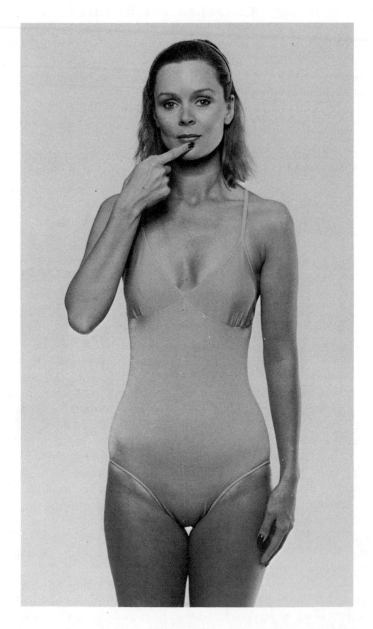

The test point for the conception vessel. Slightly below the midpoint of the lower lip.

MERIDIAN TEST POINTS

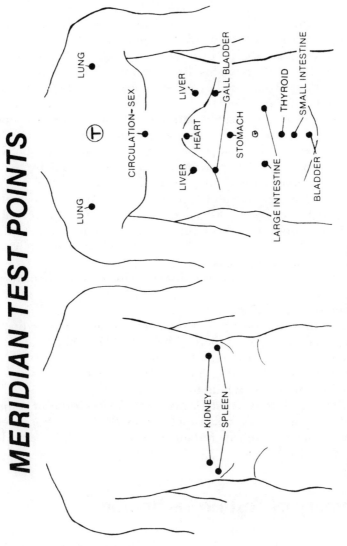

chological states is the discovery of a fact such as this: shame, chemise, and shirt all have the same origin. Here we see how, through the ages, the psychological concept and a physical correlate of that concept are still related in our psyches; this we can learn from present-day psychological techniques. Then, on investigating the history of the words, we find that they came from the same source. What we discover today psychologically, the etymologist can discover through his discipline. Words that are connected at their root are connected even today, and those distant roots are connected in our psyches.

Shyness also is a negative attitude relating to the conception vessel. This may imply that shy people are often those who hide themselves lest their shame be seen. This connection between shame and shyness has previously been pointed out by Sydney Smith, "The most curious offspring of shame is shyness."

Bernard Shaw in *Man and Superman* says, "We live in an atmosphere of shame. We are ashamed of everything that is real about us; ashamed of ourselves, of our relatives, of our incomes, of our accidents, of our opinions, of our experience, just as we are ashamed of our naked skins."

Perhaps the timidity and the distrust which are so characteristic of shyness are a result of a fear of punishment—the "sin" has been revealed through the shame.

There are many references to shame that imply public display. From Shakespeare, *King John*, "You but make it blush, and glow with shame of your proceedings, Hubert." Edward Spenser in *The Faerie Queene*, "Relenting Sorrow did in darkenesse lye, / and Shame his ugly face did hide from the living eye."

As Darwin wrote in *The Expression of the Emotions of Animals and Man*, "Under a keen sense of shame, there is a strong desire for concealment." And in Jeremiah 51:51 we read, "Shame hath covered our faces."

Summary of Testing Techniques

The testing process is far from difficult. In fact, it is incredibly simple, and is now being carried out by thousands of doctors and lay people. However, it requires experience and practice to do it accurately and reliably. The procedure is:

1. *Test the thymus.* If the thymus tests strong, then you know that the person's life energy is high, and he is, at the moment, invulnerable to many stresses. You need go no further in your testing because, if the thymus is testing strong, his cerebral hemispheres are balanced and he is now creative, productive, and able to solve his problems. His emotional states are balanced and neutralized and there are no major negative emotions interfering with his life energy at that time. (You have seen from the photographs how someone's looks can affect you; therefore, you must make yourself neutral when you perform the test.)

   Note: There are certain instances in which the testing can produce false positive results, that is, the subject may test strong when he really should be testing weak. In severe cases I have even found that certain people may test strong for refined sugar! They also may test strong for hateful thoughts and, paradoxically, weak for loving thoughts. These false results can easily be prevented by having the subject chew a ribonucleic acid tablet (readily available at any health-food store) just prior to the testing. (For details on this refer to "The Umbilicus Test" in my *Collected Papers,* Volume II.) While the incidence of these false positive results is not high, if you want to be absolutely sure of the results it is always best to give a tablet prior to testing. I do it routinely in my practice.

2. If the thymus tests weak, do the *hemisphere test.* This will indicate which cerebral hemisphere is dominant at this time, and the subject will then know that certain corrective measures are required to alleviate this general imbalance.

3. At the same time you will learn from the hemisphere test which set of meridian test points to challenge. If the person is left-hemisphere dominant, you test the "midline" meridian points; if he is right-hemisphere dominant, you test the "bilateral" points. (With the bilateral points, you usually need to test only one side. If, as occurs occasionally, you do not find anything on the initial test side, then test the other side.)

4. Now that you have found the specific meridian weakness, simply have the person repeat several times, with feeling, and visualizing the appropriate positive affirmation.

5. Retest and you will find that the meridian is now energized, the hemispheres are balanced, the person is therefore creative, and the thymus is testing strong. The blockage of the flow of life energy has been corrected.

   That is all you need to do to find out and to correct the predominant emotional state affecting anyone at the time of testing. Isn't that simple—and isn't it of vital importance?

As pointed out previously, experience and practice are required to do the testing reliably and accurately. It is simple, but it must be done precisely. There are a number of variables which must be controlled, such as whether you are standing under fluorescent lights, whether a television or radio is on while you are testing, or other environmental factors.

As an example of a hidden but important variable, consider the following incident. Amy has never really had a boyfriend, but currently has a crush on a young man in her class. In the three years that they have been in the same class he has never asked her out, so recently she summoned up all her courage and sent him a note saying that she would like to go out with him. Now she is concerned because she realizes that she has been forward. She is worried that he may take her message wrong and think that she wants to have sex with him, which was not her intent. I tested her for "I like Tom" and she tested weak. I asked her to say, "I don't like Tom" and she tested strong. She protested, "But this is impossible. Of course I like him. Why else would I ask him out?" Then I remembered her concern that he may become sexually involved with her, so I asked Amy to say, "I want to have sex with Tom," and before I tested her she replied, "Of course I don't!" I felt that she was telling the truth, but she tested strong for the statement. Everything was *reversed*. She tested as not liking Tom and yet she wanted to have sex with him, the opposite of what she and I believed. Then she asked me, "Do you think the results would be different if I took off my digital watch?" Routinely I have all my students remove their digital watches before we begin any testing. But in Amy's case, I had overlooked it because it was concealed in a bracelet. After she removed the watch, the results were the opposite of those we obtained initially. She tested strong for "I like Tom" and weak when she said, "I want to have sex with Tom." We then reviewed some earlier testing and found that all the results had been reversed because of the digital watch.[40]

Another way to test for the underactive meridian is to have the subject say the positive affirmation *once* for each meridian. The one for which he tests weak is the meridian with the problem. For example, you may find someone says, "I am humble," and he tests strong. For "I am happy," he tests strong. But suppose when he says, "I am content," he tests weak. This indicates that he has a basic underlying stomach meridian problem (discontent) to be corrected.

THE MERIDIANS, ASSOCIATED ORGANS, AND NEGATIVE EMOTIONAL STATES

MERIDIAN	ORGANS	NEGATIVE EMOTIONAL STATES
Lung	Lungs	Disdain, Scorn, Contempt, Haughtiness, False Pride, Intolerance, Prejudice
Liver	Liver	Unhappiness
Gall Bladder	Gall Bladder	Rage, Fury, Wrath
Spleen	Spleen Pancreas	Realistic Anxieties about the Future
Kidney	Kidneys Eyes Ears	Sexual Indecision
Large Intestine	Colon Rectum Appendix	Guilt
Circulation-Sex	Adrenals Reproductive Glands	Regret, Remorse, Jealousy, Sexual Tension, Stubbornness
Heart	Heart	Anger
Stomach	Stomach Sinuses	Disgust, Disappointment, Bitterness, Greed, Emptiness, Deprivation, Nausea, Hunger
Thyroid (Triple Heater)	Thyroid Pericardium	Depression, Despair, Hopelessness, Grief, Despondency, Loneliness, Solitude
Small Intestine	Duodenum Small Intestine	Sadness, Sorrow
Bladder	Bladder Urethra	Restlessness, Impatience, Frustration

THE MERIDIANS, ASSOCIATED ORGANS, AND POSITIVE EMOTIONAL STATES

MERIDIAN	ORGANS	POSITIVE EMOTIONAL STATES
Lung	Lungs	Humility, Tolerance, Modesty
Liver	Liver	Happiness, Cheer
Gall Bladder	Gall Bladder	Reaching Out with Love and Forgiveness, Adoration
Spleen	Spleen Pancreas	Faith and Confidence about the Future, Security
Kidney	Kidneys Eyes Ears	Sexual Assuredness
Large Intestine	Colon Rectum Appendix	Self-Worth
Circulation-Sex	Adrenals Reproductive Glands	Renunciation of the Past, Relaxation, Generosity, Abjuration
Heart	Heart	Love, Forgiveness
Stomach	Stomach Sinuses	Contentment, Tranquility
Thyroid (Triple Heater)	Thyroid Pericardium	Hope, Lightness, Buoyancy, Elation
Small Intestine	Duodenum Small Intestine	Joy
Bladder	Bladder Urethra	Peace, Harmony

TEST IMAGES FOR EACH MERIDIAN

Lung	You are with someone who you feel is very silly or ignorant. You feel much smarter and you are very aware of the contrast between your genius and his stupidity, and you feel superior.
Liver	You are very unhappy because your lover has left you. Everything would be perfect if only he would come back to you.
Gall Bladder	Someone has just done something very infuriating. He has just read your most personal letters and your private diary without your permission. You are shouting at him. You want to hit him.
Spleen	Next month's bills are before you. You do not have the money to pay them, and you can see no way of coming up with it.
Kidney	You are having sex with an acquaintance—someone you are not particularly attracted to, yet are not totally turned off by.
Large Intestine	You have just done something over which you feel extremely guilty. Use an example from your own life.
Circulation-Sex	• You are in the midst of a long project, and it seems that the project will never be completed. You sincerely regret that you ever began it. • You are thinking of a person who really turns you on, and the more you think about this person, the more excited you become.

TEST IMAGES FOR EACH MERIDIAN— Continued

	• You find your lover with a rival and you are trying to figure a way of getting your lover away from the rival and back for yourself.
Heart	You come back from a walk in the neighborhood and catch a vandal in the act of letting the air out of the tires of your car.
Stomach	• You are walking down the street and see your lover strolling arm-in-arm with someone else. You realize that you have been displaced. • You have been in line for a promotion for some time. When the vacancy occurs, someone else is given the job.
Thyroid	You are at home, you have no energy, and you have nothing to do worth doing. You feel heavy and weighed down. Everything is just too much.
Small Intestine	You feel full of tears, as if you could cry.
Bladder	You are standing on a bus that is caught in a traffic jam. The bus is moving very, very slowly. You are in a great hurry to get home. You are becoming very upset.

THE MERIDIANS AND THEIR EMOTIONS ■ 199

Meridian Correlates

Each "bilateral" meridian has a corresponding relationship with a "midline" meridian and vice versa

"Bilateral" Meridians	"Midline" Meridians
Lung	Thyroid
Liver	Stomach
Gall Bladder	Heart
Spleen	Bladder
Kidney	Circulation-Sex
Large Intestine	Small Intestine

The following case history will illustrate how these meridian relationships may be manifested.[41] Bill's wife called me one morning to tell me that a few hours earlier he had been taken to the hospital in an ambulance. He had been having pain around the upper abdomen and chest. He was obviously in great distress. I told her that in view of his history of angina he almost certainly was having a coronary occlusion. She replied, "No, the doctors could find no evidence of a heart attack." They thought there must be something wrong with his abdomen.

They continued to hold this opinion for twenty-four hours—and then evidence of a coronary occlusion was found, or perhaps to put it another way, the evidence of a coronary occlusion developed and was found.

It puzzled me that with Bill's long history of heart pains, the doctors did not immediately find evidence of the coronary occlusion. Why were they so insistent, at least initially, that the problem was not cardiac but abdominal. And afterwards he did have obvious cardiographic signs of a myocardial infarction and was treated accordingly.

Some months later Bill's wife called me again to report that he was having another attack similar to the previous one. I drove over to his home and came to the conclusion that he was not having a coronary attack, for many reasons, not the least of which was the fact that his cardiograph was unchanged, and that his heart meridian was testing strong. When I examined his abdomen I could feel some tensing and guarding of the muscles of the right hypochondrium. As I pushed in more, there was a point of deep and quite painful tenderness. He was having a gall bladder attack! We drove to the cardiologist, who confirmed that, in his opinion, this was not a heart attack. I worked on him physically and relieved the gall bladder tenderness with marked improvement in his general well being.

It now seems quite obvious that Bill was having a gall bladder attack when he was first admitted to the hospital, but that at some point he did also have a coronary occlusion. I am sure that the terrible fear Bill had had for many years that he was going to have a heart attack, as well as the frightening situation in the hospital itself, helped to precipitate it. In a medical text I found the following information: "When the heart is the seat of a proclaimed or a latent disorder, vagal reflexes from a diseased gall bladder may bring about decreased coronary blood flow, arrhythmia or heart-block; the 'cholecystic heart.' " This is what I believe happened to Bill. He was predisposed to a coronary occlusion because of his impaired circulation, which had been a problem for years, but the precipitating factor may have been a result of his diseased gall bladder. The text further stated that "electrocardiographic abnormalities without other evidence of cardiac disease often revert to normal following removal of a diseased gall bladder. Likewise, patients with angina pectoris and pseudo-angina have benefited."[42]

The bilateral meridian that relates to the heart meridian is the gall bladder meridian. There are good psychological reasons why this should be so. The negative emotional attitude associated with the heart meridian is anger and for the gall bladder meridian it is rage. The difference between the two states is that rage is the acting out of the anger. One may feel anger, but one does not just feel rage, one expresses it. In a sense, the gall bladder emotion of rage is a more violent and more primitive attribute of the heart meridian, and the two are intimately related.

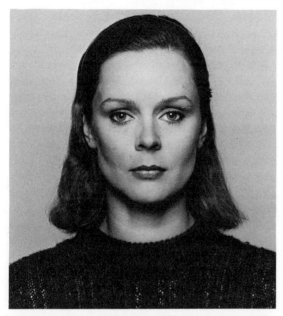

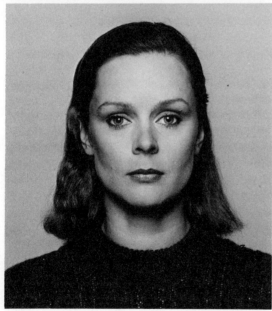

The facial expressions appear to be identical but are subtly different and therefore affect different meridians because the model was thinking different negative thoughts.

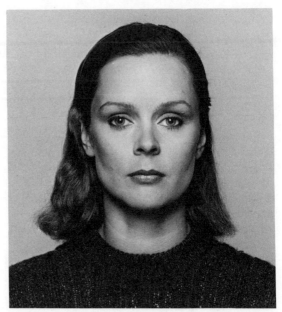

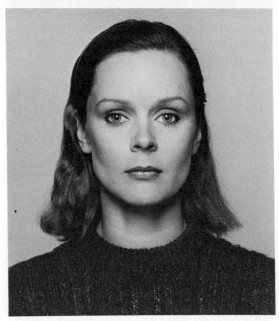

The Deeper Layers

Based upon what you have learned to this point, you now know how to determine your own predominant emotional attitude or that of anyone with whom you come in contact. As you can see, this can be incredibly beneficial in terms of reaching our goal of high life energy, positive health, creativity, and positive emotional balance.

We can now take the technique further and discover the deeper unconscious emotional attitudes that are affecting us. Remember that we are aware only of a small part of our mental functioning. While the emotional attitudes of which we may well be aware (i.e., those in our pre-conscious), those that we have already tested, are of great importance, they are, as it were, the end results of all the unconscious emotional attitudes that lie beneath them. To get closer to our goal, it is desirable to correct these underlying unconscious layers.

One of the most incredible findings, as you will learn when you do this testing in layers to reveal the unconscious, is that meridians that tested strong will later be revealed as weak after the meridian which is currently testing weak is corrected. Then you correct that meridian and test again, continuing until the thymus tests strong. For example, suppose that at the first level of testing (that is, the level described earlier in this book) you discover that you have a spleen-meridian energy problem. You can test all the other meridians and they will be strong. Now say two or three times with conviction the positive affirmation for the spleen meridian, "I have faith and confidence in my future." As you would expect, the spleen meridian will test strong, but it is now likely that some other meridian that previously tested strong will reveal itself as being

203

weak. It is only after you uncover and correct that first layer of meridian energy imbalance that the second meridian problem reveals itself. There is a definite order in which these layers reveal themselves.

For example, the second layer may have revealed unhappiness (liver meridian). Perhaps you felt that your worries and anxieties about the future were really based on the fact that you wanted someone else to help you, yet this other person had not helped you at all. Your unconscious feeling was, "If only (liver) he would provide me with what I need, then I wouldn't have to worry about being able to pay the rent (spleen)."

To correct the liver-meridian energy imbalance, say with feeling the appropriate affirmation, "I am happy." Another meridian energy imbalance may now reveal itself. It can come to consciousness or pre-consciousness *only* after the layer of unhappiness has been corrected. This may be, for example, a thyroid meridian imbalance. Perhaps underneath you felt depressed, heavy, and hopeless about the whole situation. This is a deeper feeling than the more superficial unhappiness. You correct that with the affirmation, "I am light and buoyant." Now when you test the thymus it is strong, and all meridians also test strong, i.e., spleen → liver → thyroid → thymus.

By implementing this technique you can rapidly reach the unconscious and peel it off in layers, just as occurs in psychotherapy and psychoanalysis.

Isn't it wonderful how these layers reveal themselves? Each emerges only when the more superficial imbalance has been corrected. You continue to go back as in psychotherapy. Every time I have done this, I am amazed that this occurs as it does. It never ceases to thrill me and surprise me. This tool gives us the opportunity to learn many wonderful things about our minds and bodies.

The last, or deepest, meridian imbalance that is corrected prior to the thymus being corrected is the one most affecting it. This type of meridian imbalance frequently tends to be more difficult to correct, and tends to recur. This basic one is, in a sense, the Achilles heel. It is, at least for this period of time (it does change) the deepest, most unconscious psychological factor holding you back. It will often be the lung or thyroid meridian. This occurs because, as I have pointed out, these are the two basic meridians involved in our early development. (The lung meridian relates to Klein's first stage or "position"—that of envy—and the thyroid meridian to her second stage—the depressive position.) Thus ultimately, the lung meridian is the basic meridian involved.

When this is corrected, great changes can occur.

The basic premise here is that you correct the meridian energy imbalance with the affirmation, and then you continually retest and reveal the meridian that is more deeply affected. You do this, like peeling layers off an onion, until you come to the point where the thymus tests strong and continues to test strong. Then you know that both consciously and unconsciously you are balanced and your life energy is really high.

(Very occasionally it will be found that there is more than one meridian testing weak at the same time, but only one of these is the one that "matters"; the other one is what we call static in the system. It is easily abolished or neutralized by taking two or three relaxing breaths. Then we find that this superficial static will disappear and the meridian that remains is the significant one.)

Let me give you an example: A patient of mine—a very attractive career woman in her mid-thirties—was single and having an affair with a married senior executive at the firm for which they both worked. When she first consulted me, she had a liver-meridian energy impairment—she was unhappy. I asked her what she was unhappy about, and she said, "I'm unhappy because my lover is not with me all the time. If only he could be with me all the time, then I would be happy. I know this is what I need for me to be happy, but I also know it is most unlikely to occur because he is too much involved with his wife and family ever to give them up for me." She said the appropriate affirmation with feeling, and her liver meridian tested strong. But her thymus still tested weak. I knew we had more work to do.

Next we discovered a kidney-meridian energy imbalance. I explained to her what this meant—basically, sexual indecision. She agreed. She said, "Yes, that's very true. I was brought up by very strict religious parents and I am concerned about my present sexual relationship with this man. I want to have sex with him; on the other hand I don't know whether I really should, for moral reasons. I also know that perhaps if I do not have sex with him, if I hold out on him, he may be more likely to come around to living with me and giving up his wife. Yes, I definitely am in two minds sexually." Then she said the appropriate affirmation and the kidney meridian tested strong, but her thymus still was testing underactive. We discovered that it was her heart meridian that was imbalanced. I pointed out to her that this meant anger. She suddenly slapped her hand with her fist and said, "Yes. You are right. I am angry with him. I am angry because he has shilly-shallied around with me for years. First he says that he will leave his wife for me, and then he says that he can't. It goes on and on, back and forth. Although I love him very much, I am definitely angry with him." And at this point she became red in the face and her voice grew loud and she said, "You are right—*I am angry!*"

Then she said, "But I can see how it's not really his fault, the poor man is undecided himself. He doesn't know what to do." So I asked her to say, "I love him, I forgive him." Her heart meridian energy imbalance corrected itself. But her thymus was *still* testing underactive. This time we found it was the stomach meridian. After we discussed what that meant, she agreed that she was feeling extremely disappointed. She stated that she felt disappointed every time he left her, that it was as if "he closes the door on me and opens it to his wife. Every time he leaves, I feel disappointed. I have a gnawing pain inside my stomach and I tend to overeat. In fact, in looking back over my life, I would say that disappointment has always been a problem for me. I often feel that I have been let down or that someone else has been chosen and deprived me of my favored position with a lover. And this is when I go on my eating binges." We retested and her thymus tested strong, i.e., liver → kidney → heart → stomach → thymus. The stomach meridian was her Achilles heel.

We had finished our work for this session. Now it was her responsibility to continue to use the appropriate affirmations. I saw her again a few weeks later and she said she felt considerably better and had decided not to see this man anymore. I heard from her a year or so after this; she wrote to me telling me that she was happily married. She told me that she felt that what she had learned about herself in that first session had really enabled her to change her life.

Sometimes it is a good idea to wait and retest in an hour or so, or possibly the next day, after a procedure such as the one outlined above. I remember a patient who went through a similar "unlayering," but in her case, I suggested that she wait for a while in the office.[1] I found on retesting her an hour later that the thymus, which had tested strong at the end of the session, was now testing weak. That is, there was more work to be done. This is not always required, but such a "mopping up" procedure can be very valuable.

In the case of the latter patient, we found that her small intestine meridian test point was testing weak. I asked, "This whole thing has made you very sad, hasn't it?" She replied that it had. At that point she burst into tears and cried for a long while. When she finished, she thanked me and said that it had been many, many years since she had cried and that she really needed to get it out.

Not long ago, I received an urgent call to see a young man who had suddenly come down with violent abdominal pains. He was gripping the right side of his abdomen and writhing on the floor. He was moaning in pain. He was white. His pulse was racing. He looked like an acute surgical emergency. I was relieved to see that his appendix had already been removed. In fact, the first thing he said to me was, "This is just like when I had my appendix out." He grunted to me between episodes of pain. As I examined him, I became perplexed. I could feel the tension of his abdomen and the spasms of his bowel, but somehow it just didn't "smell" like a surgical case.

I gradually helped him to settle down. His pulse came down to about 90 and he said that the pain was easing off somewhat. Then I tested him and found that the meridian of involvement was the heart meridian. I asked him, "Who are you angry with?" He said, "I'm not angry with anybody." So I asked him to say, "I forgive my father," and he still tested weak at the heart meridian. So it was not his father, nor was it his stepfather. But when he said, "I forgive my mother," the heart meridian tested strong and almost immediately he began to look relieved. He got to his feet. Some color returned to his cheeks and he said the pain had nearly gone.

I asked him why he was angry with his mother. We discovered that the previous day he had been going through his old school reports, which were far from satisfactory. He was angry because, in his estimation, his mother hadn't done enough to help him at that time. In fact, he felt that she was responsible for the psychological problems that had led to the bad reports and to his having to see numerous psychologists, as well as for his dismissal from a number of schools. It was the anger that had whirled up in him which had precipitated the spasm of the colon. After he transmuted his anger, I tested him further and found a large intestine meridian problem. It was the guilt arising out of his anger toward her that affected him most deeply.

I am not implying that once an unlayering procedure is carried out, there is nothing else to do. I suggest that each day, whenever you can, you have yourself tested to find out what problem you are having at that time so you can instantly correct it before it gets out of hand or develops into a pattern. This way you can keep yourself "up"—full of life energy, not drained by meridian energy imbalances—when reinforced by the daily program.

I had a patient who had experienced a terrible tragedy. His best friend was killed in an accident in which my patient was also involved and from which he is still severely injured. The accident had occurred only a few weeks before. Because my patient was driving the vehicle at the time of the accident, it would be reasonable to expect that the predominant emotions affecting him at the moment would be guilt—a feeling that perhaps he could have avoided the accident and his friend would still be alive; or possibly grief over the loss of his friend; or perhaps worry about what he was going to do now that he was injured and unable to work. Bringing my psychiatric experience to bear on the case, these were the predominant emotions that I expected to find with him. But as soon as I tested him, I found otherwise. The predominant emotion was anger. Most surprising. When I discussed this with him, however, he readily agreed, and said, "Yes, I am very angry that the accident ever occurred, and I am really angry with the owner of the car. He lent it to me in a condition that predisposed me to the accident."

It was only after the anger was alleviated by the appropriate affirmation that another emotion—depression, grief (thyroid meridian)—revealed itself and could then be confronted and corrected. To have attempted to deal with this emotion (which I suspected at the outset) initially would not have been as effective as dealing with the emotions that were actually present in consciousness and pre-consciousness. At a deep level there was grief, but it had to be dealt with as it arose, as it revealed itself. The way to uncover the grief was to release the anger. This way he was helped far more quickly and thoroughly.

Unconscious Determinants

The art of living is to stay in the present. If my wife does something and I get upset, it should be because what she has done upsets me. But we often find that we carry over patterns of expectation from previous experiences into present ones. We often find, for example, that a husband or wife who has been married previously gets unreasonably upset with what the second spouse has done—not because the current spouse has done something so upsetting, but more because of the memory triggered by the incident. It could and often does even trigger unconscious memories from early childhood and parent-child relationships that were unsatisfactory. To oversimplify, this is what we mean by the *unconscious determinants* of our present activities. So it is important to evaluate any situation in its true present context, rather than invoking past patterns. By peeling off and eradicating those unconscious emotional and meridian energy imbalances that affect us in the present, we can be in a better position to deal with the current situations.

Let me reiterate. One definition of complete psychological normality could be that, regardless of what happened, we would not be extremely negatively affected (stressed) by whatever came along. In other words, our life energy would be high enough that the events that occur in daily life would not interfere with thymus activity and cerebral balance. Of course there is much more to "psychological normality" than that, but for our present purposes it is an adequate description. If we carry out our daily program we should be able to maintain an energy level that allows us to "bounce back" from each little stress to keep all our troops in the armory prepared for the big battle rather than having them scattered throughout, continually occupied with little skirmishes. A present problem will perhaps affect a meridian only at the superficial testing level and will not trigger a chain of historically emotionally related reactions. In other words, there are no hang-ups at this time. The achievement of such a state is the major purpose of testing in the various layers and levels—by correcting the unconscious imbalances operant, we are maximizing our ability to function harmoniously in the present.

Let us review the general technique of the deeper layer testing and correction.

1. As previously, test the thymus. If it is underactive, then test the hemispheres. If the person is left-hemisphere dominant, test the "midline" meridian test points; and if he is right-hemisphere dominant, test the "bilateral" meridian test points.
2. Find the meridian that is underactive. Have the person repeat the appropriate positive affirmation. On retesting you will find that the meridian tests strong now.
3. Repeat the thymus test. If it is strong, you need go no further. You are probably working with a relatively emotionally healthy

person capable of living in and working in the present. If the thymus tests weak, repeat the hemispheres test. Find the involved meridian, correct it with the affirmation, and retest the thymus. If it is testing strong, you have finished. If it still tests weak, then repeat the hemispheres and meridian tests and correct what you find. It is generally only necessary to repeat this procedure two or three times until you have found the Achilles heel and corrected it.

A man came to see me and he was obviously very tense. His voice was tense, he gripped his hands tightly together, and when I touched his body to test him I could feel the tension within him. He complained primarily of back pains and chronic constipation. On testing I found, as expected, that his thymus was underactive. I tested each hemisphere and discovered that he was left-hemisphere dominant at this time, so I then tested the meridians with midline test points. I found that it was the circulation-sex meridian that was devitalized. I was not surprised, knowing that this meridian is often involved in cases of tension such as this.

  I had three major categories of emotions to discuss with him relative to this meridian involvement. I suggested that, in view of his overall picture, it was probably the aspect of tension that was most affecting him. With this he agreed and said, "Yes, I am very tense, and I even know deep down that if I could only relax, this back problem would go away." We then discussed the possibility that his tension might have a sexual problem at its source. He was in his mid-fifties. He said that he had never been married, never had a serious affair, and actually had had only a few sexual experiences in his life. He had no close female friends. He had been troubled by persistent sexual thoughts and he was constantly trying, usually unsuccessfully, to push them out of his mind. I suggested that he repeat the affirmation, "I am relaxed," and that he visualize himself in a very relaxed state. On retesting the circulation-sex meridian, we found that the imbalance had corrected itself. But his thymus was still testing weak. Even so, he suddenly said, "My back feels easier than it has in years!" On palpating the involved area, I did find that the muscle tension had relaxed somewhat.

We retested his hemispheres and found a right-hemisphere dominance. On testing the "bilateral" meridians we found that the large intestine meridian (guilt) was affected. Remember, this meridian had not tested weak in the first procedure. It had revealed an imbalance only after the sexual tension problem had been recognized and corrected. I asked him if perhaps he felt guilty over sex in general or over a specific sexual incident, to which he replied, "No, not really." However, you will recall that the deeper layers of imbalance are generally unconscious, that is, not within the subject's conscious knowledge. After he considered this possibility, he then said, "You know, that's a very reasonable question. I am a strict Catholic and I know that it is wrong to masturbate, and wrong to have sexual intercourse before marriage. So every time I consider one of these activities, suddenly I am overwhelmed with guilt. Yes, I can see that this is what has been happening to me over the years."

He then repeated the affirmation for the large intestine meridian, "I am basically clean and good. I am worthy of being loved." He had a look of amazement on his face when we tested and found that now his large intestine meridian test point was strong. He said, "Well, you have helped me to face something about myself that I had kept hidden all these years. That is really amazing."

On testing his thymus again we found that there was more work to be done. He was still right-hemisphere dominant, and on testing we found the lung meridian was now involved. With the correction and release of energy in the large intestine and circulation-sex meridians, his body was now able to express its "problems" with the lung meridian. Now, as you might have discovered for yourself by this time, it is often difficult to discuss the emotional attitudes associated with lung-meridian energy imbalances with a person without appearing to insult him.

I began carefully to outline what the emotional concomitants of the lung meridian were, and this man was quite surprised at what was revealed. Now in psychiatry every patient is different, but after twenty or more years of practice, one soon assesses a situation and knows where the problem areas are. So I suggested to this man that although his appearance was one of meekness and humility there was a fair amount of superiority operating—and I suggested that perhaps because of his sexual aloofness he had developed this feeling. He thought about this and agreed. When he said, "I am humble" with a clear understanding of the true meaning of the word, he tested strong. He said that he found little difficulty in accepting these findings after considering them. "After all," he said, "my own body is telling me these things." Now his thymus tested strong, and he left knowing what work he had to do.

When I saw him several weeks later, he was a changed man. He came in smiling; he seemed much more at ease with himself in general. He was far less tense and he reported that his back had given him minimal problems. The most remarkable thing for him, he said, was the change in his bowels. He had been constipated for many years, normally having a bowel action only every three days or so. Since that first session, he was having regular bowel actions once and sometimes twice each day without laxatives. He was very pleased that he now understood himself better, and said that he realized why he had such difficulty in finding some-one to whom he would like to be married. But he was confident that with continued work he would soon attract the type of per-son with whom he could easily establish a long-term relationship. He re-emphasized that the most important thing for him was that he understood himself better. He saw very clearly the interde-pendence of the functions of his body, mind, and spirit and now he was able to work toward the development and achieve-ment of his goal.

Let's take another example. I once had to make a decision as to which of two assistants to hire on a full-time basis. They were both students and part-time assistants and were both very helpful. After I had made the decision and one assistant had started her full-time job, the other one came to me and asked that we test her, as she felt that something just wasn't right. She had been a student long enough to be aware when something was out of balance. Her thy-mus tested weak and we found left-hemisphere dominance. On testing the "midline" meridians, we found the stomach meridian was involved. She was already familiar with this work, and she exclaimed, "Well, obviously I'm disappointed! I am very upset that you chose the other student for the job. I feel that I deserved that job, and I do feel literally *dis*appointed. I feel that I had developed a relationship with you that has now been broken in some way. You have transferred your trust to someone else." We then took some time to discuss my reasons for employing the other student and I reassured her that our relationship, from my standpoint, was as good as ever. I expected to find then that her thymus tested strong, and that would be the end of the discussion. Instead, though, we found her thymus weak and her left hemisphere was still dominant. On testing, a circulation-sex meridian problem was revealed. She said, "I know why. It's because I'm jealous. I feel that the appointment was *mine* and that the other student has taken it away from me." She thought for a moment and said, with great insight, "You know, this is identical to the situation I have always had at home. I'm the younger sister and I have always felt that my older sister is given preferential treatment, that she is given things and attention that are rightfully mine." She repeated the appropriate affirmation with conviction, and we found that her thymus was strong.

She has remained a student and part-time assistant for some time now, and she has maintained a good relationship with the rest of my staff, including her "rival." She had recognized and corrected her disappointment first and then her jealousy. As a side benefit, she recently reported that since our discussion her relationship with her sister has been remarkably better and that she feels much more comfortable in her family in general.

In view of what you have just read, you may begin to wonder how significant a first-layer meridian imbalance is in developing a long-term program for yourself. It depends on how often that meridian imbalance is operant. If it was only of short duration, then it should not be a cause for concern. But if you are experiencing physical symptoms such as a headache or upset stomach or the like and you find a meridian imbalance, then it is significant. By relieving the emotional concomitant you will help to relieve the physical symptoms (I am not implying that you will cure it). On the other hand, if you consistently find one meridian testing weak, that indicates an area for work. Long-term imbalances in the meridian will ultimately affect the organ it serves. So by correcting the imbalances at an emotional level, at an energy level, we are practicing prevention. We may be able to prevent a physical problem from developing.

In most cases where there is meridian energy imbalance, laboratory tests show no evidence of abnormality. It is often too early for that. And this is a wonderful aspect of our research. It often allows us to practice primary prevention.

Another point to be considered in assessing the value or importance of a first-layer meridian imbalance is that what you find on testing indicates the predominant emotional state operant at that time. You can learn what is holding you back right now. You can then correct it and release the energy that is blocked in that meridian and get yourself back in order. You are in a better position to achieve your full potential, to function with maximum life energy.

The Double-Bind

Soon after I first obtained my driver's license, I was driving alone when I came to an intersection controlled by a traffic policeman. He looked straight at me and put his hand up in a "stop" gesture and said in a loud commanding voice, "Come on!" Immediately I felt tremendously anxious. I didn't know what to do. Did he mean for me to come on, or did he mean for me to stop? What was I to do? Whatever I did would be wrong. If I went with his verbal command, I would be disobeying his gesture. If I went with his gesture, I would be disobeying his verbal command. All I could see was disaster, whatever I did. If I went forward, I was wrong; if I didn't go forward, I was wrong. My panic increased. Worst of all, I had no one to turn to to ask for advice.

This is what we mean by the double-bind. This phrase was coined by Gregory Bateson, who felt that this communication process was one of the most important factors in the causation of schizophrenia.[1]

One of the models that the advocates of this theory proposed was that the mother had mixed feelings toward the child and when she would, for example, ask the child to come close because she loved him, as he got closer, she would start to push him away. Her own heightened mixed feelings became intolerable as he approached. The child given this conflicting message does not know what to do. He wonders, "Do I go with what she says, or do I go with what I feel she is saying with her gestures?" The important aspect of the double-bind is that there is a *contradictory communication being given simultaneously using two different modalities.* It is not saying to someone, "I love you," and then following this with, "I hate you," because that is not simultaneous and it is the same modality of communication. But when you say, "I love you" but the expression on your face is one of anger, this is a double-bind. The transmitter of the message is in two minds. Does the mother basically like or dislike the child? Her own confusion is transmitted to the child, and now he becomes confused.

The other important ingredient in the model is that there is no external authority to whom to turn and ask, for example, "What did Mommy mean? Did she mean 'I love you,' or did she mean, 'I hate you'?" Just as I had no one in the car to ask, the child has no one to use as a point of reality reference. Further, the model has the strong, dominant, double-binding mother along with a very weak father. The father says, in essence, "I have enough problems with your mother myself. I don't understand her either. Don't come to me with your problems about her." This is the basic conceptual model for the factors leading to the double-bind.

A psychiatrist or anyone listening to people discussing their problems begins to realize that this situation is not reserved for schizophrenics or even for psychotics. It is occurring to each of us every day. What of the government that declares it believes 100 percent in peace yet engages in provocative acts, for example? Or what of the agency that is established solely for the purpose of implementing energy conservation programs but which daily condones activities that mitigate against it? A company may advertise that its sole purpose for existence is to serve the good of the people —while it reports windfall profits. Or what of the advertisements that indicate the appeal of smoking while quoting the surgeon general's warning on the ad? Or the pretty, coquettish girl who leads the boy on and then says, "Whatever gave you the idea that I would want to have sex with you?" Her body is saying yes, her voice is saying no. What is he to believe?

Think of the double-binds a politician may be capable of giving when he makes statements such as, "I think that the free enterprise system is absolutely too important to be left to the voluntary action of the marketplace." (*Environmental Action*, December, 1979)

Consider the stereotyped situation. The husband comes home from work and can sense by the way his wife is walking around the house that something is not right. He hears her heavy, aggressive footsteps, hard on her heels. She is clattering the cooking ware, saying little, and has a disturbed expression on her face. He says to her, "What's wrong, honey?" and her standard reply is, "Nothing." Now what is he to believe? He can *sense* from her every gesture and "vibration" that she is upset, but she *says* nothing is wrong. He is now caught in a double-bind situation.

And what of the husband who comes in at 3 A.M., exhausted after an obviously heavy night. His wife asks, "What have you been doing?" and he replies, "Nothing." These are all double-bind situations. They destroy our life energy; they will drive us crazy, perhaps not psychotic, but certainly in the loose sense of the word, crazy.

To test your response to a double-bind, use a sample situation such as the one described at the beginning of this chapter. Have someone test you in the clear. You should test strong. Now have a third person say to you while looking at you, "Come here." You should again test strong. Then have the third person remain silent but put up his hand in a "stop" gesture. You should again test strong. But now, have your partner test you while you are experiencing both messages simultaneously. The third person says, "Come here," while at the same time he has his hand up in the "stop" gesture. Now you will find that, if you are like 90 percent of individuals, your life energy has been depleted by this stress and you will test weak. You, like most of us, are vulnerable to this double-bind. Of course, if your life energy were higher, you would not be vulnerable, and it is my hope that what you learn from this book will give you this capacity.

The next question that arises is, which of the two messages in this communication are you believing? How do you respond to this ambiguous, simultaneous love/hate message? First, test to see whether under this type of stress you tend to become left- or right-hemisphere dominant. To determine this, simply test for hemisphere dominance as you are being given the double-bind message. If your response is left-hemisphere dominance, it means that you are basically accepting the "good" part of the communication. You realize that the message is a mixed one, and you choose to ignore the "stop" and accept the "come here." Conversely, if your response is right-hemisphere dominance, then you again recognize the contradictory nature of the message, but you respond to the "stop" portion.

I have tested many patients and students using this system, and I have found that those who test left-hemisphere dominant in response to the stress of the double-bind communication tend to be able not to be upset by a form of rejection. These people will try again, recognizing that the communication is mixed and hoping that the next time the response will be positive. They are basically optimistic. Those individuals whose response to the stress of the double-bind transmission is to become right-hemisphere dominant are more likely to be put off by the rejection and not try again. They tend to be more pessimistic.

Note: You may test right- or left-hemisphere dominant in a situation that is double binding, but for it to be a true double-bind, the specific meridian involved must be the primary one for each hemisphere. Lung is the basic meridian for the right hemisphere, and thyroid for the left hemisphere. This is in keeping with Klein's first position (paranoid-schizoid) and second position (depressive).

Listen to what your friends, your relatives, advertisements, government reports, tell you. You may begin to realize how we are affected by all communications, and how binding communications tend to lower life energy. After all, it takes a great deal of energy just to interpret the message and to determine what portions you will believe. But recognize that if you can activate your life energy sufficiently, you will not be affected. In this world of increasing "binds," this can be a comforting and reassuring thought.

THE DOUBLE-BIND
The model's contradictory message will cause you to test weak unless your life
energy is high. Are you able to overcome it? If not, which hemisphere becomes
dominant?

The eyes say "yes," the hand says "no."
The eyes say "come," the hand says "go."

The Daily Program for Life Energy

You have learned how you can correct the negative emotional attitudes that are affecting your life energy as a result of stresses to which you have been subjected. You can correct these whether they be caused by past or recent experiences, whether they be conscious or unconscious.

In order for you to enjoy a more healthy, harmonious life, I suggest a simply daily meditational program to activate and vitalize your meridians. It is not necessary to test for individual meridian imbalances—and this is of particular benefit if you do not have a test partner.

Use this program several times each day routinely, and especially when stressed. This is a way of practicing true prevention—abolishing problems at an energy level before they have a chance to develop physically.

If possible, this program is best carried out if you adopt the Alexander horizontal position,[1] a position for general postural improvement. It is taught as part of the Alexander Technique that was developed by F. Matthias Alexander, and it can be extremely beneficial. It aligns the body, thereby permitting a free flow of energy throughout and enabling the thymus to monitor and correct imbalances. The position is as follows: Lie down with your knees bent, your feet flat on the floor, and the outside of your thighs parallel to your hips. Put a book or two under your head so that your spine and neck are aligned. In this position you will be relaxed and receptive to energizing influences. And in this position, your body is in balance and your body energies are balanced; you are in an optimum situation to benefit from your meditational experience.

219

Put the tip of your tongue on the rugae, and breathe in and out through your nose until you begin to feel relaxed.[2]

Now go through each meridian in turn, saying with conviction the positive affirmations for each. It is helpful, although not essential, to touch the test point(s) for the particular meridian at the time you say the affirmation. Say them in any order you find comfortable, finishing with the affirmations for the thymus. Say them either aloud or to yourself, and at the same time visualize the associated positive feelings.[3] Allow your breath to flow on its own. Say each affirmation three times, with three successive breaths, and continue until you end with the thymus affirmation. As you do the final affirmations you may wish to tap your thymus area for reinforcement. Think of your energy being balanced and flowing smoothly and lovingly into all your organs. Imagine them all working in complete harmony for the total enrichment of your health and well-being. Close with the affirmation: "My life energy is high. I am in the state of love."

This is a very simple meditational program. I have taught it to hundreds of students over the years. Many have said that, just as a final positive reinforcement, they like to concentrate on their homing thought before ending the meditation. This simple procedure can be very rewarding, and it can assist you in achieving your goal.

DAILY AFFIRMATION PROGRAM

I have love,
    faith,
    trust,
    gratitude,
  and courage.   Thymus

I am humble.
I am tolerant.
I am modest.   Lung

I am happy.
I have good fortune.
I am cheerful.   Liver

I reach out with love.   Gall Bladder

I have faith and confidence in my future.	
I am secure.	Spleen
My sexual energies are balanced.	Kidney
I am basically clean and good.	
I am worthy of being loved.	Large Intestine
I renounce the past.	
I am generous.	
I am relaxed.	Circulation-Sex
I have forgiveness in my heart.	Heart
I am content.	
I am tranquil.	Stomach
I am buoyed up with hope.	
I am light and buoyant.	Thyroid
I am jumping with joy.	Small Intestine
I am in harmony.	
I am at peace.	Bladder
I have love,	
faith,	
trust,	
gratitude,	
and courage.	Thymus

close with:
My life energy is high.
I am in the state of love.

We have found that the therapeutic power of the positive affirmation can be increased if it is said in an impersonal way. For example, if instead of saying, "I am content," Bill says, "Bill is content," there will be, on deeper levels of testing, a greater increase in energy. The reason for the heightened effect of the impersonal positive affirmation is that it involves the act of thinking, of putting out a message into the world which then comes back to you. Whenever we direct our communication out into the world, whether it be speech, writing, poetry, music, or the like, there will always be a greater increase in life energy than if we keep the message to ourselves. In this context, it is very important to listen intently to the words as they come back to you and focus on taking them in.

Overcoming Fears and Phobias

All of us are troubled in particular circumstances by apprehensions and fears concerning a future event. It is now possible to discover and easily correct these with the knowledge that you have already acquired. Consider the following examples: A woman told me that she knew she wanted to get married but she also knew there was something holding her back, always preventing it. She found it difficult even to talk about it. I asked her to think about being married—exactly what she thought about I do not know, but it was what marriage meant to her. On testing her, we found that the small intestine meridian was weak. When we discussed the emotions related to this meridian, she said, "Yes, that's appropriate. I think what I fear about marriage is that it is going to make me sad and tearful. I'm afraid I will end up crying throughout my marriage as my mother seemed to do throughout hers."

A student recently told me that she was very frightened about going to the dentist for her appointment the next day. She said that in fact whenever she goes to the dentist she is in a state of extreme distress. She asked if I could help. I asked her to think of being in a dentist's chair. We found that her thymus tested weak. As we continued testing we found that in her case the particular meridian involved was the stomach meridian. We were unable to find a conscious reason why this meridian should be involved, so I suggested to her that she continue repeating the associated affirmation, "I am content," reinforcing it with the thymus thump. I suggested that she do this as often as she could before she saw the dentist and then while she was being treated by him. Both she and the dentist later told me how much better that session had been than any of her previous ones. She reported that she felt very little fear and apprehension and the dentist told me that for the first time he could really do proper work on her as she was no longer so tense and fearful.

We have been able to reduce stress and anxiety with many students about to undergo any form of operative procedure, dental or surgical, with gratifying results.

Whenever you are approaching a fearful situation, such as going to the dentist, perhaps taking a trip on an airplane, being interviewed for a new job, sitting for an examination, attending court, or whatever, visualize the situation strongly in your mind and then test to find the impaired meridian. Work on keeping that meridian as activated as possible prior to and during the stressful experience. You could be quite surprised at the help this will give you.

In the same manner you can help yourself to overcome, for example, the smoking habit. Think of smoking and you will find that your thymus will test weak. A specific meridian, usually the lung meridian, will also test weak. You will find that you can help yourself to stop smoking by concentrating on the lung affirmation to ease the withdrawal.

At times when you think of highly stressful situations, and smoking is one, you will find that you will be so weakened that your indicator muscle will test weak. Just thinking of it, without test-touching the thymus, is stressful enough to cause the muscle to test weak. In such cases, you will find that test-touching one and only one meridian will cause the muscle to stay strong when you think of the highly stressful situation. This is what we call double-negative testing. The meridian that causes the muscle that is weak in the clear to test strong is the involved meridian. This double testing applies when the stressful situation is so great that it diminishes your life energy and causes the indicator muscle to test weak even before the thymus test-touching procedure is carried out.

This method can also be beneficial in terms of goal direction. Another friend told me that he had always wished he could strike it rich with one of his wildcat oil-drilling schemes. So I asked him to think of striking it rich. We found that this thought weakened his liver meridian, strange as this may seem. When we asked him to think not just of striking it rich with oil, but also of using that money for philanthropic purposes (which he really wants to do, and which would be more important to him than any personal material wealth), he tested strong. He thanked me and said, "Well, I realize my goal is not to get money through oil. My goal is to do something for other people when I have the money, which I hope to get through the oil." Thus he has the beginning of his homing thought.

A patient told me that she had great difficulty swallowing. As soon as she put something solid in her mouth to swallow—like a pill—she would become extremely apprehensive and fearful and would choke. Because of this, she was unable to take vitamins and food supplements, which she truly needed for her health, and was on a soft diet for many years.

I asked her to think of swallowing a pill. Immediately, her circulation-sex meridian test point was weak. As soon as she said the appropriate affirmation and kept it clearly in her mind, she was able to swallow with ease. Since then, she has had very little difficulty with her swallowing, and whenever she does have problems, she just reinforces the affirmations with the thymus thump, and her problem is once again resolved.

Elena was born in Hungary, and she lived there until a tragedy occurred when she was fourteen years old. Within a short period of time, right at the end of World War II, her father and mother were imprisoned (as she was herself for a brief period of time), tortured, and beaten. For three months after Elena's release from prison, she was anxiously searching for her father (who was, in fact, dead), and desperately trying to get her mother out of prison. Her mother eventually was released, but within two weeks of that both of Elena's maternal grandparents died in front of her.

Since that time, she has had terrible memories, nightmares, and thoughts of her Hungarian experience. That period affects her so much that whenever she thinks anything in her native Hungarian language, let alone says it aloud, she becomes extremely stressed and apprehensive.

What could we do about this? First, we had to find out which meridian was predominantly affected when she thought of her Hungarian experience. We found that Elena's gall bladder meridian was affected—that she was feeling rage. So she said and incorporated with deep feeling the affirmation as part of her daily program. Soon she was able to talk more freely about the experiences, and she overcame most, but not all, of her apprehension and stress when speaking or hearing her native language.

A student told me that he had a fear of heights that was extremely debilitating and distressing to him, and it greatly interfered with his functioning. He was a sane, rational man, a scientist, very logi-

cally oriented. Tranquilizers and psychotherapy had failed to relieve him of his fear. When he consulted me, I asked him to think
of being on top of a very tall building. Instantly his thymus tested
weak. We found that the specific meridian involved was the circulation-sex meridian. (With true phobias it is almost invariably this
meridian which is involved.) I then showed him, to his own amazement, that if while thinking of this phobic situation he also said to
himself with conviction the affirmation, "I am relaxed," he no
longer tested weak. I pointed out to him that now he could see just
how powerful positive thoughts could be in helping him to overcome his phobic situation. "Well," he said with a smile, "I'll think
about it." It was obvious that he was not at all confident that such
a simple technique could be of any benefit.

When I next saw him, he came into my office with a huge smile
on his face. He shook my hand warmly and said, "You won't believe what happened. My wife bought tickets to the opera for us.
When we arrived there, I discovered that our seats were in one of
the back rows right at the top of the theater. I immediately became
very stressed and apprehensive and thought, 'I can't possibly sit
there. It will kill me!' But I decided to try what you said. While
walking up the stairs I said the affirmations. To my amazement I
was able to sit through and enjoy the total performance. You've got
a believer."

Most of us have had fears and phobias at some point in our lives.
Many people become extremely frightened when they are about to
have an injection or have blood drawn. Some people refuse to get
into an elevator or to go into a room with no windows. Others are
afraid of developing a specific dreaded disease. Whatever the fear,
it drains life energy. Now we have a way to take care of such energy
drains. With the energy that is gained, we are free to pursue our
goal of positive health.

Transmutation

"To become renewed, transfigured, in another pattern."
—*T. S. Eliot*

Modern psychiatry often reinforces our feelings of helplessness and dependency by neglecting the role of the patient's will. Of course we all know there are many people who seem to want to stay in the negative, but this may be because they don't realize that they are in the negative—that there can be a "positive!" I believe that if they did, they would make the change.

One of the problems with psychiatry is that we have become obsessed with finding out *why* we are upset. The important point is not what has made us upset, but in which way we are upset and how we can overcome it, and how to raise the vitality, the life energy. The *why* has to do with left-brain investigation, but the true change within the individual comes when both brains and the thymus are involved in the decision. And it comes from discovering the exact emotional state involved, as you can do with the techniques described in this book, and then working to transmute, to turn that emotional state into the specific positive. So it is not a question of *why*. It is a question of identifying the state and then activating our life energy, our wills to be well, to turn it into the positive. This is the dual-hemisphere, creative approach to the problem.

By transmutation I mean the ability instantly to turn the negative into the positive. As an example, let us say that you are tested by a friend and it is found that your liver meridian is weak. Your first step toward turning this into the positive is to recognize that you are unhappy. Then choose to give up the unhappiness and take on the positive feeling of being happy and blissful. Just say the appropriate affirmation with conviction, and visualize it strongly and clearly, and the negative becomes positive. This is transmutation.

To want to do this, and to want to continue to do it, your will to be well must be present. This is your active contribution to your health, to your life, to attaining your goal. You must want to be well, and then you can easily go about achieving it.

Let's be very clear as to what is meant by transmutation. If you are angry, for example, I am not recommending that you push your anger down inside you. That only hurts you in other ways. Nor am I suggesting that you act out the anger. That hurts both you and the other person. What I am suggesting is that you transmute it. Recognize that you have the anger, recognize that it is hurting you and others, and then say the appropriate positive affirmation with conviction. You will then activate your will to be well and you will overcome the anger with positive emotions. Your anger no longer exists. It has been transformed, transmuted, into something positive and productive, and your life energy has been stimulated.

All this has important implications for psychosomatic medicine. We know, on the one hand, that negative emotional states ultimately lead to physical illness—heart disease, cancer, diabetes, asthma, and so on. But we also now know precisely which emotional attitudes may lead to precisely which diseases, because we know the emotional states that are related to each meridian, and therefore each organ that becomes diseased.

Thus, you can see how psychosomatic illness begins. The mental attitudes and emotional states interfere with the energy supply through the meridian, and to the specific organ. That is how the mind affects the body. In most psychosomatic conditions, there is an "interaction between psychological factors and a physiological predisposition to the illness."[1] You can also see that if we correct the emotional attitudes, if we continually buoy ourselves up by transmuting negative into positive, we can keep our energy balanced and practice primary prevention.

What happens if an individual already has a disease? We know that there are physical diseases that feed back and cause emotional problems. These are called somato-psychic diseases. Again, we know what specific emotional problems will tend to be caused by or to accompany the various physical diseases.

Thus, even if we do not subscribe to the belief that the emotional state causes the illness, at least when people have illness we can then identify the accompanying emotional states. Even if it is too late for an individual to correct his emotional imbalances and prevent the occurrence of disease, at least the emotional component can be stopped from feeding back into the disease. This can be done with the use of the appropriate positive affirmations, among many other things.

In these chapters I have outlined a new approach to preventive and psychosomatic medicine, as well as to psychiatry. But more importantly, I believe it is a major breakthrough for *you*. You, as an educated layman, can now carry out important research into psychosomatic medicine. You do not require a laboratory, and you do not need multi-million-dollar grants. All you need is some people to test, some inquiring minds, and the facts presented here. You can do some very important work just by testing yourself and your friends and seeing time and again the relationship between specific emotional states and organs.

It is incredible to think that each organ has a specific corresponding emotional state, but this is our finding. We can now begin to understand certain personality types—the asthmatic and the lung meridian, the diabetic and the spleen meridian, and so forth—and to open up tremendous vistas.

It is my hope that in some way you have learned how to be well —and how to identify the specific problems and attitudes that were holding you back. Now you can easily, positively, and simply work to turn them around, to transmute the negative into positive states of love, faith, gratitude, trust, and courage. This is the reason I have written this book.

Our goal is to function as much like an adult as possible in life, free of encumbrances of past problems and stresses. This we can accomplish by peeling back the layers and then correcting specific emotional problems that are affecting us. When these are corrected, we will be invulnerable to most stress and our energies will be released to be devoted to our true purpose in life. Our *thymos* will be active and our energies will no longer be dissipated fighting stressful battles throughout the body and mind. We can begin to discover our deepest homing thoughts, our true selves, and to mobilize our energies to achieve our positive goals. Our life energy will be free and detached from the negative and will be moving into the sunshine, into positive health. While I do not believe that this book alone will make possible the full achievement of our potentials (would that that were the case!), I do hope and believe that it will be a beneficial tool in achieving development and maturation.

As I stated at the beginning of this book, in my years in psychiatry and preventive medicine I was often very disappointed and unhappy to see myself and my peers falling so short of our potentials, not going where our endowments and heritages could lead. Now I know that if you carry out the procedures that we have discussed, much less of your life energy will be drained in trying to cope with negative attitudes and debilitating stresses. You will be liberated, your own master. You will know your purpose in life and can set about achieving it. I hope and pray that you reach your goal, your home.

"Love is the lesson which the Lord us taught." (Edmund Spenser)

Epilogue

My hope is that now you have an understanding of the supreme importance of your life energy for your mental and physical health. You also now know about the function of each of the hemispheres of your brain, and you have learned that the balanced activity of both hemispheres is required for problem-solving and creativity. You have learned how to correct any imbalance so that you are now able to be one of that 5 percent or so of the population that is truly creative. You can now find new solutions, the proper solutions, to the problems of life. You can use your whole brain to help yourself and everyone around you. You now have the equipment and the knowledge to understand yourself as has never before been possible.

You have also learned about each of the emotional states and how each is related through the specific acupuncture meridian to particular organs of the body. This is the basis of the mind-body link and the foundation of a holistic understanding of our total functioning, mental and physical. You have learned how you can assist your life energy to help overcome any physical problem you may have by invoking the power of your thoughts to correct the accompanying specific negative emotional state. And more importantly, you have learned how every physical illness starts with a particular negative emotion. Thus by frequently monitoring ourselves and correcting these early negative states, the precursors of physical disease, we can keep ourselves healthy. We can practice the positive prevention of disease.

You have learned a simple technique of affirmations that may be carried out on a daily basis and also whenever you are stressed.

230

This simple technique will help to keep you emotionally balanced, with all your emotions in the positive. Thus your life energy will be high and you will be healthy. Now all your emotions can be positive and the life energy that courses throughout your body and your soul can be uplifted with love. This is what I mean by psycho-biological harmony. And through these simple procedures, it is yours.

I hope as well that you have now learned a love for your language and a respect for the myriad psychological insights within it, especially the power of the word. I hope you feel humble and awed in the presence of what you have learned about the incredible richness and subtlety of our mental and physical functioning.

You have learned how to find out what is really going on inside you, what you really feel and believe and desire, by the application of a simple technique. You have learned the wonderful world of mental and physical functioning that is now at your fingertips for investigation as a result of this simple test. You now have a most powerful research tool to use on yourself and your friends. Now you can learn what is really right for you—not just what you *think* is right—in all aspects of your functioning. Now and only now can you make the right choices for your life. You can elicit information from your deepest unconscious and find out what you really feel and what you are really thinking, and what you really want in life. This can be of incredible benefit to you. Used with care it will change your life. You will be able as never before to develop and unfold and to achieve your own personal evolution.

I could have written a more scientifically rigorous book, one which might possibly have won acclaim from my professional colleagues. But that would have been another left-brain book. As my purpose has been to help you change your life, it is important that I address your right brain as well. Your left brain is already so overwhelmed by your day-to-day living that it is deaf to the new message. It cannot hear anymore, and if it cannot hear it cannot be helped. Hence I have written this book to talk to your right brain as well as to your left. I want to help you to understand, to "see," and thus to grow and to learn—to learn who you were created to be and then to grow into your true self—by at all times keeping your eye on your homing thought, your true goal in life.

You have learned the supreme power of your thoughts. Over the centuries philosophers and psychologists have speculated on this, but now you have been able to experience something previously undemonstrable: the immediate power of your thoughts to influence your physical state. Your thoughts have the power to alter the physiological response of your muscles. A thought or a word can change the energy of the organ. This you can prove for yourself. Thoughts have the power to cause or cure illness in your body. You can now use them for health.

What I hope more than anything else is that from reading this book you have learned the supreme power of love and can now demonstrate it. It is love that banishes all the negative emotions. It is love that invokes the spirit and activates the life energy. It is love that balances our brains and makes us creative. And it is love for our true self, for the self that we can be, that drives us on to want to be better and want to be healthier and to want to be more evolved. Love is health and life.

Appendix I

MAJOR
ETYMOLOGICAL
REFERENCES

Some of these books have been my friends for many years. I have grown to love them, as they have given me many hours of quiet satisfaction. I hope that this work may stimulate you to explore these monuments of our society and to treasure and value them as they deserve. To know our language is to know ourselves, and to love our language is to love ourselves.

Perhaps the best place to start is with Partridge's *Origins* and the *American Heritage Dictionary*. Most importantly, please do not be overwhelmed by the size of the *Oxford English Dictionary*. To me, it is the greatest inexhaustible treasure house.

American Heritage Dictionary of the English Language. New York: American Heritage Publishing Company, 1969.

Benveniste, Emil. *Indo-European Language and Society*. London: Faber and Faber, 1973.

Buck, Carl D. *A Dictionary of Selected Synonyms in the Principal Indo-European Languages*. Chicago: University of Chicago Press, 1949.

Crabbe, George. *English Synonyms*. New York: Harper Brothers, 1890.

Johnson, Samuel. *A Dictionary of the English Language*. New York: AMS Press, 1967. (reprint)

Klein, Ernest. *A Comprehensive Etymological Dictionary of the English Language*. Amsterdam: Elsevier, 1967.

Lewis, Charlton T., and Short, Charles. *A Latin Dictionary*. Oxford: Clarendon Press, 1879, 1969.

MacDonald, A. M. *Etymological English Dictionary*. Paterson, N.J.: Littlefield, Adams, 1964.

McDonell, Arthur A. *A Practical Sanskrit Dictionary*. Oxford: Oxford University Press, 1958.

Morris, William, and Morris, Mary. *Morris Dictionary of Word and Phrase Origins*. New York: Harper and Row, 1977.

Onions, C. T. *The Oxford Dictionary of English Etymology*. Oxford: Clarendon Press, 1966.

Oxford English Dictionary. Oxford: Clarendon Press, 1933, 1961.

Partridge, Eric. *Origins—A Short Etymological Dictionary of Modern English*. 4th ed. London: Routledge and Kegan Paul, 1966.

Pokorny, Julius. *Indogermanisches Etymologisches Worterbuch*. Bern: Francke, 1959.

Shipley, Joseph T. *Dictionary of Word Origins*. New York: Philosophical Library, 1945.

Skeat, Walter W. *An Etymological Dictionary of the English Language*. 4th ed. Oxford: Clarendon Press, 1910.

————. *Principles of English Etymology*. Oxford, 1887.

Smith, Charles John. *Synonyms Discriminated*. London: George Bell and Sons, 1910.

Webster's New International Dictionary. 2nd ed. Springfield, Mass.: G. & C. Merriam, 1944.

Weekley, Ernest. *An Etymological Dictionary of Modern English*. New York: Dover, 1967.

Wyld, Henry C. *The Universal Dictionary of the English Language*. London: Routledge and Kegan Paul, 1961.

For additional information on Dr. Diamond's research findings, write to:

John Diamond, M.D.
% The Institutes for the Enhancement
of Life Energy and Creativity
P.O. Box 566
Valley Cottage, New York 10989

Appendix II

NOTES
INTRODUCTION

1. Plato wrote in *Symposium* (186D), "[The doctor] ought to be able to bring about love and reconciliation between the most antithetic elements in the body. . . . Our ancestor Asclepius knew how to bring love and concord to these opposites, and he it was, as poets say and I believe, who founded our art."

2. *Fragments Of Empedocles,* trans. William E. Leonard, (LaSalle, Ill., 1973).

3. Wright, M. R. ed. *Empedocles: The Extant Fragments.* (New Haven: Yale University Press), 1981, pp. 30–34.

4. Of course, the concept of the interaction of the mind and the body is not new. Consider the definition of *emotion* as "a strong excitement of feeling, tending to manifest itself by its effect upon the body." Charles John Smith, *Synonyms Discriminated.* (London, 1901), p. 429.

5. The Chinese correlated the organs and meridians with certain emotions. This is a comprehensive and verifiable approach. See Dr. Felix Mann, *Acupuncture: Cure of Many Diseases.* (London: Heinemann, 1971), p. 51.

THE GOAL

1. It is not without significance that the ancient Chinese believed that the Chi first entered the lung meridian and from there traveled through the body to the various other meridians and channels of energy. (See chapter 3.)

2. For more on the concept of breath and spirit, see Ron DelBene, *The Breath of Life: A Simple Way to Pray.* (Minneapolis: Winston Press, 1981).

3. James Hastings, ed. *Encyclopedia of Religion and Ethics.* (New York: Scribners, 1920), Vol. XI, p. 784.

4. John Diamond, *The Collected Papers of John Diamond, M.D.* (Valley Cottage: Archaeus Press, 1977), Vol. I, pp. 34–49.

5. Xanthippe was the wife of Socrates, "notorious . . . for the stories of her bad temper." This phrase was used by Franz Josef Haydn to describe his wife. Unlike my patient, Haydn fortunately had his music.

THYMUS GLAND

1. Denis and Joyce Lawson-Wood, *The Five Elements of Acupuncture and Chinese Massage.* (Northamptonshire: Health Science Press, 1973), p. 20.

2. Hans Selye, *The Stress of Life.* (New York: McGraw-Hill, 1978).

3. For details on the intricacies and subtleties of testing, refer to *Behavioral Kinesiology Report,* No. 10, December 1977.

4. Friedrich Hoffmann, *Fundamenta Medicinae,* trans. Lester S. King. (New York: Science History Publications, 1971), p. 47.

5. In studying the etymology of *retaliation,* we find that it means returning like for like, especially returning evil for evil. The Latin *talio* means reciprocal punishment in kind.

6. See, for example, *Beyond the Pleasure Principle,* Vol. XVIII, Standard Edition, 1920.

7. Samuel Schwartz, M.D., "Incidence of Cancer in Patients with Thyroid Dysfunction." Presented to 1979 Spring Conference of the International Academy of Preventive Medicine, Dallas, Texas.

8. Adrian Stokes, *A Game That Must Be Lost.* (Cheshire: Carcanet, 1973), p. 68.

9. *Ibid.,* p. 30.

10. Sources for Biblical quotes throughout this book are the Authorized King James version and the New English Bible.

11. The I.E. root, *leubh* (to love) gives rise also to *leave* (permission), *furlough,* as well as *belief* and *libido.*

12. Bernard Leach, *The Potter's Challenge.* (New York: Dutton, 1975), p. 35.

13. Octavio Paz, *Newsweek,* November 19, 1979, p. 137.

14. Luke 17:19 "And he said unto him, Arise, go thy way: thy faith hath made thee whole."

15. John Henry Newman, *Parochial Sermons* (1837).

16. Jonathan Swift, *Sermons Trinity* (1744).

17. For further discussion of the Indo-European roots see pp. 99–100. For a list of major dictionaries consulted, see Appendix I.

18. In a book written in 1901, *Etymologica Parerga,* H. Ostoff states that the German word *treu* is related to the Indo-European name for the oak; to be loyal means to stand as firm as an oak.

19. Erik H. Erikson, *Childhood and Society.* (New York: W. W. Norton, 1963), second edition, pp. 247–251.

20. Frederick Leboyer, *Birth Without Violence.* (New York: Alfred A. Knopf, 1975).

21. Melanie Klein, *Envy and Gratitude.* (London, 1957), p. 17. Klein says, "One major derivative of the capacity for love is the feeling of gratitude. Gratitude underlies also the appreciation of goodness in others and in oneself."

22. Hanna Segal, *Introduction to the Work of Melanie Klein*. (London: Heinemann, 1964).

23. William G. Sutherland, *The Cranial Bowl*. (Mankato: Free Press, 1939). Also Harold I. Magoun, *Osteopathy in the Cranial Field*. (Kirksville: Journal Printing Co., 1966).

24. Hebrews 2:15 "And deliver them who through fear of death were all their lifetime subject to bondage."

25. *Complete Psychological Works of Sigmund Freud*. (London, 1910), Vol. XI.

26. See also Richard Whately, *Bacon's Essays: With Annotations*. (London: Longmans, Green, Reader, and Dyer, 1867), pp. 101–110, Essay IX, "Of Envy."

27. Segal. op. cit., p. 27–28.

28. Helmut Schoeck, *Envy: A Theory of Social Behaviour*. (London: Secker and Warburg, 1969), p. 162.

29. Segal. op cit., p. 27.

30. Klein. op. cit., pp. 8, 20.

31. For more on this, see Diamond, *Your Body Doesn't Lie*.

HOW TO SOLVE YOUR PROBLEMS

1. You can also think the phrase, but it is better to say it aloud. Extra reinforcement is given to the thought when it is vocalized.

2. In clinical practice I test in many layers through which we are able to achieve a deeper understanding that is beyond the scope of this book.

3. John Diamond, M.D., *Some Contributions of Behavioral Kinesiology to Art*. (Valley Cottage: Archaeus Press, 1979).

4. And, of course, this is what most advertising, for example, is directed toward—changing our unconscious attitudes, not our conscious ones.

5. John Diamond, M.D., *Speech, Language, and the Power of the Breath*. (Valley Cottage: Archaeus Press, 1978).

6. John Diamond, M.D., *Lectures on a Spiritual Basis of Holistic Therapy*. (Valley Cottage: Archaeus Press, 1979).

7. One of the Brampton Lectures at Columbia University, 1964. [I wish to thank Professor Derek Freeman of the Australian National University for bringing the anthropology of choice to my attention. The interested reader is referred to Professor Freeman's paper, "A Precursory View of the Anthropology of Choice," Canberra: Australian National University, 1978.]

THE HOMING THOUGHT

1. John Diamond, M.D., "Lectures on a Spiritual Basis of Holistic Therapy" (Valley Cottage: Archaeus Press, 1979).

2. Herbert Read, *Essays in Literary Criticism: Particular Studies*. (London: Faber, 1938, 1969), pp. 45–46.

3. Yehudi Menuhin and Curtis W. Davis, *The Music of Man*. (New York: Methuen, 1979), p. ix.

4. Consider the opposite of the homing thought in this quote by James Beard: "I think there probably is a lingering desire in many of us to give into the delicious self-indulgence . . . made even more enjoyable by the guilty sense that one is misbehaving." *Travel and Leisure*, December 1978.

THE CEREBRAL HEMISPHERES

1. The word *creative* comes from the Latin *creare*, meaning to make or produce. In modern English it has come to mean being original and innovative.

2. John Gardner, *The Poetry of Chaucer* (Carbondale, Ill.: Southern Illinois University Press, 1977).

3. John Diamond, M.D., *Speech, Language and the Power of the Breath* (Valley Cottage: Archaeus Press, 1979).

4. Curt Sachs, *The History of Musical Instruments* (New York: Norton, 1940), p. 52.

5. Kermit Shafer, *Blooper Tube* (New York: Crown, 1979).

6. For a full description of these the interested reader is referred to Freud's *The Psychopathology of Everyday Life,* Standard Edition, Vol. VI (London: Hogarth Press, 1971).

7. Kermit Shafer, *Blunderful World of Bloopers* (New York: Bounty, 1973).

8. M. M. Mahood, *Shakespeare's Wordplay* (London: Methuen, 1957).

9. Bob Aylwin, *A Load of Cockney Cobblers* (London: Johnston & Bacon, 1973).

10. Standard Edition, Vol. VIII, 1905.

11. John Diamond, M.D., *Behavioral Kinesiology and the Autonomic Nervous System* (Valley Cottage: Archaeus Press, 1978).

12. Although these results correlate closely with encephalographic studies, we are not testing the electrical properties of the brain as an electroencephalogram does, but rather the "magnetic" properties of the brain. If you doubt that the body has electromagnetic properties, then use a pole of a magnet instead of the test hand. You will quickly see how much we are affected by magnetism. This property will become even more important when we discuss acupuncture.

INTRODUCTION TO ACUPUNCTURE

1. See, for example, Mary Austin, Acupuncture Therapy, ASI Publishers, New York, 1972, and Felix Mann, The Meridians of Acupuncture, London, Wm. Heinemann Medical Books, 1971. These are called *meridian alarm points.*

2. Of course, if he says the positive affirmations for the thymus, then all meridian imbalances will automatically be corrected.

3. Temporarily relieved by the "cocktail hour"

4. It is not necessary in most cases to test both sides of bilateral points, although in some instances when you experience difficulty in arriving at a conclusion it is required. This is not a frequent occurrence.

THE MERIDIANS AND THEIR EMOTIONS

1. You may find as you begin to undertake some of the testing in this chapter that some subjects are strengthened by what appears to be an inappropriate affirmation. For example, when you should be strengthened by saying, "I am full of joy," you may be strengthened as well by saying, "I am happy." These responses are not common, but when they occur it is often because the subject's own understanding of the meaning of the word is very generalized and perhaps confused. Merely explain the specific definitions to the subject and retest. Considering how imprecise our language has become, it is surprising how rarely this situation occurs.

2. "An Introduction to Psycho-Etymology," *Collected Papers of John Diamond, M.D.*, Volume II, (Valley Cottage: Archaeus Press, 1980), pp. 139–157. For an example of the psychoanalytic approach to etymology, refer to Ernest Jones, *On the Nightmare* (London: Hogarth Press, 1949).

3. Owen Barfield, *Poetic Diction: A Study in Meaning* (New York: McGraw-Hill, 1964), pp. 63–64.

4. When testing these meridian types, you will find that most people will test strong in the clear and weak when they test-touch the point for the specific meridian involved. Some people who are more vulnerable to the particular stress being introduced may test weak in the clear. It will be found for those people that touching the test point at the same time, through some mechanism which is not well understood, will cause them to test strong. This indicates that the specific meridian is involved, but that the energy loss has been greater than usual.

5. For a comprehensive list of dictionaries consulted for definitions throughout this chapter, see Appendix I, p. 233.

6. Richard Crashaw, "The Hymn of St. Thomas in Adoration of the Blessed Sacrament."

7. Carl D. Buck, *A Dictionary of Selected Synonyms in the Principal Indo-European Languages* (Chicago: University of Chicago Press, 1965).

8. Vol. V, 15th edition, 1978, p. 179.

9. Aeschylus, *The Agamemnon*, tr. Gilbert Murray (London: Allen & Unwin, 1961), p. xiv.

10. in Melanie Klein, *Envy and Gratitude & Other Works 1946–1963* (New York: Delta, 1975), p. 280.

11. E. R. Dodds, *The Greeks and the Irrational* (Berkeley: University of California Press, 1951), p. 31.

12. Adrian Stokes, *Greek Culture and the Ego* (London: Tavistock, 1958), p. 22.

13. William Whateley, *Prototypes or the primarie precedent* (1639).

14. *The Philosophy of Spinoza* (New York: Modern Library, 1927), p. lxviii.

15. You may recall in this context the frequency with which alcoholics develop liver disease. We now see how we must deal with their emotional factors in addition to their nutritional deficiencies.

16. The word *splenetic* has no relationship to the emotional states that accompany the spleen meridian. Its first usage was to do with depression,

and then later it evolved to its present usage—to have "an irritable or morose or peevish disposition or temperament; given or liable to fits of angry impatience or irritability; ill-humoured, testy, irascible," related to the heart meridian emotions. (see p. 149).

17. John Diamond, M.D., *The Re-Mothering Experience* (Valley Cottage: Archaeus Press, 1981), pp. 63–68.

18. John Diamond, M.D., *The Life Energy in Music* (Valley Cottage: Archaeus Press, 1981), Vol. I, pp. 124–131.

19. Hanna Segal, *Introduction to the Work of Melanie Klein* (London: Hogarth Press, 1973), p. ix.

20. Acts 18:6 "I am clean." Joshua 2:19 "We will be guiltless." Luke 11:41 "And, behold, all things are clean unto you."

21. But, as we now know, sorrow and disappointment are not functions of the circulation-sex meridian at all, but they are related to the small intestine and stomach meridians respectively.

22. William Cowper, *The Task*.

23. Percy Bysshe Shelley, *Queen Mab, a philosophical poem* (1813).

24. Robert Burton, *The Anatomy of Melancholy* (1621).

25. Owen Meridith, *Lucile* (1860).

26. See also "A Psychological Notation on the Root Gn, Kn, Cn," by Henry A. Bunker and Bertram D. Lewin, in *Psychoanalysis and Culture*, eds. G. B. Wilbur and Warner Muensterberger (New York: International Universities Press, 1951), pp. 363–367.

27. The *Oxford English Dictionary* defines resentment as "a strong feeling of ill will or anger against the author or authors of a wrong or affront."

28. Charles Darwin, *Expression of the Emotions in Man and Animals* (New York: Philosophical Library, 1955).

29. People who are bitter themselves often suffer from "sour stomach."

30. Segal, op. cit., p. 40.

31. Theodore Reik, *The Haunting Melody* (New York: Grove Press, 1953).

32. John Bowlby, *Maternal Care and Mental Health*, Monograph Series, no. 2, World Health Organization, Geneva, 1951.

33. Morris B. Parloff, "The Me Degeneration", *Psychology Today* (December 1979), p. 92.

34. Simultaneous contradictory messages. see pp. 214–217.

35. In the Editor's Note to the introduction of Freud's "Mourning and Melancholia" (Vol. XIV of the Standard Edition of the *Complete Psychological Works*), we read that Freud included under the term melancholia "what are now usually described as states of depression."

36. Eric Partridge, *Origins—A Short Etymological Dictonary of Modern English* (London: Routledge and Kegan Paul, 1966).

37. Lady M. W. Montagu, *Letter to Miss A. Wortley* (1709).

38. The interested reader is referred to C. S. Lewis, *Studies in Words* (Cambridge: Cambridge University Press, 1960, 1967), chapter 3.

39. Of course, one can also have tears of anger (heart meridian).

40. Excerpt from *Diamond Report* No. 66, August 1982.

41. From *Diamond Report* No. 56, October 1981.

42. H. Bailey and M. Love, *A Short Practice of Surgery* (London: H. K. Lewis & Co. Ltd., 1971, fifteenth edition), p. 848.

DEEPER LAYERS

1. We must remember that frequently, for proper deep testing, we go through many levels to reveal what is beneath each layer. Here we are concentrating upon revealing successively deeper layers, not levels, of the individual.

THE DOUBLE-BIND

1. Gregory Bateson, et al, "Toward a Theory of Schizophrenia," *Behavioral Science*, 1:251, 1956.

DAILY PROGRAM

1. See Diamond, *Your Body Doesn't Lie.*
2. Put your tongue against the roof of your mouth, with the tip about a quarter of an inch behind the upper front teeth. This is a strengthening position. (See Diamond, *Your Body Doesn't Lie*).
3. It is preferable that you say the affirmations aloud. Your own voice will strengthen and reinforce the affirmations.

TRANSMUTATION

1. The New Columbia Encyclopedia (New York: Columbia University Press, 1975), p. 2236.

Appendix III

It has been found, primarily through the work of Dr. George Goodheart, the originator of applied kinesiology (from which the use of the muscle test discussed in this book is derived), that certain food supplements can be beneficial for specific meridian imbalances. If you find that one or two meridians are consistently testing weak over a period of time, then it may be advisable, with proper nutritional guidance, to help reactivate these meridians with appropriate support. Of course, these should always be tested individually to ensure their effectiveness in each specific case.

A number of vitamin companies now market concentrated extracts of whole glands in tablet form. These are quite distinct from hormone preparations, which may be derived from the glands.

Nutritional support can be very valuable, but it is just that—it is a support. I believe what is basically required is on the one hand working with the underlying psychological factors that produce the meridian weakness, and on the other, getting nutritional information and other guidance and therapy from the appropriate health professionals.

MERIDIAN	SOME BASIC SUPPLEMENTS
Thymus	Thymus concentrate.
Lung	Lung concentrate. Vitamin C.
Liver	Liver concentrate. Bile salts. Vitamins A, "F." *
Gall Bladder	Bile salts. Vitamin A.
Spleen†	Spleen concentrate. Vitamins C, "F," G, or Pancreatic concentrate. Betaine hydrochloride. Vitamins A, B_1.

* Qualitatively derived unsaturated fatty acids (arachidonic, linoleic and linolenic), sometimes unofficially referred to as "Vitamin F."
† Spleen meridian relates to both spleen and pancreas.

243

MERIDIAN	SOME BASIC SUPPLEMENTS
Kidney	Kidney concentrate. Chlorophyll. Vitamins A, B$_1$, B$_2$, C, E, "F."
Large Intestine	Lactobacillus acidophilus. Chlorophyll. Wheat Germ Oil. Vitamins A, B$_1$, C, D, E.
Circulation-Sex‡	Adrenal concentrate. Vitamin C.
	or (male) Prostate and testicular concentrates. Vitamin E.
	or (female) Ovarian and uterine concentrates. Vitamin E.
Heart	Heart concentrate. Vitamins B$_1$ and/or B$_2$,§ E.
Stomach	Stomach concentrate. Betaine hydrochloride. Vitamins B$_1$, B$_2$, B$_3$, B$_6$.
Thyroid	Thyroid concentrate. Sea vegetables. Iodine. Vitamin C.
Small Intestine	Duodenal concentrate. Vitamins B$_1$, D, E.
Bladder	Wheat germ oil. Vitamins A, B$_1$, C, E.

TISSUE SALTS

The twelve tissue salts are low-potency homoeopathic remedies. Dr. Schuessler suggested over a hundred years ago that these twelve salts were essential to the life of a cell.* His theory was that when the salts in the cells were balanced, then health would be facilitated. While medical science may not approve of his biochemical principles, nonetheless, each activates a specific meridian. Thus, life energy may be enhanced through the re-balancing of the acupuncture system of the body, which these tissue salts can help achieve. Again, as with the food supplements, it is not recommended that they be used for transitory imbalances, but rather when a consistent pattern emerges, such as persistent underactivity of a meridian over a period of time.

While these tissue salts are available in health food stores, it is of course always best that they be used with the guidance of a qualified health practitioner. I usually recommend that tissue salts be taken for not more than a few weeks.

MERIDIAN	TISSUE SALT
Lung	Silica
Liver	Kali. Sulph.
Gall Bladder	Calc. Phos.
Spleen	Kali. Mur.
Kidney	Ferr. Phos.

‡ Circulation-sex meridian relates to both adrenal glands and reproductive glands.
§ Should be tested individually.
* J. B. Chapman, *Dr. Schuessler's Biochemistry* (London: New Era, 1961).

Large Intestine	Nat. Mur.
Circulation-Sex	Nat. Phos.
Heart	Nat. Sulph.
Stomach	Calc. Sulph.
Thyroid	Calc. Fluor.
Small Intestine	Kali. Phos.
Bladder	Mag. Phos.

Index